In the Defense of This Flag

The Civil War diary of
Pvt. Ormond Hupp,
5th Indiana Light Artillery

Transcribed and annotated by
John Lee Berkley

McGuinn & McGuire
PUBLISHING, INC
Bradenton, Florida

 For information, contact McGuinn & McGuire Publishing, Inc., Post Office Box 20603, Bradenton, Florida 34203.

Library of Congress Cataloging-in-Publication Data

Berkley, John Lee.
In the defense of this flag : the Civil War diary of Pvt. Ormond Hupp, 5th Indiana Light Artillery / transcribed and annotated by John Lee Berkley.
p. cm.
Diary previously published: My diary / Ormond Hupp. – Odessa [Mo.] : Ewing Printers, 1923.
Includes bibliographical references and index.
ISBN 1-881117-06-5
1. Hupp, Ormond, 1840-1926 – Diaries. 2. United States. Army. Indiana Light Artillery Battery, 5th (1861-1865). 3. United States – History – Civil War, 1861-1865 – Personal narratives. 4. Indiana – History – Civil War, 1861-1865 – Personal narratives. 5. Soldiers – Indiana – Diaries. I. Hupp, Ormond, 1840-1926. My diary. II. Title.
E506.8 5th.B47 1994
973.7'472'092 – dc20
[B] 94-5270
CIP

Printed in the United States of America

This book is dedicated to my beloved mother,
Margaret Lyons Berkley.

CONTENTS

The Diary

The Narrative

Beat! beat! drums! – Blow! bugles! blow!
    Through the windows – through the doors – burst
        like a ruthless force,
Into the solemn church, and scatter the congregation;
Into the school where the scholar is studying;
Leave not the bridegroom quiet – no happiness must he
    have now with his bride;
Nor the peaceful farmer any peace, plowing his field or
    gathering his grain;
So fierce you whirr and pound, you drums – so shrill you
    bugles blow.

Walt Whitman: *Beat! Beat! Drums!* I.

Preface

I have known about my maternal great-grandfather's diary almost as long as I have known anything. In my family, its author was a somewhat mythical character, larger than life, a man of indomitable strength of character, who was also a "character". These impressions come from my mother who delighted my brothers and me with stories about visits to her grandfather's house as a young girl. After writing this book and researching the historical aspects set forth in Great-Grandfather's Civil War diary (or "journal", as he called it), I feel that I now know "Grampa Hupp" in a different way. He has stepped down from the clouds, so to speak, and become part of the family again. If the written word engenders a sort of immortality on the writer, then Ormond Hupp's accounts of wartime pain and loss, love and glory help to bring him and his times back to life, if only in the imagination. So in addition to a challenging intellectual adventure, the writing of this book and the transcription of the diary have been an emotional experience. I have gotten to know Ormond Hupp in a very special, even affectionate sense. This work, then, is an attempt to make public what, for me, has been a very personal journey.

Ormond Hupp's diary is not great literature. One should not anticipate the rich prose of Elisha Hunt Rhodes or the biting eloquence of a Mary Chesnut. Hupp was a young Indiana farm boy with one year of college behind him when he set down his wartime thoughts and observations. The style is generally stiff, abbreviated, and maddeningly short on descriptive detail. He neglects, for example, to state the name of his military unit anywhere in the document, and commonly allows phrases like, "it was the most wondrous sight I have ever before seen", to substitute for in-depth description. Nevertheless, what I find splendid about his writing is its raw unvarnished honesty and lack of pretention. His diary is just that, a diary. It is not Gone With the Wind. Under the most trying of circumstances, this young, thoroughly 19th century American of the northern Indiana prairies found words enough to paint a portrait of wartime America that succeeds admirably in drawing us into its scenery. In the process, not only do we view these critical historical times through the eyes of the common man, but, more importantly, we also become acquainted with the man.

This book is really two books in one: Hupp's diary comes first with footnote annotations, followed by an eight chapter narrative that qualifies as a complete biography. Although mostly devoted to placing Ormond Hupp's Civil War observations in historical perspective, the narrative also examines his pre- and post-war life, as well. It is unfortunate that he left no journals of these periods, for surviving documents and reminiscences show him to have lived at least as remarkable a life in peacetime as he did in war.

My intent in combining Hupp's diary with my own narrative is two-fold:

First, the narrative documents the larger historical framework of events, people, and places contained in the diary. Quite frankly, readers who are not familiar with Civil War history may struggle at times to understand the larger significance of the diary's contents. Consequently, I have attempted to weave the diary within the fabric of history by using footnotes in the diary, and by including the more detailed narrative. The narrative section, arranging events in more-or-less chronological order, will be most effective in putting things in perspective. Because Hupp's unit, the 5th Indiana Light Artillery, was involved in most of the major battles of the western theater, a reading of the narrative not only depicts Hupp's personal adventures, but stands as a fairly complete history of western theater campaigns east of the Mississippi River;

Second, the narrative also serves as a comprehensive biography of Ormond Hupp, the man. Although Hupp's experiences as a soldier deserve special consideration, other aspects of his life also warrant examination. To my mind, how the average person came to participate in a momentous historical event like the American Civil War – and how they fared afterward – are just as significant and worthy of telling as the momentous event itself. Thus, the narrative follows one man from childhood, through the cataclysmic drama of war, to the ultimate fulfillment of the American dream in the Gilded Age. Those who participated directly in the mid-century eruption of internecine slaughter we call the Civil War were first and last, flesh and blood, feeling human beings. They suffered pain, raised families (usually large ones), paid bills, and fretted over the future, just as their descendants do today. Reading their own words transmitted across time from the thick of battle helps to put back the flesh on their bones, and reminds us of their humanity.

Reference sources for the narrative include recent popular accounts of the battles and general Civil War history written by Shelby Foote, James

M. McPherson, Peter Cozzens, Albert Castel, Kenneth Hofendorfer, and others of similar stature. I have also made use of appropriate volumes in the monumental compendium of Civil War documents known by the long title of *War of the Rebellion: A Compilation of the Official Records of the Union and Confederate Armies*. Most authors refer to this set as the *Official Records*, the practice followed here. I have also made extensive use of the 10-volume set *Photographic History of the Civil War* which contains some of the most well-known war photographs taken by Matthew Brady and other pioneering field photographers.

I have also used relevant state regimental histories and other documents, genealogical reports, National Archives records (muster, pension, and medical), family papers files, and pages from the Ormond and Laura Hupp family Bible. Library research was augmented by numerous visits to battlefield parks, cemeteries, former Hupp homesteads, and interviews with living relatives.

At all times, I have tried to veer as close to the truth as possible in telling this story. Where conflicting scenarios have emerged, I have used my feeble judgement of such matters to present the side that I believe is most accurate. Where the facts lay jumbled in controversy – as, for example, in deciding which of several artillery batteries killed General Polk (see Chapt. 7; Narrative) – I have presented the competing sides for the reader to sort out. I apologize for unforgivable errors or omissions. I welcome and appreciate any and all reader feedback about this book.

Acknowledgements

I owe an extreme debt of gratitude to all those persons and institutions who have provided aid, comfort, and resources for this project. This work would have been impossible without the willing and gracious help I received from numerous libraries, historical museums and societies, state and Federal archives, not to mention relatives and friends.

People and institutions who helped include Robert Horton, Indiana State Archives; Betty C. Menges, Stuart B. Wrege Indiana History Room, New Albany and Floyd County Public Library; LaPorte County Public Library; Cindy Stuart, Western Historical Manuscript Collection, University of Missouri, Columbia; Marie Concannon, The State Historical Society of Missouri; Curt B. Witcher, Allen County Public Library, Fort Wayne, Indiana; Louise A. Arnold-Friend, U.S. Army Military History Institute; U. S. National Archives, Washington, D.C.; Sally Newkirk, Floyd County Museum, New Albany, Indiana; William Clark, Ringgold (GA) Historical Society; Hazel Young, Perryville Battlefield State Historic Site; Gettysburg National Military Park, Pennsylvania; Mary A. Beck, Missouri State Archives; W. S. Horn, Saline County (MO) Historical Society, Marshall, Missouri; Stuart McConnell, History Dept., Pitzer College, Claremont, California; Marshall (MO) Public Library; Fairfield Bay (AR) Public Library; Margaret Pabst, Janet Ferry, and Jack Ericson, Reed Library, State University of New York, College at Fredonia; and Service Print, Dunkirk, NY.

Friends and relatives who have provided valuable aid, support, and information include Gary Lash, C. Gary and Shirley Brown, Wesley and Martha Johnson, Roscoe Hupp, Jim Franklin, Greg Carroll, Dale Berkley, Robert Berkley, Jr., Pat Tasker, Barbara and Dan Cornell, my sons, Jory and Alex, and wife, Mira Tetkowski Berkley. To the last three, I promise not to drag them through any more cemeteries or libraries – at least for a while.

A Note on Editing

Ormond Hupp's diary was written when he was young, mostly under very trying conditions. He made many errors in spelling and punctuation (among others) that are mostly reproduced here without correction for historical purposes. Some misspellings are noted with the [sic] designation, for some the correct spelling is noted in brakets [brackets], and other obvious clinkers are left with no change or comment. Punctuation errors were probably printer's errors, but others probably originated in his original journal (now lost). I have corrected glaring punctuation errors, especially where they contribute to confusion.

MY DIARY

Ormond Hupp

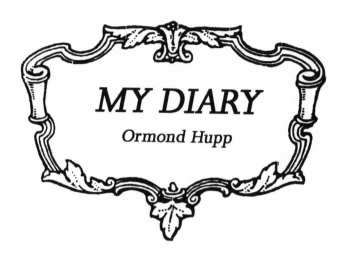

The Ewing Printers, Odessa
1923

VOLUME I

To my children
and my children's children
this little record of my
experiences in the
defense of this
flag is
dedicated.

VOLUME I

New Albany, Ind.
February 1, 1863

Feeling very desirous of keeping a brief record of events while in the service and having lost my journal at the Battle of Perryville – concluded to write it over as well as my weak memory would admit. I will merely sketch it off in a brief style until I reach the period of the present time.

Signed
Ormond Hupp

My Diary

Enlisted Sept. 16, 1861 in the city of Laport, Indiana, by Mr. Allen, citizen of the above named place; was sworn in on the 22nd, staid in camp at Indianapolis from the 18th of Sept. till the 25th of Nov. and employed most of the time in drilling Infantry drill; went to Louisville, Ky. and there we stayed in camp till the 8th of Dec. under Capt. Merrill and were taking our first lessons in Inf. drill.

On Dec. 8 went to Bacon Creek; here we practiced target shooting and drill till the 11th of Feb. – the muddiest place I ever saw.

A great deal of sickness existed among the troops while at this place; every soldier was sick of the biz.

On the 11th of Feb. we started under Michael for Bowling Green, Ky. at which place we arrived with but little opposition on the 14th; we suffered considerably on this march and here our first soldiering commenced.

On the 22nd we started for Nashville, Tenn., at which place we arrived after a tedious march on the 25th; here we lay in camp till the 25th of March, when we started for Huntsville, Ala., where we arrived to the great astonishment of the citizens on the sudden appearance of the Blue Coats, as they called us.

The ladies kept very dark and could be seen only through a crack in the door, but they got over this in a very few weeks and many of the fair sex could be seen enjoying an evening promenade with the Yankee boys.

Several of the boys of our Company became intimately acquainted with many in the place, but I heard of none proposing marriage.

The country in the region is hilly and mountainous, what farming land there is nearly worn out and worthless: they have always been accustomed to raise cotton and scarcely anything else, as it would pay better to buy corn and other necessities from the north.

Their manner of cultivation is about 50 years behind Indiana; in nearly every case they use nothing but a single horse and wooden plow and they never pretend to remove the stubble of a last year's crop of corn or cotton, but merely furrow it out, plant their seeds and commence tending it in the most slovenish manner you could think of.

The timber here is mostly oak, very little chestnut.

The evening of the day we arrived an expedition was sent on the cars to go as far as was possible, two of our officers accompanied them and when within 4 miles of Decatur they ran off the track which had been torn up for the purpose by the Secesh here; they were forced to retreat with the lone engine and one car.

We left one gun but not without spiking it.

Next morning the whole force advanced and ran into Decatur, found the Tennessee bridge on fire and succeeded in putting it out without its doing much damage.

The rebels left us a good breakfast, well cooked and left for parts unknown. We captured all their tents and equipment, also 100 stand small arms and there were several boxes of nice things in the depot on their way to Jeff. These we went into with hearty good will and got a great many trophies which will be memorials in after years.

We left Decatur for Tuscumbia after a stoppage at Decatur for 3 days.

From Decatur there was a brigade of us; had several skirmishes on the way andreached the place on the night of the 15th of April; here we expected a fight but the Gray Backs got afraid and were making tracks for the mountains where we found a great many Secesh, but they kept still; a great many left their homes and all furniture and made tracks.

One of these I will mention as the house was but a short distance from our camp.

A man by the name of Nelson (he was aide-de-camp in the rebel army) left one of the finest mansions in the south; the house was richly furnished from garret to cellar; he took no time to remove anything but the family.

I chanced to get in the house next day after we got there and I never saw finer furniture, dresses, books and everything belonging to a house; the cellar was full of all kinds of wines, brandies, and preserves, which the boys pitched into as they would have rebels.

I took from the house three books and a 5-gal. demijohn of wine; most of the boys got something.

On the plantation we were encamped on there were 75 slaves; they had the largest crop of corn I ever saw in cribs which we helped ourselves to at the expense of the C. S. A.

The country around this place was rich and productive; quite level after leaving the mountains about 6 miles behind.

The timber was mostly, some chestnut and hickory, and along the mountains considerable persimmon.

Tuscumbia contains, or did contain before the rebellion, 1000 inhabitants, is situated on the M. & Charleston R. R. 3 miles from the Tennessee, noted for having one of the nicest springs in the south.

Women were a scarce article in this place, at least while we were there.

On the 20th [of April, 1862] we were attacked by an overpowering force and forced to retreat; they kept close to our heels and the morning of the 21st, a skirmish ensued near Courtland, Ala. which resulted in the capture of 20 of our stragglers.

We killed several of them, but how many we never knew as we were in a hurry to reach the Tennessee Bridge before we should be cut off on the 23rd.

All was safe across the river at 11 a. m. the bridge was fired; it looked awful to see such a vast deal of labor consumed by flames on purpose.

Such is the wages of war!

On the 25th we arrived back at camp at Huntsville, after an absence of nearly a month; on the 27th our section went in camp on the Hill, commanding the road from Decatur with the 15th Ky. to guard us.

Here we spent our honeymoon in the south.

During the time we stayed here the weather was very warm with but very little rain.

The people were mostly Secesh in the vicinity, but became more friendly the longer we stayed.

On the hill above named we could have the finest view of the town and surrounding country I ever beheld.

The cornfields (for such they were when we were there as cotton was not a profitable crop) could be seen for miles around almost filled with niggers tending the crops; they would get out at daylight in the morning and work till dark, only allowed an hour for dinner.

A quarter of a mile from the camp lived a family by the name of Green with two grown daughters that J. W. and I became very much attached to; their names were Adelaide and Josephine.

We would slip the guard lines and be with them nearly every night.

Shortly after we left Josephine died with typhoid fever.

Huntsville was the handsomest place I ever saw while in the south and contained the most splendid buildings my eyes ever beheld.

It lies at the foot of the Cumberland Mountains and is noted for its wealth and fine buildings.

The Huntsville Spring is the largest and best spring in the south; it furnishes ample water for the town which is supplied by the waterworks.

The Cemetery is situated on the east side of the town and contains many of the most splendid monuments that I ever saw erected.

There are several seminaries in the place and every convenience for educating the rich, but the poor are obliged to rear their children without even the benefit of a school room.

The wealthy think it a disgrace for the poor to be educated and so they are kept under.

While here I often went over to Clement's plantation, which was a mile distant; here was an octoroon lady, as white as any of our northern ladies, and as sensible as any girl I ever met with.

For some time I made several presents and in turn she gave me milk and did my washing and mending and often talked over her condition; she declared she would have her freedom sometime.

About the first of June the black berries commenced ripening: they beat those of the north by odds, in size and in quantity.

We had them at our pleasure from then till the first of September.

The uplands and mountains were covered with the delicious fruit of which I gathered at one time about six quarts, and made some excellent wine.

On the 25th of June the middle section of our battery with the 19th Ill. was ordered to Winchester, Tenn.

On our way we passed through splendid farming country mostly and some as well located farms as I ever saw.

On the third day we reached the place, the distance being sixty five miles: the weather was very warm and the roads miserably dusty; the reader therefore can judge we were ready to stop.

Winchester is situated on Duck River, on the west bank and is a beautiful town containing about 1000 inhabitants noted for the several Female Academies, and the beautiful farming country surrounding it.

At the time we were there the two schools were closed but there were 400 young ladies that were obliged to stay on account of communications being cut off from their homes.

The second day we arrived at Beckner and I went in the country four miles to a tobacconist for the purpose of purchasing some cigars. We found the folks to be northern people of the cleverest sort; we were invited to take tea but declined as it would make it too late: they then had us eat a pie and smoke and after buying 300 cigars of him we parted probably to meet no more, but promising to make another visit should our stay in the place admit.

He was true union, but was obliged to keep cool to save his neck. The name was Harris, and a more sociable family I seldom met.

We returned to camp, as we supposed, to enjoy a good night's rest, but not so: at 3 o'clock next morning the bugle sounded Boots and Saddles call, we were ordered to Stevenson, Ala. and at 5 a. m. were all on the road and with much regret left the beautiful place, for when we came it was the intention to remain sometime as a guard to keep at bay S_________'s Cavalry which numbered 2000 and had been doing much to our trains between Shelbyville and Murfreesboro.[1] I'll speak of a lady before I entirely leave this place – one that I borrowed a knife of to butcher a beef. Her name was Johnson, she had a family of six children, two sons and four daughters, all away from home and married but her youngest son who is in Mississippi employed on a R.R.: her husband has been dead eight years.

She was the owner of twenty slaves, little and big, and they did all her work and rendered her a comfortable living.

She was awfully afraid we'd steal some of her slaves and thus be the ruination of her.

She showed me some twenty daguerretypes, those of her family and several others.

She was hard to beat for talking – and after passing an hour or so with her and eating a splendid apple pie, I bid her goodbye and returned to camp.

I will now return to our march.

Our road was what was called the Paint Rock Valley Road which reached the M & Charleston R. R. at a station by that name.

On the morning of the second day we were attacked by some guerillas which we routed after a short skirmish – we had one man wounded but none killed.

That same evening our advance cavalry attacked another party, capturing four men, their horses and arms.

One of the horses afterward sold for $400.

We took up our march next morning at 8, and all that is worth

---

[1]This is a reference to Colonel John A. Scott, who commanded the 1st Louisiana Cavalry. However, Scott was operating farther east from the rail line indicated (Murfreesboro to Shelbyville, TN). It is more likely that the harassing cavalry in this case was led by Nathan Bedford Forrest, John Hunt Morgan, or both. Scott later operated in the Green River region of KY, through which Buell's army would pass on the way to Louisville.

mentioning of this day's march is the burning of eight houses owned by guerillas.

One we burned I shall always remember, as the woman and children hid in the mountains till we passed and they were discovered by some of our men.

She came down crying and begging of them not to kill her.

It is a horrible thing – she had no place to go, all she had in the world was burned up and what she did afterward I know not as we moved on and left her crying with her three children by her side.

On the way we passed the roughest country and along the most outrageous roads I ever saw.

Very little of the country between Winchester and Stevenson is any account for farming; the timber is mostly oak, some little beech and chestnut.

On the 24th we stopped to rest at Belfont, fifteen miles from Stevenson.

Belfont is a small place of about 600 inhabitants, Secesh to the backbone – we killed a couple of cattle and rested for the next day's march.

The country around here for a short distance is of a rich quality and very productive.

We reached Stevenson the next day and went in camp.

Stevenson is a railroad station where the Memphis and Charleston R. R. intersects with the Nashville and Chattanooga road, laying off the Tennessee four miles.

The only thing worth mentioning is a large spring which affords all the water theyhave in the place which contains about 200 inhabitants and about half of them are black, but it is about as pretty a place as I ever saw.

We received five months pay here on the 30th of June.

On the 1st of July we went under Col. T__________[2] acting then as Brigadier Gen. and a better or more able commander has never been in the field.

To Bridgeport on the Tennessee – Bridgeport is situated on the east side of the river, a small town on the M. & C. R. R. ten miles from Stevenson, containing about a dozen old rickety buildings, among them was the best saw mill I saw while in the south.

---

[2]This may refer to Gen. George Henry Thomas, second in command to Buell at Perryville. Thomas was promoted to major general in April, 1862. One of the more able Union generals, he later (fall 1863) took command of the Army of the Cumberland. He was known as "The Rock of Chickamauga" for his exploits in that battle.

There were but two families living in the place at the time we were there.

Our main force was at Battle Creek four miles below, the Gen. Commander was M. C. Cook of Ky. who was under Gen. Buell whose headquarters were at Huntsville, Ala.[3]

After we were changed from O. M. Michael [Gen. Ormsby Mitchel] to Buell we were put on half rations and kept so during the time we were in Ala.

All the flour we were to receive he sold to the citizens at reduced prices, hardly leaving first cost.

I believe if the said Buell had made his appearance at two or three different times, when the boys were throwing themselves on the subject, he would have been hung, which he richly deserved, for his conduct afterwards as well as on that occasion.

Here we were attached to the 9th Brigade commanded by Col. [Leonard A.] Harris afterwards made Brigadier Gen. for his gallantry and daring deeds at the battle of Perryville, Ky.

The brigade consisted of the 10th Wisconsin, 38th Indiana, 33rd and 3rd Ohio with our battery [5th Indiana], and we thought it the best Brigade in the service, but there were many more as good.[4]

The country around the place and from the Tennessee to Stevenson is very broken, there is but very little of the soil that will produce good corn, most of the fields are so stony that a person can walk from one end to the other without touching the ground. For my part, I can't see how people can ever make a living by farming on such lands, but then they live on almost nothing, many of them never tasted wheat bread and I doubt whether they were ever ten miles from home.

Most of the water through the country is spring water and in some cases they get their water a mile from the house when a well might be dug and water obtained in twenty or thirty feet, but there are some of them actually too lazy to live.

The crop of peaches proved to be nearly a failure in the vicinity where we expected to feast very heavily on them, but the weather was too dry and but few came to maturity.

During the time we were there nothing of importance occurred - we had several little skirmishes but never brought on a general engagement.

---

[3]"M. C. Cook" is actually Major General Alexander McCook, commander of the 1st Army Corps, which included the 5th Indiana Light Artillery (Hupp's company). Major General Don Carlos Buell was commander-in-chief of the Army of the Ohio.

[4]The 3rd Ohio was actually with the 17th Brigade; Hupp means the <u>2nd Ohio</u>. His brigade also included the 94th Ohio under Col. J. W. Frizell.

The rebel pickets were stationed on the opposite side of the river within talking distance of ours; they would often exchange whiskey with our men for salt and coffee.

I often went out six or eight miles to forage for apples, green corn, chickens, and whatever I could find that was fit to eat.

A family by the name of Williams has three daughters who attracted the attention of many of the northern boys.

They were strong Secesh but cared but little about talking on the subject.

The only union people I met while there was a McFarlin family who had settled there from New York in the year 1848 and had the best farm and the only profitable one I saw in the vicinity.

Their orchard was of the best quality and afforded me many a good apple and peach.

Matilda, the wife, could make an excellent pie, for I have tasted of a many a one of her manufacture.

McFarlin said that they were all Secesh that he knew of in that neighborhood and he was actually afraid of his life sometimes.

There was a great chance for Bush Wackers in those parts and they exercised themselves to no little degree.

I have often wondered when I look back and see the number of times I was exposed to these band of murderers and outlaws, that I never fell into their hands, but I was always prepared for the worst and would have stood a brush at any time before giving myself into their hands.

An instance occurred while we were here in camp worth mention. We were scarce of meat one evening and there happened to be three or four hogs running around camp. So several of us armed ourselves with knives and pistols and resolved to have some fresh meat.

We succeeded after sometime in butchering two of them, large and fat, and of course we knew how to dispose of them.

Occurrences of similar nature occurred frequently in our company, as we had but little mercy with rebel property of that kind when hungry.

The 4th of July, '62 we spent in this desolate place.

A salute of thirty two guns was fired at 12 m., the balance of the day the boys lay in the shade conversing over past scenes, and a more lonely day I never experienced.

I passed a day in a very agreeable manner while here with the Boys of the 21st Ind. at Battle Creek; had a good long chat with all my acquaintances, took supper with a Mr. Green and then bade them all goodbye to return to my desolate quarters.

I happened to drink a little too much Catawba wine while with them and was sick all night.

On the 15th of Aug. four of our pieces were ordered to Stevenson to guard the Fort, the only troops there at the time was the 13th Michigan and here we made preparations to remain some length of time.

We built a nice bowery over our horses to protect them from the scorching sun, which at the time made both man and animal seek shade of some trees until its disappearance in the evening.

We had our water to haul one and one half miles from a spring situated in the wood to the west of the place; water could have been had at the Stevenson spring which was only a quarter mile from the Fort, but the water was deemed unhealthy by the physicians and the water from the one we used was the purest and best water I ever saw.

There was but little good farming land in this vicinity the enterprise of the people here is very little; they merely supply the wants of the body and drag their lives away regardless of any future period.

Very few slaves are owned in these parts by any one person; a quack doctor had thirty all told.

His name was Giles and he appeared to be a gentlemanly sort of a man.

I patronized his orchard several times and found some very fair apples.

He had a daughter, Mary, who could put up a very good pie, and took several dimes from the boys for her good things.

They appeared to be good Union people and I don't doubt their profession for I know not their hearts.

There were 400 negroes working on their fortifications.

The Fort was a beautiful structure 250 feet square and was made to command eight guns; walls eight feet thick, at the bottom, four on the top.

It was built of timbers two feet in thickness and then packed with dirt; a ditch ten feet wide and eight feet deep was cut all around it making it eighteen feet from parapet to bottom of ditch.

At the entrance there was a large gate three feet thick and a bridge over the ditch which could be raised during action; this bridge was ten inches thick making the passage three feet ten inches thick in time of action, which would stand considerable battering with small guns before an impression could be made.

There were four stockades in the place for musketry purposes, which were very neatly constructed and would have been hard to be taken by infantry but were not designed to stand artillery fire to any extent.

Back of the town (if so it may be called) was a mountain a half mile high on the top of which we kept a picket watching for any approaching danger which was anticipated all the time we were in there.

This hill is covered with a thick growth of cedar trees which renders it impossible to distinguish a person any distance; on the top is a clean spot of about a half acre from which you can see many miles.

This hill will never be fit for anything after the little cedar timber is taken off, as it is almost solid rock.

A person would think it a great place for wild game, but all that can be found is a few rabbits and once in a while a red squirrel, but in the timbered land are a great many fox squirrels, some deer and any amount of o'possums.

I never spent an hour hunting while there.

On the 20th of Aug. our other three pieces, which were left at Bridgeport as a guard came to us.

They had been expecting an attack for several days and had had two or three skirmishes as the rebels had got across the river to a considerable number and kept picking up foraging parties sent by our men.

On the 22nd a small party of our boys went out under our captain on a scout: at a small place by the name of Bolivar they burned several houses belonging to guerillas.

In one two story house resided an old blind lady who said her husband was dead, but we found out better: her husband and son both out with their guns at the time.

The boys moved her and her things into the street, then set fire to the buildings which burned but a short time before a couple of kegs of powder which were under the floor exploded and tore the house to the grounds.

Such were most of them at heart; they would face you and talk Unionism and all such stuff while at the same time they were ready and only watching for a favorable opportunity to kill you.

After learning all they could the boys returned to camp with the news that an attack might be expected soon, so preparations were at once made for the same.

The line of pickets was strengthened, the water casks in the Fort were all filled, provisions were taken from the depot and stored in the Fort; but nothing of note happened till the 31st.

We had been ordered to evacuate and at four in the morning we started our caissons and all ammunition chests, but the ones on the limbers of the guns, with the sick and convalescents were put on the cars for Nashville; the rest of us were to await the train from Huntsville bringing the 10th Wis. which regiment had been guarding the M. & C. R. R. between that place and Stevenson for some time.

We then took the mountain road across the Cumberland while the train was to take what supplies were left and the remaining sick and leave for Nashville.

News came in at 10 a. m. that a large number of Cavalry was close to town so a small party of cavalry from our Co. started out to see what was up with one of our Howitzers commanded by Serg. English [Cpl. John J. English] in the rear of the company.

After leaving the place about a mile a party of cavalry was discovered and they immediately opened on them with their piece, sending a messenger back at the same time for another.

They kept them at bay for some time and drove them to the main body which was marching rapidly forward to the engagement.

On seeing the great number marching on to us, our Captain ordered his brave little band of soldiers back to the front; they followed up the attack and we were soon engaged in fighting in earnest.

The engagement lasted from 11 a. m. till 3 p. m. when our ammunition was nearly all shot away, and we were ordered by Gen. Buell to leave the place.

During the time we were fighting, the train from Huntsville arrived and everything being ready we loaded what stores could be put on the cars, destroying the remainder and left the place forsaken.

In this fight nothing but our battery was engaged and we didn't lose a single man; our

Captain later learned from a reliable citizen that their loss was four killed and fifty six wounded, which did very well considering the circumstances.

Had it not been for Buell's stringent order the Infantry would have gone out and given them a few of Uncle Sam's pills, but as it was we were obliged to obey orders.

The Reb Cavalry followed in our rear for seven miles when two companies from the 10th Wis. came to a halt and gave them three or four rounds when they dispersed and troubled us no more that day.

We traveled fourteen miles that night; here some guerillas had torn up the R. R. track and the train ran off, but did no material damage, although it took us until noon the next day to get the locomotive on and repair the track.

One of our baggage wagons broke that night and was left with all its baggage and while we were waiting repair of the road the Captain sent its driver back to recover it., but he never returned – we heard afterward he was captured.

On the night of the 2nd of Sept. we reached the foot of the Cumberland Mts. and fully 500 negroes followed us from Stevenson, men, women, and children, and a more disgusting sight I never saw in the Union Army.

If I ever felt like deserting it was then, but I bore it with patience as I have many a thing since I enlisted.

We had good success in crossing the mountains and reached Tullahoma, Ala. [TN] that night, a small inland town situated on the N. & C. R. R. with about 1500 inhabitants.

There is a nice stream called Goose Creek running through one end of the place which affords water the year round.

There is very little enterprise among the people, altho' the country on this side of the mountain to the above named place is mostly good productive land.

On the opposite side very little farming is carried on as it is so stony and rolling.

At Tullahoma we overtook Gen. Smith who had 10,000 men marching for Nashville and next morning joined him and on the evening of the 5th we reached Murfeesboro where we overtook several more divisions which were all on their way back to Kentucky for the purpose of routing Bragg who was trying to get in the rear and cut us off from Nashville on the night of the 6th.[5]

We reached Nashville at 12 m. and remained two days, during which time we got the rest of our battery, that was started on the cars from Stevenson, together and considered ourselves once more a complete battery.

J. Blink returned from LaPorte and came to us here, bringing me several letters from home with several necessary articles of clothing which were all welcome and he gave me great consolation.

We left six of the company at this place on account of sickness.

As I neglected a description of this place on our way down I will now fill a few lines of my journal with a very brief description.

Situated on the south side of the Cumberland [River] it contains about 14000 inhabitants mostly Americans who are fully two thirds Secesh, but I think Union feeling is becoming more prevalent every day.

---

[5]Officers mentioned are Brig. General William S. Smith (4th Division, Second Army Corps, Army of the Ohio) and General Braxton Bragg, Commander of the Army of Mississippi, CSA.

A splendid Court House stands in the public square, as fine a one as I have ever seen, and educational advantages are good.

There are some of the most beautiful dwellings in the borders of the city there can be found in the south.

Edgeville is on the opposite side of the river from Nashville and has 1000 inhabitants and is much handsomer than N. V.

On the 9th our line of march was taken up for Bowling Green, Ky. where we arrived on the morning of the 11th and I met an old friend, E. Simpson, and had a long talk over the past and old times.

On the 15th we learned that Bragg had cut the L. & N. R. R. at Green River and thus destroyed our communication with Louisville and intended giving us battle there.

Every preparation was made for battle and on the 16th we were ordered forward.

I was taken sick here and was not able to be with the battery until within eight miles of Mumfordsville [Munfordville] and then not able for duty, but as a battle was expected I was on hand and would have participated in it had Buell, who was at our head, moved on, but here he lay three days within eight miles of Bragg, with a third more men, only for him to get out of the way and such a dissatisfaction among the men never prevailed in any army.

When we moved on the night of the third day, Bragg was gone with everything toward Louisville.

I will here describe Mumfordsville [sic] and Green River Bridge there.

A small town of about 1000 inhabitants situated on the north side of the river; this river is not navigable for large boats, small ones often come and go as far as the bridge which is one of the finest structures in the U. S. built mostly of iron at a cost of $275,000.

It is 170 feet above the surface of the water and has been one of the greatest curiosities to the soldiers that has ever been seen while in this department.

Since the war broke out it has been entirely destroyed and seriously damaged several times.[6]

Our march was continued after Bragg the next day and at noon we took dinner (if such it may be called) at the old stamping ground at Battle Creek which looked as natural as life.

---

[6]Munfordville was the site of an important rail bridge (Louisville and Nashville RR) across the Green River. After beating back a determined attack by Confederates under Colonel James Chalmers on Sept. 14th, the Union garrison under Colonel J. T. Wilder was attacked again on the 16th by Bragg and forced to surrender. Buell's approach from the south (and lack of food for the rebel troops) forced Bragg to evacuate Munfordville on the 20th.

The ground was not cultivated but was barren as a desert.

The corduroy that we had made roads out of had been taken up and laid into fence, but Bragg and our army finished them the second time – the land will be fit for nothing in the vicinity of this old camp for years to come – if it ever is.

All the timber fit for wood within two miles has been consumed and what they will do for fencing when they come to fence up their farms is hard telling.

Within a half mile of our old Camp is a beautiful cave in which I spent a half day last New Year, looking at the many curiosities that are to be admired by all who see them.[7]

There are two entrances half a mile apart, the distance through is something more as it is considerably winding.

In it are many chambers filled with sights worth seeing.

I came very near losing my way but succeeded after some time in finding the open air and I then returned to my tent to worry the rest of the day away as best I could.

After resting here we again moved forward, nothing more transpiring worth mention until the next day when our advance attacked the rear guard of Bragg's forces, killed several men and over twenty horses.

We kept pushing on with such speed that Brayton [Braxton Bragg], not wishing to bring on an engagement, turned off the Louisville pike at Elizabethtown and made his way in the direction of Bardstown.

We were kept marching on toward Louisville.

Elizabethtown is a beautiful town situated at the junction of the L. N. and Bardstown pikes, contains about 800 inhabitants and is noted for the productive country which surrounds it.

On the 25th we took dinner at West Point, a small town of 1400 inhabitants, situated on the South bank of the Ohio eight miles from Louisville.

While we were resting here two boats came in from Louisville with supplies which were distributed among the half starved soldiers.

For three weeks previous to this we had had scarcely anything to eat as our communication had been cut off for near two weeks.

We started from here at 3 p. m. that day with considerably more energy than when we arrived and marched till 10 that night and stopped, as we supposed for the night.

---

[7]The cave mentioned here is in the general area of Mammoth Cave, located a few miles southwest of Munfordville. Many caves occur in the region, and the identity of the one described here is uncertain.

It as 12 o'clock when we got our horses tended to and our coffee and crackers swallowed and were making preparations for a few hours rest, when an order came that we had to make Louisville that night.

In a half hour we were again on our way and so near worn out that many would fall asleep traveling.

At sunrise next morning we found ourselves once more formed in a park in the city of Louisville, and for the first time in ten months in sight of our native state, Indiana.

This was the morning of the 26th and we had then been marching with the exception of a very few days since the 31st of August, most of the time night and day, often not having three hours rest out of twenty four.

The first two days after our arrival there was but little stir; the majority were well satisfied to stay in camp and rest their weary limbs, as they were confident their stay was short.

We were all furnished new clothes and every necessary article needed in the battery and they had been greatly needed for some time: in fact, everything was furnished us but pay, which had been overdue for some time.[8]

On the 29th of Sept. Gen. Rousseau's[9] Div. in which our battery was) appeared on a grand review and were marched through all the principal streets of the city.

The General was much pleased with the discipline of both officers and privates and it was said of him that his command was the best organized and best drilled of any review had ever been in the place.

After spending most of the afternoon showing ourselves we returned to camp and found that rumors were afloat that we were to march in the morning; this we dreaded, as we wanted our pay in order to purchase a few necessary articles which had been needed for some time.

Preparations were going on all night for our departure, but I laid down my blankets and rested easy for such I needed as I was near worn out.

Our camp, while in this place, was on Broadway nearly opposite the L. & N. R. R. depot.

This is the finest street in the city, the inhabitants mostly men of wealth who have erected some of the most magnificent buildings for dwellings I have ever seen.

---

[8]Muster records show September 1, 1862, as the last date of pay. Apparently, Hupp had not received this payment in late September.

[9]Brigadier General Lovell Rousseau led the 3rd Division under McCook's 1st Army Corps. This division suffered the greatest number of casualties among Union units involved in the battle of Perryville in which Hupp was wounded.

Louisville contains 60,000 inhabitants mostly of American descent.

On the morning of the 30th of Sept. Lieut. Allen, who had been absent on a sick furlough for some time returned to the battery.

His section was all glad to see him return as we all fared much better when he was with us.

On the first of Oct. Buell started for Bragg through Kentucky.

We left in the Third Division, 9th Brigade, commanded by Gen. Rosseau [sic].

We all thought him the best man we had been under.

Little did we think the morning we started that we were going any further than the suburbs of the city to camp, but our minds were changed in a few hours.

That day we made sixteen miles, went in camp on a Secesh farm, and had orders to burn all rails we could make use of.

The General remarked that he had no mercy for the D. S. and their rails but he would not burn those of Union men.

We left Louisville with nothing to eat and no commissary wagon and many of the boys suffered in consequence of it.

I started out and got my supper a mile distant and left a piece of bread in my haversack for by breakfast, but some lucky fellow nabbed it while I was gone and my breakfast came up minus with the rest.

We travelled on that day to Taylorsville; the afternoon was very rainy and as we had no tents we were obliged to lay in the rain all night with but very little grumbling.

Our commissary team reached us that night at 12 o'clock and since we had had nothing to eat but what little we begged and drafted since leaving Louisville, tired as the boys were they crawled out from under their blankets and got a cracker and a piece of raw bacon and went to bed as contented as many at home with their well filled tables.

The sun came out next day and dried up the ground; we moved over the river and went in camp as we supposed to remain several days.

Taylorsville is a fine little place with about 500 inhabitants, the country from Louisville here is beautiful and well adapted for farming.

The people are all enterprising but a good share of them Secesh.

There is plenty of timber of nearly all kinds to supply necessary wants.

On that evening (the 3rd) we were ordered out on a scare a lay in line of battle all night, as it was said Bragg was in a few miles of us with the intention of making an attack, but it all proved to be a scare.

Next morning we marched at 9 o'clock and reached Bloomfield where we went into camp.

Nearly every fence from Taylorsville here was torn down by the advance who were doing some fighting all the while.

We remained until 10 a. m. next day at Bloomfield, situated in the midst of a beautiful country, and with 600 inhabitants and is said to [be] a Union town.

We marched ten miles with but little opposition and on the 6th we went into camp on the bank of Goose River.

We had considerable trouble getting water here as the bank was so steep a horse could scarcely climb it.

Here the country became more hilly and rough, the timber scrubby and mostly oak, the enterprise of the people much less, and it looked about twenty five miles from nowhere (how far it is I never asked.)

On the 7th we reached Maxville [Mackville], traveling through rough country all day, but found many Union people on the road greeting as we passed in an encouraging manner.

If all in the north were that way we'd soon have peace, but as it is it will be some time before the war is brought to a close.

Maxville [sic] is quite an enterprising little place of about 400, mostly Secesh. I was told by a gentleman that called himself Union who lived in the vicinity.

Here we butchered a beef and I stayed up late to roast some for the morrow, for was all we had to eat.

I happened to be lucky enough to find several pieces of crackers lying in the dirt which gave satisfaction to my hungry stomach.

It was a hard matter to find water in this vicinity and what our coffee was made of had a green scum over the top a whole inch thick, but it was all there was and of course we would use it in preference to our going without.

The way we managed it was to boil it and keep the scum off for some time before putting in the coffee: it would in this way do very well.

On the morning of the 8th we marched toward Perryville at sunrise.

It was not the day for our division to be in advance but as it was composed of old troops and a fight was expected that day Rousseau took the advance.

The cavalry and two pieces of artillery left some time before the infantry.

We had marched but a few miles when we heard the cannonading some distance in advance and we were confident that sharp skirmishing was going on ahead.

This was kept up for some time, and still we moved on, not anticipating a battle.

As we drew near Perryville, the cannonading became plainer and it was evident the advance had gone as far as they could: this was in two miles of Perryville.

By the time our battery got up Capt. Loomis[10] had all his guns at work, which were replied to with much vigor.

Here within eighty rods of where they were firing, we stopped and fed our horses, awaiting orders as the firing that was going on was merely trying their position.

At 11 a. m. we were ordered forward and in a corn field about 40 rods from the road, opened fire at once, which was kept up for two hours and was replied to with great vigor.

At the end of that time their batteries were silenced and a shout rung out along our line like distant thunder.

By this time our line was formed which was said to be three miles long; on the left of us was Gen. Jackson's Division[11], composed mostly of new troops; next came Rousseau's veterans which were composed mostly of troops which had been in service from the commencement of the war and these two divisions were the only ones that had much to do with the engagement.

But a short time elapsed before the enemy could be seen at a mile distant with their bayonets glistening in the sun (for it was a beautiful day) and advancing toward us in three columns deep.

Everything was put in readiness to receive them and at about this juncture their batteries opened a cross fire which seemed to make the earth quake, this fire from the enemy was doing much damage but we could only stand as best we could, our line reserving their fire until their infantry got within thirty rods, we then opened on them and finally after about fifteen minutes they fell back.

The came up this way the third time and did their utmost to take our batteries but met with the same results each time.

The third charge they made on our battery they came within twenty yards, but were forced to fall back with half their number.

Our battery was then ordered to fall back and we left with one man killed and four horses, also four men wounded.

We fell back on the opposite side of the road about fifty rods from our former position.

---

[10]Captain Cyrus 0. Loomis, Michigan Light Artillery, 1st Battery of the 17th Brigade. Hupp was in the 9th Brigade.

[11]Brigadier General James S. Jackson, 10th Division, killed at Perryville.

We had but just got in battery and ordered to lay on the ground, holding our fire for close action, as our ammunition was near gone, when I had to help take one of the lead horses out that had been shot with a minie ball.

The bullets and shells came thicker and faster here than I ever want to see them again.

We had just got this horse out when one of mine was shot with a minie ball which reached his heart, killing him instantly.

The battle was general and raging now all along the line, and it was plain to be seen that the enemy was too strong for us.

Reinforcements had been sent for which were within four miles, but were refused, as the General Commander [Buell] said it couldn't be possible that any musketry fighting was going on.

Gen. Rousseau sent another message for reinforcements and stated if they weren't sent his whole division would be killed, but the traitor in reply said he brought the fight on and might end it the best way he could, he would not send a man.

It would have been a very easy matter for Buell to have turned the left wing with the men he had lying idle and ruined their army what could not have been captured, but he was too much of a traitor for this and our men had to suffer the consequences.

When my horse got shot I was lying close by him on the same side.

I immediately called one of the boys to help take him out and run around to the near side in order to unbuckle the breast strap.

I had it but half unbuckled when a shell from the enemy struck me on the left arm and passing on, struck the ammunition chest, exploded and caused the cartridges in the chest to explode.

It was all done in an instant and resulted in the instant death of F. Eric [Ehrich] who was struck in the head with a piece of shell and the wounding of four others, C. Miller, burnt, A Farg [Forry], arm broken and badly burnt on head and face; A Pettit, lip cut and wounded slightly in the head and myself cut in the left arm, right arm, and face.

When the chest blew up it took me in the air about ten feet.

I had my thoughts during the operation and concluded I was torn to pieces, but after striking the ground and lying there about three minutes, I jumped up and saw that I was badly wounded, my clothes were all torn off, and the burn from the powder set me near crazy.

The smoke of the explosion was so thick I could see nothing and as I remember the head surgeon passed us before the battle and told us where the hospital would be found and to come there if we got wounded, I thought it the best policy for me to reach them as soon as possible for fear the loss of blood would weaken me so I would be unable to walk.

Leaving everything, (for I was in such pain I cared for nothing) I started in their direction.

The balls flew around me like hail as I made my steps back but lttle did I heed them.

At one time a twelve pound shell exploded within a few feet of me, tearing up the ground, in a fearful manner, and I had not gone more than a quarter of a mile when I felt so exhausted I could hardly stand.

Here a young man gave me a canteen of water which revived me and I again started and soon reached the first hospital which was a small log house within a quarter [mile] of the left of our line of battle.

Shell and shot were passing all around the house and it afterward struck by a shell, killing two men.

I went in and tried to have my wounds dressed, but the surgeon was so frightened that he knew nothing, as he wanted to take my arm off when there was no bone injured.

I left him at once and found another hospital but a short distance in a farm house: here there were about 300 wounded.

Such a sight I never beheld before and never wish to again.

I saw there was no chance here and as I felt as though I could get a little farther, concluded to find another place; the loss of blood by this time had made me so weak I could hardly stand.

When I reached the road (which was but a short distance from the house) I fell and could go no farther.

A few minutes passed in loneliness and I had given up to die and cared for nothing – I was almost crazy through pain.

After I had laid here a short time, J. Countz [Kurtz] who had been sent after water for the boys in the battery came along, recognized me at once, got off and poured some water on my head and face, gave me a drink and with some help got me on his horse and started for the hospital a half mile distant.

We had gone but a short distance when we came to a man that has a tub full of whiskey poured out of a barrel and was giving it to the wounded.

Countz [sic] handed me a quart basin full and I would have drunk every bit of it had they not taken it away from me; but for all that I drank near the quart and felt no effects from it any more than it gave me a new spirit.

We pressed on and soon came to a hospital which was a farmhouse.

I was here but a short time when Countz [sic] brought a surgeon who dressed my arm.

I felt but little easier as the greater share of the pain was from the burns, but in about a half an hour I got some sweet oil on my face which eased the pain.

Countz [sic] got me a quilt from the lady of the house which I put around me and lay down under a tree: he then left me and returned to the battery.

By this time the musketry had died away and nothing could be heard but the booming of a cannon about every five minutes, mingled with the groans of the wounded.

I was eager to hear how the battle had terminated so in the course of two or three hours he returned and stayed with me the rest of the night, telling me all he knew concerning the battle – that all my things had fallen into the hands of the enemy and that the loss in the battery was two killed, sixteen wounded and twenty horses killed and that the rebels held the field.[12]

He thought the fight would open in the morning, as preparations were being made for the same.

Morning came and nothing could be heard but the peal of a cannon every few minutes and it was evident the enemy has retreated.

Orders came that all those that could must get back about two miles toward Maxville [sic] to a large meeting house that had been converted into a hospital.

Our company ambulance happened to come along about this time and I got in and was taken back and lay under a large oak tree till 3 o'clock p. m. without any thing to eat since I was wounded.

At this time Countz [sic] came back and made me some coffee which revived and made quite a change in my feelings; I laid under this tree two nights with but the one quilt, the weather was quite cold and chilling and in consequence many suffered.

On the second morning Andrew Pettitt [sic] who had been slightly wounded came to me and wanted to take me to a barn where our boys had been collected together about a mile away, so he got a citizen's horse and helped me on: we reached the place about 10 a. m. just as it commenced raining hard.

There was plenty of straw in the shed on which I laid down almost exhausted: it was not long before the boys brought me some sheep broth and a cracker which I did not refuse.

---

[12]Officially, the 5th Battery sustained 2 killed, 13 wounded, and 6 captured or missing (Hafendorfer, 1991).

Along in the afternoon I had my wounds dressed and they had become very painful, especially my left arm.

I lay in this shed till the morning of the 13th when I got in an ambulance and rode to Perryville where I found a train of wagons going to Louisville and all that were able to ride were requested to go.

The surgeon in charge said we would only have twenty miles to ride in the wagons, the rest of the way we would have the cars.

I studied some time and concluded it was best for me to go: I thought I would stop at a farmhouse if I was unable to stand the ride.

C. V. [W.] Miller and I selected an open wagon, fixed ourselves as comfortable as we could and soon a train of ninety wagons were off for Louisville, a distance of ninety miles.

I had got a blanket of W. M. [F.] Marshall which made me comfortable and kept me from suffering with the cold.

We stopped at Shephardsville at 10 p. m. for the night, a distance of fifteen miles from Perryville and my sufferings were more than I can express, but I had made up my mind to reach L_______ if I lived.

There was nothing issued to us and all I had that day was one cracker and I had not slept a wink since the battle so of course I was well nigh exhausted, so when morning came I was glad to see it for I lay rolling in pain all night.

Charley got me a cup of coffee and a cracker which served me for that day while we travelled on and reached Bardstown about 1 p. m. when the citizens brought us out some coffee.

We were to stay here till 4 o'clock and during the time a lady came around dressing what wounds she could and I had her put a new cloth on my arm which was in a fair state of mortification.

Bardstown is a handsomely located town with 2400 inhabitants situated in the midst of a beautiful farming country and the people are said to be about half Secesh and the balance on the fence, ready to fall either way.

The greater part of the country between Perryville and here is rough and rolling but there are many good farms scattered along in different places and through this country I see the best production of stock, especially cattle and horses I have seen in many a day.

We left at the appointed time and travelled eight miles that night, then rations were issued to Charlie M. [C. W. Miller] who prepared us some coffee and meat which we took hold of with a good will.

I was very restless and did not sleep a wink during the following night: after getting some coffee in the morning we pulled out and had thirty two miles to make Louisville that day.

My wound became very sore, not being washed or dressed but once since that fight: I could hardly stand to ride and felt very much exhausted; in fact I felt as though ten cents would buy me, but Charley got me a drink of wine which gave me new courage and shortly the train moved on.

The day was hot and sultry, the roads very dusty, and at times the teams would trot, which caused the dust to rise so one could not see the team that was attached to the wagon.

I felt as though I would have to give up as my arm became so painful, but my courage was strengthened by a little whiskey we had purchased at Bardstown and as the weather became cooler toward evening I bore it as patiently as possible.

Seven a. m. found us at Louisville, but not to stop as we anticipated: we soon learned our destination was New Albany, Ind. and I, for one, felt satisfied to wait patiently for the sake of reaching my native state.

New Albany is five miles from Louisville on the opposite side of the Ohio and we crossed the pontoon bridge and arrived there at 8:30.

The hospitals had all been awaiting our arrival and were in readiness to administer to our wants in short order.

The train stopped at Headquarters which was then at No. 4 Hospital.

The train I was in was near the advance: it was not long, therefore, until I was out and waiting orders.

All that could walk were taken to the different hospitals and those that were unable stopped at No. 4.

Dr. Sloan headed a number, among which were Charley and I, and took us to No. 1, which is but a short distance from No. 4, here we were conducted to Ward 3 where we found comfortable beds.

By this time I had become much fatigued, but could not sleep notwithstanding I had not slept four hours since the battle: in by a short time we were furnished a good supper, something we had not been used to for many a day.

I was hungry and eat hearty after which I felt myself a new man.

Before 12 o'clock that night my wounds were dressed and they were found to be in a mortifying condition: another day's delay and the amputation of my arm would have been necessary to have saved my life.

Morphine was given me and I rested several hours that night, and felt much revived next morning.

The nurses in that ward were named Wilson and C. Brood and the treatment I received from Wilson while there I shall never forget.

Charley M. will also be remembered for the services he rendered me from Perryville here without which I can't see how my wound would have escaped mortification: all that saved it was the administering of cold water, he being the only one who could get around.

News had reached home that I was mortally wounded, to correct this, I had Charley write the next day stating my condition, that I was out of danger that might come from the wound, unless erysipelas [streptococcus infection] should set in.

I will now return to the battery which I left on the battlefield.

As was suspected, Bragg had retreated during the night, of the memorable 8th with our Army following as far as Crab Orchard, Ky. capturing many stragglers and a vast amount of stores.

Here Buell deemed it prudent to lead his army toward Nashville as it was the intention of the rebels to march and take the place to render any succor to the small party that had been left there under General Negly.[13]

After a tedious march our Army reached the place about the middle of November and opened communication once more to Louisville.

He found Negly's men in a starving condition: they had had scarcely anything to eat for near a month, but as Negly was a true patriot, he would sacrifice all rather than give up his post.

Out captain [Peter Simonson] left the company at Bowling Green and came to see his boys here and at Louisville and take some necessary articles to the battery.

I was never any more pleased to see any of my folks than him.

He saw that I was well cared for and after making out my descriptive roll, I bid him adieu.

On his return to the battery he took two Napoleon guns in exchange for his smooth bores and twenty two horses: this was about the 22nd of Nov.

He brought me a trunk full of eatables which lasted for a month.

On the 30th, with much regret, he took my hand to bid me adieu, probably for the last time, but I trust not, however the fate of a soldier, surrounded as they are with many dangers in such a life, can look ahead and picture himself one of the most miserable of human nature.

The result of the battle of Perryville was on our side, 3000 killed and wounded; the enemy lost according to their statement, 3000 killed and a great number more wounded than our number.[14]

---

[13]Brigadier General James Negly held Nashville with a small garrison force. Hupp is correct in his assessment of Bragg's intentions to attack Nashville, and Buell's determination to counter that move. However, Bragg later changed his mind and retreated to Knoxville.

[14]Casualties for Buell's army were 845 killed, 2851 wounded, and 515 captured or missing for a total of 4211 losses. Bragg lost 510 killed, 2635 wounded, and 251 captured or missing, for a total of 3396. In both cases, incomplete reporting suggests that casualties were actually higher than reported. As at Antietam in the east, neither army could claim a decisive victory at Perryville (Hafendorfer, 1991).

It was considered a draw battle as they held half of the field during the night, the cause of their loss being more than ours was their having four lines while we had but one.

It was said men were never known to do better fighting than Rousseau's Division.

Many of the new troops on our left became demoralized and ran like wild sheep; such was the case in nearly every regiment under Gen. Terrill.[15]

For the first month after I came to the hospital my sufferings were great, very seldom would I sleep over one hour during the night and often not shut my eyes.

Charley got along remarkably with his burnt face, but the chills took hold of him which kept him reduced very much but he finally became master of the disease and again recovered to more than his former weight.

* * * * *

It is now the first of March [1863].

Time has passed rapidly since I came here.

I have been able to run around through town some time, but my arm is still weak, pains me considerable at night.

The battery has passed through another hard fight at Murfreesborough [sic], Tenn. [Battle of Stones River] where their loss was much greater than at Perryville.

After the battle the captain [Simonson] came up to this place on his way home on a twenty day furlough, looking well and feeling proud of the conduct of the boys that were engaged.

It is now the 10th of March, time is passing rapidly; I have been at Headquarters and found I need never return unless I want to.

New Albany is the worst laid out town I ever saw and is noted for its many foundries and shops built for the construction of boats.

There have been several boats finished and gone since I came here.

The gunboat, Tuscumbia, bearing five guns which was built here during the past year at a cost of $250,000 left here with her crew for Vicksburg the fore part of last week.[16]

The town contains about 14,000 inhabitants, mostly American de-

---

[15]Brigadier General William R. Terrill of the 33rd Brigade, 3rd Division (Hupp's division) was killed in the battle.

[16]The strategic Mississippi River city of Vicksburg was finally taken by U. S. Grant's forces on July 4, 1863, after a two-month siege. Gunboats played a significant role in the battle for Vicksburg. New Albany was a major ship building center.

scent and is besides a great place for girls, among whom are some of the beauties of the land.

Soldiers are, as a general thing, treated with much respect by them: a number have found partners for life, which gives rise to a considerable dissatisfaction among the young men of the city.

The country in the immediate vicinity is very broken; the soil sandy and of very poor quality, but after leaving the river five or six miles, the surface becomes more level and productive, the farms are improved and stocked in grand style.

Before the war broke out this was considered one of the best places for education in the state, now the buildings are all taken for hospitals, but as good care is taken of them the schools are likely to be as successful in the future as in the past.

Besides the River Navigation there is the benefit of the L. N. A. & C. R. R. which does a vast amount of business

They have splendid buildings for depot purposes.

It is now the 19th of March and I find myself in the hospital acting in the capacity of nurse, which business I have been at since the 12th of March; the work is not hard and much better than doing nothing as I am not able for field service.

There is at the present time a jolly lot of boys in this ward, who were wounded at Murfreesborough [sic] on the 1st of Jan. 1863[17]; they are all getting along fine and need little attention.

St. Patrick's Day was kept in memory by the Catholics of this place; they had worship most of the day.

The churches here are worthy of much praise; a person need not hesitate for want of a doctrine suitable for their belief for every denomination teaching the Christian religion can be found.

The Baptists have met with great success this winter as well as the Methodists: the former had forty new members and are still keeping their meetings up.

I have come very near joining several times, but something has kept me from it.

March 26. Nothing of importance has transpired since this month commenced.

Morgan[18] is said to be on his way to Louisville; the citizens are all in a

[17]The Battle for Murfreesboro (Stones River) took place from Dec. 31, 1862, to Jan. 3, 1863, 12 weeks after Perryville. Union armies, now commanded by Gen. Rosecrans, forced the retreat of Bragg's forces, but not before both sides suffered staggering losses: over 35,000 total casualties.

[18]Confederate raider John Hunt Morgan led an expedition into Kentucky from

bustle; considerable of the government property is being removed to this side of the river; 10,000 reinforcements are to be in Louisville this evening en route for the army of the Ohio which is in command of Gen. Burnside, who lately superseded Gen. Wright.

Gen. Burnside will probably reinforce Gen. Rosencranz [sic] who is in command of the Army of the Cumberland now at Murfreesborough [sic], Tenn.

The reinforcements are from the Army of the Potomac.

April 2. Since I last wrote in my journal nothing unusual has transpired.

Dr. Fry has issued an order prohibiting the sale of intoxicating liquors to soldiers in violation of which all spirits belonging to the violators are to be confiscated.

The order appears to trouble a great many, who think it will be too beneficial to the privates whose families in many cases are greatly in need of money to prevent starvation.

The late order preventing the selling of fire arms and ammunitions was violated here last Sunday morning by a hardware dealer and the order was carried out to the letter: all fire arms and ammunition in this shop were confiscated.

We were greeted once more on the 29th of March for two months and I have not concluded as yet what to do with the small amount I received, I think I will keep it till next pay day.

The weather has been with the exception of two cold disagreeable days (the last day of March and the 1st day of this month) quite pleasant with but little falling weather, reminding me more of spring than any weather this spring.

The panorama of the War is being shown here this week: I have not been to see it yet, but intend to go this evening providing it don't rain.

April 8. Nothing of importance has transpired since my last writing: I have occupied my leisure in opening a set of books.

Nearly every evening of the past two weeks has found me at the Baptist Church.

The weather is cold for this time of year; spring is no farther advanced than two weeks ago.

Sunday last I attended services at the First Presbyterian Church and found myself well entertained: it is the best finished church in the place.

July 2nd to 26th, when he was captured in New Lisbon, Ohio. He had violated Bragg's orders not to cross the Ohio River.

In the forenoon of Easter Sunday I attended the German Catholic and there was a large attendance.

There are some of the most splendid paintings in this church I ever saw.

I had a letter from the company last week: they are all in fine spirits and good health and anticipate a battle soon.

Their guns are to be changed for the James Rifle and they are to run a full battery in a short time; several changes and promotions have taken place.

My attention was greatly attracted the other day on visiting the City Nursery carried on by Smith and Brown whose hot house is the finest piece of structure my eyes have ever met.

They have eight orange trees filled with the delicious fruit; flowers of all kinds could there be found, many in full bloom; the India Rubber tree, the first specimen I ever saw; the vermillion was there in full bloom.

After viewing all the scenery we returned to the hospital with the intention of returning in a short time.

April 10. Weather has the appearance of rain, and we are expecting news from Charleston daily; the morning paper states the bombardment of the place by DuPont and Hunter has commenced, but I have little faith in the expedition yet.[19]

Last night the Baptist preachers of this place insulted the soldiers that were present and something is expected tonight.

Campbell's minstrels entertained large audiences here last night and the night before but I concluded it wouldn't pay and stayed in the ward and occupied the time in playing checkers and reading and writing.

One of my old acquaintances that was wounded at Perryville and laid here in the hospital till he got well and enlisted in the marine brigade com'd by Col. Ellett came back last evening.

The company he went in broke up at St. Louis and he thought it best to report here after going home for fear he had not been mustered out of the three year service.

Dr. Fry intends giving him transportation to his regiment tomorrow. His name is Dillon Turner of the 105th Ohio.

The patients in the various hospitals in town are being well cared for, but few among them are in a dangerous condition.

---

[19]After scoring major victories along the Atlantic coast, Rear Admiral Samuel F. DuPont was ordered to attack Charleston, SC, in April 1963 in concert with a land assault by Major General David Hunter. The attack failed, just as Hupp anticipated.

They are daily expecting to fill these hospitals from Nashville, preparatory to the expected battle in that vicinity.[20]

April 8 [11?]. Weather warm and pleasant, with indications of rain.

Yesterday (Sunday) I was housed up most of the day; at 12 went down and saw the baptism administered to five who made profession in the Baptist Church during the revival in the above church; there have been over forty converts.

April 13. Last evening I went out to the Cemetery and had a pleasant walk; the grounds were thronged with people, both citizens and soldiers, as it is becoming very fashionable for the soldiers to have beaux in this place, which is not a hard task if one conducts himself in a respectable manner.

During the time we were there we had the pleasure of becoming acquainted with three young ladies who were familiar with the grounds, which made our ramble much more interesting.

Sunday evening I stayed in the ward as I felt quite unwell; this was the first Sabbath eve for the past three months I missed going to church.

We got news last evening of the destruction of the gunboat Keokuk, off Fort Sumter, commanded by Capt. Rhind.

It looks rather dark on our side at that place, but our officers feel confident of success.

April 14 The weather speaks rain within a few hours this morning.

Twelve men were started to their regiments this morning from this hospital all belonging to the Army of the Cumberland.

April 17. Weather warm and pleasant.

News of the abandonment of the taking of Charleston S. C. reached us last night and many are sorrowfully disappointed, but I expected nothing else.

It is now rumored that Iron Clad Fleet is to move to the Mississippi to participate in the taking of Vicksburg. The returns of the spring election are very encouraging to the Union Cause.[21]

Charley M. [Miller] and I had a pleasant walk yesterday evening; on

---

[20]Occupied Nashville remained safely in Union hands and was never seriously threatened that year. Bragg was kept busy by Gens. Rosecrans and George H. Thomas at Chickamauga and Chattanooga (September 1863). Nashville was later attacked (Dec. 15-16, 1864) by Confederate forces under John Bell Hood who not only failed to take the city, but was routed by Union forces under General Thomas.

[21]This refers to state elections (mostly gubernatorial) in spring 1863. The Union war effort was being challenged by "copperheads" and other anti-war elements who sought compromise with the South. Results were mostly narrowly favorable to Republican candidates who, like Lincoln, favored pursuing the war to victory.

our way we came to a lot in which a man was ploughing for corn and I proposed to plough a round which was consented to by him.

This was the first ploughing I had done since leaving home.

We reached the hosp. just before supper and were blessed with a good night's rest.

Our head cook was changed yesterday and it was easy to distinguish it as there was much better cooking the next meal.

I had a letter from A. Petit [Pettit], a comrade in my Co. last eve; he states they are all well and are to receive pay in a day or two.

The battery is to be supplied with James rifles in the course of a week.[22]

April 13 [18?]. Weather cloudy and cold: we were obliged to put fire in the stove last night for the first time in a week.

Charley M. had a letter from the Co. this morning which left them in good fighting spirits.

The 3rd section is formed which has not been running since the Stone [sic] River fight.

Last evening a company of us went to hear the Continental Old Folks which I pronounced good and well worth my quarter; they displayed the oddities of modern singing: there were twelve in number each wearing a peculiar dress, worn by the upper 10s forty to 125 years ago.

There were two Misses Page (sisters) about sixteen or eighteen years of age who are hard to be excelled in singing.

War news of importance today – the running of the blockade at Vicksburg by seven of our gunboats with the loss of one transport (the Henry Clay) is cheering news, and this morning's paper stated the evacuation of that place has commenced.

Should this be so the Mississippi will soon be open and I have some hopes the General Commander [U. S. Grant] will make his words true by coming in possession of the place this month.

Night before last a private belonging to some Penn. regiment and employed on the hospital boat, Woodford, (which is being fitted out for the Mississippi Marine brigade at this place) fell through the hatchway cracking his skull and causing his death in a few hours.

Little did he think a few hours previous, enjoying good health as he apparently was, his time for this world was so limited; but such are the fortunes of the human body.

---

[22]Patented in 1856 by Gen. Charles T. James, "James projectiles" resembled modern artillery shells and had ridges and slits in the base to take rifling in the cannon barrel. James rifles came in many calibers including some smooth bore models modified with rifling to take James' highly accurate exploding shell.

We also have the intelligence of Gen. Foster's relief at Little Washington, N. C.[23]

May 4. For some time past the weather has been rainy. The day appointed for the National Worship by the President was well respected here, it being a beautiful day and all the business houses closed and the churches well filled and attended.

Services at the Hospital at 9 a. m. and at the Centenary Church at 10. Rev. Cushman and Hill were the speakers and did great honor to the occasion.

Saturday we received the news that Hooker had crossed the Rappahannock and a great battle was being fought, and a report that Rosecrans has been attacked and is doing some hard fighting: the latter is not much credited.[24]

Every paper that makes its appearance sees no rest until the news is revealed to the ward.

Bank's success at Grand Lake, La. was read Saturday.[25]

May 4. I have been employed writing letters: have just finished four and have one more to write today.

Saturday last I did the hardest day's work since I've been here: we had to whitewash and scour the woodwork and mop the floors: Wednesday we have another hard day's work to scour the windows.

Charley and I were out walking on the streets and while passing by one of the market houses saw a lady fall down on the pavement a few steps ahead and I knew she had taken a fit; we picked her up, carried her into a drug store close by and she soon began to revive; before leaving we found she was a milliner and had been subject to fits for some time.

We had several other adventures before going home but I will now

---

[23]This refers to the siege of Washington, NC, the Tar River gateway to lush agricultural resources coveted by both sides. Confederate General A. P. Hill kept General John G. Foster bottled up in Washington while his foraging teams collected food stuffs for Lee's army.

[24]The "great battle" was at Chancellorsville, VA, (May 1-4) and pitted Major General "Fighting Joe" Hooker of the Army of the Potomac against Robert E. Lee of the Confederate Army of Northern Virginia. Lee won. Hupp was right about Rosecrans. The next month, however, the Army of the Cumberland began the drive to push Bragg out of Tennessee, known as the Tullahoma campaign, after Rosecrans' headquarters.

[25]A political appointee, Major General Nathaniel P. Banks commanded the 19th Corps, Department of the Gulf. This sentence probably refers to naval engagements on Grand Lake (near the Gulf of Mexico) associated with the campaign by Banks to capture Port Hudson on the Mississippi River, a part of Grant's Vicksburg campaign.

quit writing for the day and go to the grand picnic out at the Fairgrounds for it is a beautiful day.

May 5. Weather cool and showery and this being election day we have to remain in the hospital. There is a guard placed here as well as at all the hospitals here.

I had the pleasure of receiving a letter from the Co. this morning written by my friend, Andrew Pettitt [sic], telling me the battery is in good condition and longing for a battle.

May 13. Since my last writing in my journal great movements have been made in our Armies as well as in many other things.

Hooker on the Rappahannock has had awful fighting and gained considerable.

Gen. [George] Stoneman has had great success in cutting rebel communication between Lee and Richmond and Hooker is today reported across the Rappahannock and close on Lee: Grant feels confident of victory at Vicksburg soon.

The hospitals here were all filled with sick from Nashville and the principle disease is chronic diarrhoea [sic].

I have not heard from home for three weeks and feel very anxious to hear from some of them.

A. Pettit wrote from the Co. last week and reports all hearty and well with the anticipation of a speedy battle.

The weather has been warm and pleasant for some time and the general health of the town is good, but I had a spat of sickness last week that left me with a sick headache and deafness in one ear: neither have left entirely yet.

A new order was issued by Dr. Fry yesterday, prohibiting all soldiers from the streets without passes, the cause was so much drunkeness.

May 17. Since my last lines nothing of great importance has transpired although much has been anticipated.

Hooker it is evident, lost as much as he gained in the late battle and Gen. Grant has accomplished considerable on the Blackwater in Mississippi, and a heavy battle appears to be approaching in the vicinity of Vicksburg but I don't anticipate a movement on the place for some time.

The weather is beautiful and everything is a growing condition.

The sick in our ward as well as in the entire hospital have improved much in the last week.

I am confined to the Hospital nearly all the time as medicine has to be given at all hours.

May 20. We have had most beautiful weather for some days and our sick are all improving but one who is lying quite low and I watch him night and day: last night I stayed with him till three o'clock.

May 21. Weather pleasant.

No very important news from the Army except the confirmation of the raid by ________[26] through Miss. in the evening papers, which is considered one of the most daring deeds of the war.

It is considered doubtful as to the success of Grant's taking Vicksburg.

May 28. Ward 3. All remains the same this morning. The weather is much cooler as the showers of the past two days have been very cooling.

We have no confirmation of the taking of Vicksburg, but the general opinion is that

Grant will eventually prove successful.

I had the pleasure of making the acquaintance of a Miss ________ last evening, as interesting a girl as I wish to meet for enjoyment, and I've concluded to make another call.

Yesterday I was occupied most of all day in writing letters: I also started $20 to father, making in all $150 sent since my enlistment.

I have also sent sister Ann [Anelizabeth] $20 which is not as much as I could have spared but since coming to this place I have allowed myself to spend considerable.

We had two men transferred to the Cavalry Div. Ohio.

Their names were Roseboom and Davis, both fine fellows and they have been sick for many months.

A committee started from here yesterday for Vicksburg to aid the wounded of the late battles.

June 5. Weather pleasant.

No additional news from Vicksburg: Grant still besieges the city.

This morning we have intelligence from Franklin, Tenn. which says a sharp fight took place yesterday and a considerable amount of skirmishing has been going on all along the line.[27] Yesterday a Quaker lady from Penn. by the name of Comstock addressed the patients of this hospital; her speaking made a great impression and will doubtless prove a benefit.

I intend to have a good time at the Ice Cream Saloon this evening.

---

[26]This, no doubt, refers to the famous 800-mile raid from La Grange, TN, to Baton Rouge, LA, by Gen. Benjamin Henry Grierson. The purpose of this intrusion was to divert attention from Grant's crossing of the Mississippi River below Vicksburg.

[27]This refers to action just north of Franklin, a small town about 10 miles south of Nashville. Rebel cavalry, under Nathan B. Forrest, captured a post held by Union Lt. Col. Edward Bloodgood, but was later overtaken and driven back by cavalry sent by Rosecrans from Nashville. Forrest later gained the upper hand and drove the Federal troops back to Brentwood, a town just south of Nashville.

I have very good health but suffer much pain with my arm and shoulder.

June 10. Weather warm: commenced raining at 1 p. m. spoiled the enjoyment of the large picnic that is being held at Hickory Grove, three miles from town.

I had made arrangements to accompany Miss _________ to the scene of action, but am just as well satisfied at home.

Nothing appears worth mentioning from our Armies: Grant and Banks are reported sure of success but it looks a little dark yet: we have news from Hooker that confirms his having a part of his force on the south side of the Rappahannock: we are looking for wounded from Vicksburg.

June 11. Weather pleasant with rain at intervals.

June 16. Weather exceedingly warm as this is the hottest day we have had this season.

Yesterday I had a pleasant time at the picnic held in Hickory Grove: I made several acquaintances, among them was a family of Dormans.

The papers this a. m. give discouraging news in reference to Lee and Hooker.

The President's appeal for 1,000,000 more men also appeared this morning.[28]

June 19. Since the 16th there has been more or less excitement over the northern states.

In the east Rebel Lee has everything in a bustle; it seems doubtful as to what his success may be.

Last night at 11 a dispatch came here announcing that a band of guerillas was raising thunder in the county.

All the able bodied soldiers in this place started for the scene of action at 7 a. m. this morning.

I'll not say anymore [sic] but wait for the results.

I had the pleasure of reading two letters, one from the Co. this a. m. one from C. W.

Miller and the other from A. Pettitt [sic].

R. Wilson, my partner, went out this morning and I am left alone.

There has been a picnic every day this week and I have been to two, Monday and Wednesday: the first at Hickory Grove where I enjoyed myself A No. 1, the other was given by the Universalist Church at the Fairgrounds and was conducted in a praiseworthy manner.

---

[28]By this time, Lincoln had already (March 1863) instituted the first U.S. draft (the Confederacy had instituted one previously). Due to the expiration of term enlistments and other reasons, the North suffered a serious manpower shortage, filled in part by the draft. The first lots were drawn in July.

Weather somewhat cooler today.

June 24. Since I last wrote in my journal I have been on an expedition down the river as far as Flint Island thirty miles below Leavenworth: there are several fine little towns along the bank, and at each place there are from one to three Co.s of Home Guards, who may be found ready at a moment's notice to repel any small band that is out to dash upon them.

At Rockport there was a beautiful Union Flag floating in the breeze. In most of these places I am told, strong Union sentiment prevails.

At French Island we found the Ram Monarch aground, she commands the river and

will remain there until high water.

Everybody we passed we hailed: some of them hated it desperate, but the sight of our two long toms needed no other assistance.

The expedition was fruitless as there had no rebels crossed and as our officers got out of whisky we turned around and made our steps toward home, at which place we arrived at 10 a. m., the 24th, all pretty well satisfied of such expeditions, especially under the same officers.

Our trip was made on the Ida, a beautiful stern wheel steamer, 196 feet long and 30 feet wide.

I think I ate the heartiest meal I have ever eaten in four months on arriving at the hospital.

June 27. It has been raining off and on since yesterday a. m.

We have private news this morning of a movement in the Army of the Cumberland: it is hoped it may be so for it has had a long rest while there has been more or less fighting in every other department.

It is said nothing is left behind but Van Clive's Div.; if so, it will be but a few days till stirring news may be looked for.

I have just started a box to C. W. Miller in the Co. which was filled with mdse. to the value of $25 but __________ since I heard of the movements I feel a little dubious as to its safe arrival.

This has been scrubbing day and as we got an early start, had everything done up by 8 o'clock.

July 6. Nothing of note transpired up to July 4, and so I will endeavor to give a brief account of the transactions of that day in this place.

At daybreak a national salute of thirty four guns was fired by the Montauk which has been lying here some two weeks: at 7 a. m. the convalescent soldiers, numbering 800, meet and formed in companies of fifty each and marched through the principal streets, bringing up at the Tabler Home, the place designed for the speaking and the dinner.

We were first greeted by a national air from the New Albany Choral

Association: then the reading of the Declaration of Independence by A. Stevens: singing: address be L. Howard: Star Spangled Banner by the Ass'n.

Dr. Fry, Surg. in charge of this place, entertained us for a time with one of the most patriotic speeches I ever heard.

A salute of three guns was then fired, followed with nine cheers for the soldiers in the field.

Dinner was then prepared and partaken of by the soldiers: it was gotten up expressly for them by the citizens and was deserving of much praise, taking into consideration the limited time that was given previous to the day.

Some of the boys complained they got nothing to eat, but there are those that couldn't be satisfied with the wealth of the world, if it were at their disposal.

At 12 o'clock we returned to our respective hospitals, feeling much more patriotic than when we left: the afternoon was given to the boys to choose their own enjoyment and as there were several half day picnics in the vicinity, there was no need of staying at home for want of a place to go.

I concluded to try the picnic at the Fair Ground so in company with Riley Wilson and Turner repaired there at 2 p. m. where I had one of the best times since I left home.

I enjoyed myself in dancing till 6 o'clock, made several acquaintances, among them Miss Shaw of this place.

In the evening we had $5 appropriated for fire works which made good entertainment.

The way I spent the 4th of '62 was very different from this: a Reg. and one battery lay on the bank of the Tennessee with the expectation of being attacked all day.

I received a letter from Sister Julia Saturday morning which did me more good than all the enjoyment of the day; I also received one from a lady correspondent I lately found in Ohio [Lib Taylor?].

Yesterday (Sunday) the sun came out hot enough to roast eggs: it appears we were blessed with weather suitable for marching on the 4th, for had it been as hot as yesterday half of them would have been obliged to fall out.

This morning is clear and warm and I have been busying myself reading one of Harper's Magazines most of the time but have just been disturbed to sign the payroll.

The news from the Army of the Potomac is glorious if it can be relied upon; we have it that Gen. Meade has captured 20,000 of Lee's army, most of his artillery and is pursuing his flying columns with Cav. capturing great numbers.[29]

Now if this can be relied upon it will prove a death blow to – the Rebs.[30]–

I'll not forget to mention the two sermons I heard yesterday at the Baptist Church, delivered by Rev. ______ of Madison, this state: the one in the evening I admired the most as it was especially for young men.

July 8. Yesterday at 2 p. m. a dispatch arrived telling of the fall of Vicksburg on the 4th, with 24,000 prisoners: and a grand jubilee was held in the evening: speeches were made by the Adjutant, Dr. Fry, and several others whose names I am not acquainted with, the Choral Association sang several patriotic songs and during the time the air was filled almost continually with fire works.

Prof. Hall added to the merriment by sending up several paper balloons: the audience retained the grounds until 11 o'clock when they returned to their different places of abode feeling that Rebeldom had commenced to play out.

Last night and the night before and at morning word was passed that Morgan was coming, which proved to be one of the biggest scares of the day, although it appears evident this evening that he is not far off and may take a notion to pay us a visit.

We all say let him come as we are all well armed and ready for service at a moment's notice: doubtless we will be called out tonight, if it be for nothing else but to deprive us of a third night's sleep in succession.

July 20. I have neglected some days having anything to say in my journal, but the weather has been so warm and I am alone as Riley, my partner, is out after Morgan.

The news of the taking of Port Hudson on the 8th has been here some days: Lee, the yesterday's morning paper stated, had crossed the Potomac and was making for Richmond with a demoralized army.

---

[29]As Pvt. Hupp and his friends celebrated the 4th of July, survivors of one of the pivotal battles of the war, Gettysburg, were licking their wounds from the three day battle (July 1-3). Meade's forces had succeeded in turning back Lee's northern offensive with staggering losses to both sides: over 23,000 casualties for Meade and over 20,000 for Lee. It was to be Gen. Lee's last offensive operation of the Civil War. Lee, incidently, lost only two artillery pieces in the whole campaign.

[30]This assessment would have proved more prophetic had Gen. Meade ordered a more timely and vigorous pursuit of Lee's devastated army. Meade's diffidence lay in the battered state of his own forces on July 4th and heavy rainfall in the afternoon which made further military operations that day difficult at best. However, Meade's cavalry harassed Lee's forces to the rain-swollen Potomac River where Lee dug in at Falling Waters and Williamsport. On July 13, Lee managed to slip across the river before the ever cautious Meade could attack him.

Meade has his cavalry close in their rear and is picking up stragglers in great numbers and it is thought he will be forced to fight at the Rappahannock.

The bombardment of Morris Island commenced on the 10th and continued eight hours, when most of the island fell in our possession: the bombardment was opened next day and terminated in its entire capture.[31]

This morning's paper states that a breach has been made in Sumpter [sic], but its reduction is thought to be accomplished before leaving.

The cry in southern papers is that Richmond is in danger - fall out women and children and defend your homes.

John Morgan was in Ohio at last accounts and 1000 of his men and his artillery are reported captured.

This place has been relieved from martial law for some days: the citizens are required to drill two hours each day and be ready for any emergency.

My health is not very good, my time is mostly spent in hospital.

July 21. Weather cool and cloudy: have occupied most of the day in reading the life of Marion[32], find it to be very interesting.

I have been troubled with the headache all day, caused by being struck on it accidentally.

Have been waiting with eager interest for the evening mail, thinking I might get a letter from home, but only met with disappointment as usual.

On reading Vanlandingham's address to the people of Ohio this morning I got mad enough to cut the rope for the last one of his followers. (This address was written at Niagara Falls, Canada, West, July 15, 1863.)[33]

July 25. Since I wrote last in my journal, nothing of note has transpired: I have been occupied most of the time in the ward.

It is now 10 a. m. and we've just finished Saturday's work: as our

---

[31]Morris Island, on the southern lip of Charleston Harbor, was not completely occupied until September 7, as part of the siege of Charleston. This operation was one of the first to rely on black combat troops, including the famous attack on Battery Wagner by the 54th Massachusetts, depicted in the movie *Glory*. Charleston was finally occupied in February of 1865.

[32]This probably refers to Gen. Francis Marion (1732-1795) of Revolutionary War fame, called the *Swamp Fox*.

[33]Clement L. Vallandigham, preeminent "copperhead" and Democratic candidate for the gubernatorial nomination in Ohio, denounced the war as ". . . a war for the freedom of blacks and the enslavement of the whites." Exiled to Canada for treason under a wartime edict, he slipped back into Ohio in July 1864. Failing in politics after the war, he practiced law before accidentally shooting himself during an 1871 trial while showing how an alleged murder victim could have shot himself. He won the case.

bedsteads were found to be full of b. bugs we've had a happy time using them up.

They threatened to cut off our supplies and break up the hospital, but it looks very evident their plans have been frustrated.

I had a pleasant time at prayer meeting last night and this afternoon I have agreed to go blackberrying and as it has ceased raining more than likely my desire for blackberries will be gratified.

July 28. Wednesday morning and all is well.

I have been employed in scrubbing and cleaning up the ward generally: got an early start and finished up at 8 o'clock.

Charlie Hall and I then took a walk at the lower end of town where the ruins of a fire were found: it was of a wood house that had been set afire with the intention of burning out a doctor but failed: the loss was $800, mostly in edged tools.

Yesterday at 12 I had a chase after a woman that had stolen $100 from a lady near the Ferry: after a sort chase she was caught, the money found in a market basket and she was taken to jail to await trial.

News of Morgan's capture reached us yesterday morning: with all his force he was overtaken by Col. Shackelford when a short fight ensued which resulted in the capture of Morgan and his force.

The prisoners are to be held as hostages in retaliation for those held by the enemy in Georgia under __________.

Morgan and staff are at Cincinnati waiting orders from Burnside.

We are anxiously waiting the paymaster who has been coming for the past three weeks and is said to be in town.

The inspector has just been here and he gave the hospital fits: had fault to find in every nook and corner, there was nothing to suit his fancy.

Last evening I attended the Christian Church: didn't think much of the sermon.

Aug. 3. The weather has been showery for some days but it is awful hot between showers.

My health is good.

Saturday last I went to Louisville, and had a very pleasant time: saw all I wanted to and returned at 5 o'clock well satisfied with the day's adventuring.

Yesterday (Sunday) Fowler and I had a good ride in the country and found some splendid people who treated us to a good dinner and all the apples and plums we could eat.

On the 20th of July we were paid two months pay: and today I was lucky enough to get a letter from C. Miller with the returns of the box I sent him on the 28th of May.

Aug. 8. Weather fair and warm.

Since I last wrote several things worthy of note have transpired.

On the morning of the 1st there was $50 stolen from one of the boys in Ward 2 and after a close watch a Tennessean was strongly suspected and the man the money was taken from jumped on him and made him confess the whole thing before he let him up and the money was found as he said.

The convict was taken to Louisville Military prison.

Wednesday I went blackberrying and got about sixteen quarts: gave half of them away and had plenty left to treat the whole ward.

Everything is in a bustle in town today.

Big show is in town and everyone is agoing but me and I have concluded as my Duck had no desire to go, there was nothing but what I had seen time and again and I would get my photograph taken with the money.

Last night I had a pleasant visit at Mrs. Miller's whose acquaintance I formed last Sunday in the country four miles n. e. of town: her husband and son are in the Army of the Mississippi.

I had the pleasure of receiving three letters yesterday from friends but to my great dismay none from home.

The war news is still encouraging, Gen. Gilmore, who has command of the Union forces off Charleston says the place must fall before he withdraws: he has made a good commencement and I hope he may be successful.

Aug. 11. Weather warm with frequent showers.

I have been employed most of the day scrubbing and cleaning up the ward: yesterday what time I had, I was writing letters: just before dinner I went down and had a plate taken for photographs which are to be taken tomorrow.

There is nothing to write today and will lay down my pen for items worthy of note.

Aug. 15. Weather today is exceedingly warm: got our work done at 10 o'clock.

We have one very sick patient: his two brothers came down to see him this morning and he appears to be much better this evening but his chances of recovery are slim.

I have had seven letters this week: one was from home, which I got last eve, and the reader may know it was pleasing, as it informed me my sister would be to see me the 1st of Sept.

Yesterday in the afternoon, I was out to see some friends and before returning home called on Mrs. T. and squared things before leaving.

They had been talking very mean about me and my calling was for the purpose of informing them that I knew of their abusive talk and that I was done with such people.

There have been several ladies to visit the hospital yesterday and today and they all appear willing to do all in their power for the comfort of the sick soldiers.

Aug. 18. Weather clear and warm.

I have commenced writing in my journal with nothing to write but as I find pen in my fingers will endeavor to take a few notes before closing the book.

Sunday I had a pleasant visit at Mrs. Monroe's in the evening: the rest of the day was spent in the Hospital.

Since Sunday I have, with the exception of going down in town a couple of times, been confined to the ward.

We had a case of the typhoid fever which requires close attention.

I have been lucky the last few days in receiving mail: many more letters have come in than expected; this evening I got two, one from C. Miller which was very gratifying as it announced the arrival of a box I sent him some days ago.

It is now 11 p. m. and I'm getting sleepy but can't go to bed before 2 in the morning, so I will occupy the rest of the time by writing a letter to a friend in the army and reading one of Brough's speeches.[34]

Aug. 22. Weather warm and clear.

My head has troubled me very much for two days: I suppose caused by sitting up so much at night.

For the last three night nights I have had scarcely any sleep.

It took us till 10 o'clock the forenoon to finish the work: our beds got so full of bugs we could scarcely stay in the ward. Consequently we had to take advantage of the water system to get rid of them, and it worked admirably by supplying a little turpentine.

No excitement today except the Army of the Cumberland is on the move and watermelons are cheap and plenty, range from 5c to 25c: we eat on an average from four to six per day in our ward.

I have made preparations to visit Mary Ellen's this afternoon.

Aug. 25. Weather cloudy and cold, the most resembling winter we've had since last spring.

I have been busy this morning filling up straw ticks.

---

[34]John Brough (1811-1865) was publisher of the Lancaster *Eagle* and joint owner and editor of the Cincinnati *Enquirer*. He was a staunch Union supporter and vigorously attacked Vallandigham, whom he defeated in the 1863 election for Ohio governor. He died in office in 1865.

Our ward looks the nicest this morning it has since I've been here.

No particular news seems to be on the travel this morning: I have just filled myself up with watermelon and will be obliged to give way to a stroll to relieve the body of its misery.

One Peter Stone of St. Clair, Mich. got his discharge and started for home this morning with $250 in his pocket: his disease was chronic diarrhea and our surgeon thinks his recovery is almost impossible.

I have just discovered that I caught a bad cold last night by leaving the window open at my head.

Aug. 30. The weather has been uncommonly cold the past three days: last night there was considerable frost in places: today it has cleared off and has moderated down considerably and has much the appearance of gaining the natural temperature for this time of year.

My thoughts have been very melancholy since Thursday last brought on by the death of Willy Rice, a little boy four years old who lived but a few steps from the Hospital and was very frequently in: consequently I became very much attached to him, he being one of the finest little fellows I ever met with.

Our Hospital received iron bedsteads on the 27th and got them set up yesterday but we don't like them as well as our wooden ones, and were it not for the bugs wouldn't make the change.

I have felt very unwell all day today, never felt more like the ague and not have it in my life.

This morning I heard a sermon at Wesley Chapel M. E. Church delivered by Rev. C. Hayes on the salvation of the soul.

Sept. 5. Weather foggy in the morning but cleared off about 9 a. m. and was warm the rest of the day.

On the 2nd I had the pleasure of seeing my sister and aunt: the reader can imagine the enthusiasm that prevailed on the occasion.

I took them to the Depaw House till morning, then I had them go to Mrs. Miller's where they will stay until Monday morning when they intend leaving.

Yesterday I took them to Louisville, drove through all the principal streets, they appeared very much delighted with the place and considered themselves in Dixie, but they were sadly mistaken.

Yesterday we got the news that our hospital is to be closed within ten days: I am as easy as a hog on ice for I don't give a hoot which way the wind blows, so it don't molest my gal.

Sept. 6. Weather fair and warm.

Yesterday morning we had the hardest wind storm since we've been here: I could fill a half dozen pages with yesterday's operations but as I have but a few moments to devote to my journal will be as brief as possible.

Preparations were made to spend the day at Mrs. Rogers' 4 mi. from New Albany, consequently Mr. Turner and I arrived at Mrs. Miller's at the appointed hour (9 a. m.) where sister Julia and Aunt Eliza were boarding and at 10 we found ourselves on the road.[35]

Our enjoyments were good on the way out.

As there were only eight of us and one horse to draw it was 11 o'clock before we arrived there.

I never was better pleased with a visit in my life: they were expecting us and more hospitable treatment is due no person than we received.

After dinner the boys put one of their mules in the wagon and six of us took a ride and of all the pleasure rides I ever experienced it put the cap sheaf on.

It was 5 p. m. when we got back to Rogerses so the horse was at once got ready and after bidding all a cordial goodbye our chabang was again steered for [New] Albany where we arrived at 7 p. m.

I had promised Mrs. Dottson to call before the girls went home and as they were willing, four of us, Sister Julia, E. Turner, Aunt Eliza and myself called before going home.

The evening was spent very agreeably, before leaving Mary Ellen passed us some of the best blackberry cordial and jelly cake that has passed my notice since leaving home.

We paid our respects to them at 9 p. m. and made our way for Mrs. Miller's: after disposing of the women, Turner and I made tracks for the hospital where we arrived in short order, steering straightway for bed and were soon overtaken by sleep.

This morning I got up at 5: went down to the stage office and made arrangements for the girls to go to Jeffersonville at 6 o'clock when I was obliged to bid them goodbye, probably nevermore to meet them: and now I am as lonesome as a lost sinner.

We are making preparations to close our hospital.

Sept. 8. Yesterday afternoon will long be remembered by the occupants of Ward 3.

The picnic which was held at the Fair Ground was largely attended and nearly all the soldiers were tight, Lager Beer being the countersign.

The weather today is sultry with some appearance of rain.

---

[35]Julia Hupp was one of Ormond's sisters, four years his junior. Aunt Eliza must be a sister of his mother (Louisa Gardner); his father, Abram Hupp, had only male siblings. Ormond's older sister, "Ann" (Christened "Anelizabeth"), may have been named after this aunt.

Sept 11. I intended to write some in my journal yesterday as it was my birthday, but owing to the uncertainty of our remaining another day had business of more important nature.

Turner and I accepted an invitation to take dinner with Mrs. and the Misses Dowerman: so after we had finished our morning's work our steps were directed thitherward where we met with the most hospitable treatment that has been shown me for two years: the dinner they prepared was excellent, I came very near foundering myself on succotash.

We continued our visit till 4 p. m. and after drinking wine to the prosperity and long life to all the family we took the parting hand, promising to write often and if we ever returned, to call.

We got home just as the supper bell rang: I partook and rested at my quarters during the evening.

On the 9th I made three calls thinking I would leave next morning: I first went to bid adieu to Miss M. C. Dottson: was well pleased with the interview: as I had promised Mrs. Monroe to see her before leaving I soon bent my steps toward her house.

I could hardly get away without supper, but I finally made my escape and reached the hospital in safety.

In the evening I went up to Mrs. Miller's, found Nan at home, had a good sociable chat till 9 o'clock and after promising them to write, I bade them goodbye.

The weather today is warm and sultry, considerable sickness is manifested throughout the city.

We hourly expect orders to close the hospital as has been the case for several days: have my things allright [sic] to leave at a moment's notice, but while I stay am resolved to enjoy myself.

Sept. 14. Had orders to clean our ward and transfer the men to another ward: this a. m. at 11 we were all ordered to get ready to transfer: soon after dinner, at 2 p. m. all the transfers were made.

I got a very good bed in Ward 3, No. 4 Hospital: felt much dissatisfied especially when we were summoned to supper, as the fare was very much inferior to what we'd been accustomed to: spent the evening at Shaw's.

Sept. 15. Felt drowsy all p. m., laid in bed and read the Louisville Democrat: stirred around through the town in the afternoon, started a box home and felt very much disappointed in not receiving a letter in the evening mail.

To make out the day and fulfill promises I called on Miss Fannie Bird in the evening, in whose company I enjoyed myself remarkably, she being skilled in the several games with cards, and I being a soldier, a game of euchre was soon started, and we played several different games.

Not wishing to brag on myself – but she couldn't hold a candle to me.

After we got through playing she told our fortunes, after which she played on the piano a few pieces and sang; the curtain then dropped on the evening.

Sept. 16. Feel very well but am still disappointed at not receiving letters.

Was detained at No. 1 Hospital today until 10 a. m.: moved my duds back after dinner and have been packing goods all afternoon.

Went in to see Annie Stokes who is one of the most agreeable girls in the place: on leaving she loaned me the works of E. A. Poe to read.

The clock struck 9 as I got in: the boys were all seated around Fowler who was playing the fiddle.

After getting a snack from the kitchen my thoughts were soon swallowed up in deep sleep, for I was awful sleepy.

Sept. 17. Waited patiently for the morning mail only to be disappointed; have been packing goods all day and am waiting patiently for a peach cobbler which is being prepared by Nate Zimmerman, our old cook.

We concluded 4 p. m. was late enough to work and consequently we are all engaged at our own pleasure.

I occupied a part of my time in writing in my journal I have no place to go tonight, and what to do with myself till bedtime I am at a loss to know.

Sept. 18. I have been on the go all day and accomplished but little: had one drink of muscat wine: was well suited in a boot that I had footed: had to put on underclothes on account of the sudden change in the weather.

It is now 8 p. m. and as I have no particular place to spend this evening I will take a game of euchre and retire for the night.

My stomach is sour as the result of eating onions.

No letters today!

I have resolved not to write till I receive some in return for those I have already written.

Sept 19. Have been packing all day.

Went out this evening and had a dish of oysters with Frank Fowler and brother. A gay time was no name for it.

Afterwards I stepped in to Miss A. Stokes' and had some grease extracted from my hat: got in at 9 and found the boys enjoying dancing, playing bones, banjo, and fiddle.

It is now 10 and high time to retire.

Sept. 20. This being Sunday I've had no work to do till 3 p. m.: have been employed writing and reading: then went over to Annie's where I remained till 6: then sought the company of Mary Ellen D________ where I found it difficult to leave till 9 o'clock or such matter: would have stayed latter had circumstances not forbid.

A heavy day's work tomorrow caused me to retire immediately.

Sept. 21. We have awful news from Rosecrans: he is said to be badly whipped: much excitement prevails throughout the city in consequence.[36]

I feel uneasy about the battery as I heard they were all cut to pieces.[37]

Have been at work all day: was down to Shaw's to get a basket of delicacies for Serg. Hill who is very ill with lung fever.

I'll take a smoke now and retire for a season.

Sept. 26. Have been fixing up my clothes today and put a box in order that I intend to send home; think of leaving for the front Monday next.

The news from our armies is encouraging today – weather warmer and pleasant.

Charley Hall and I have been to an oyster supper this evening at the Miss Shaw's.

Last night I went to a party and didn't get home till 4 this morning: got into the old woman's vineyard and got her after me with a broom: got into the kitchen about 10 and made the pies and ham suffer.

Sept. 28. The Army of the Potomac is on the move again: orders came last night for us to open No. 1 Hospital and be ready for wounded any day.

We have, after a long day;s work, prepared the house, but up to 9 p. m. this evening there had been no arrivals.

Last night I had one of the sweetest little times with Miss _____ that a person could ask for, with but one previous meeting.

Yesterday afternoon I spent at Miss Dottson's: she was well supplied with delicacies and an agreeable afternoon was put in.

I consider she is one of the nicest gals in the place, and if it wasn't for existing circumstances, the results of our meeting might be different.

Oct. 5. Sunday: weather has been broken and cold for several days.

Nothing of note appears in my mind.

Friday the city was favored with a menagerie and I had the misfortune

---

[36]Rosecrans' Army of the Cumberland was indeed "badly whipped" at the Battle of Chickamauga Creek, TN (Sept. 19-20). Forced to retreat back to Chattanooga by Bragg's forces, Rosecrans was soon replaced by Gen. George H. Thomas on orders from U. S. Grant.

[37]The 5th Indiana battery was engaged at Chickamauga and the siege (by Bragg) of Chattanooga. Official Records, however, show their casualties to have been relatively light, although they lost some armaments.

of losing $1.50 through the ticket agent and in consequence I could not attend yesterday.

I passed a lonely day as there was no excitement in town: after supper I called on

Miss Stokes, where I stayed till 9 o'clock and engaged her company for tomorrow evening to go into the country for church.

Remained at home during the day: weather cold and cloudy.

Dr. Green [asst. surg. A. S. Greene] and lady came in on us and heard some smutty talk while we were eating supper: after supper Fowler and I got our gals and repaired to the country church where we were permitted to listen to a worthy minister of the M. E. Church.

It was generally understood that we were to enjoy ourselves and the clock struck 1 before we landed in the city.

Oh! that I could spend such a night often!

Arrangements were made to go on a nutting expedition Saturday and a gay time is anticipated.

Oct. 5 [6?]. All quiet on the Potomac: weather cloudy and cold: took my position as Assistant Ward Master.

Oct. 7. It commenced raining last night and rained hard all night.

Just as the rain commenced falling I called on Miss Bird to spend the evening and in consequence of its falling in such torrents I refrained from venturing home until a late hour, thinking it might slacken, besides the evening were very tempting.

I must say that since leaving home I have never had more enjoyment in such a length of time.

In the forenoon yesterday it happened to be in the way to call on M. D. where I had an interview (one not very agreeable) of three hours.

No patients admitted yet, but are hourly expecting them. The air is cool today, but much pleasanter than for several days past, with the wind in the northeast.

Sickness is very common in the city, especially chills and fever: it is not uncommon to see from two to eight funeral processions daily.

Oct. 10. I feel rather down in the mouth today: probably owing to the late hours which I kept last night: but I had such good company the clock struck 11 before I was aware of it which brought our evening's amusement to an end.

I promised Mary to return some future time and peruse her beautiful album.

The weather today is clear but quite cool.

It is now 9 a. m. and I have my washing to do before dinner therefore this will have to suffice for today.

Oct. 11. I did up my morning's work with the intention of going to church but had an invitation to ride in the country, went out to Rogerses, five miles from town and enjoyed myself hugely for several hours: gathered the first chestnuts in my life: made arrangements to go nutting on Wednesday and hope it may be so I can go for I am certain I can enjoy myself.

Spent evening with E. S. and had an interesting conversation on novel reading.

Monday: weather cold and rainy.

Cleaned up my room and read an interesting story in Harper's Magazine, entitled The Three Voyages, which occupied the forenoon: in the afternoon of today I wrote two letters, one from Miss S. and the other to Sister Ann, spent the first evening home for a week.

Oct. 13. Rained most all night: wet underfoot and have deemed it prudent to stay in all forenoon.

This afternoon went down to No. 5 with Charley Hall, had a chat of 1½ hours, and returned to find Nathan Zimmermann waiting for some one to go down to vote.

I went down to the polls and as I expected, couldn't vote: it was now 2½ p. m. when it commenced raining and is raining up to the present time, 8 o'clock.

I have put in the rest of the day reading.

I came to the conclusion not to write another letter home until they wrote me if it be six months, but I have a letter to write Miss S. before going to bed.

Oct. 14. Cleaned up room in forenoon: yard being very wet, concluded to let it be until it dries off: got a hold of a piece in Harper's Monthly that occupied most of the afternoon: after supper took a walk with Frank through the city and saw many living curiosities.

Oct. 15. Helped get Billy off in the morning to Madison: went down to Tom's and got some apples with Riley Wilson: made out a requisition for rations and was until dinner getting them.

In the afternoon drove Fowler's team to Camp Joe Holt and to several places around town: after tea called on Miss Mary Ellen for the purpose of exchanging some books: spent most of the evening at home.

Oct. 16. Weather fair and pleasant: did up morning's work and passed the day mostly in reading.

Went up to Mrs. Miller's in the evening and had a gay time with Nan and a lady from Bloomington, Ind.

Oct. 17. Weather cloudy with a good cool breeze from the southwest.

Went a nutting with Mr. Mann's folks and had one of the gayest times that could be talked about: got acquainted with El Neate, one of the most noble looking girls I ever saw.

Didn't get back till night and had no luck getting nuts.

Got a letter from home which caused me more grief than I've had for years.

Beautiful day to feel so bad! Can't enjoy it: remained alone in solitude all day.

Oct. 20. Have been no place since Saturday evening: feel rather serious as to how the forward move by the Rebs will result.

Got a barrel of apples from the Sanitary Com.[38] last eve.

Weather pleasant: am going to Dowerman's after tea to get a pr. of shirts Alice is making.

Got a letter from the Co. the first since the battle of Chickamauga: sorry to hear they lost their guns.

Got a letter from C. W. Miller which was very interesting: gave me full details of the great fight: wrote one to Sister Julia and one to J. Fargher.

Stayed home all day and went to John Street church in the evening.

Weather rather cool wind in the s. w.: news from the front encouraging.

Oct. 23. Wrote a long letter to C. Miller and read the papers, also several pieces in

Godey's L. Book: in the evening went to prayer meeting at 3rd Presbyterian Church.

Oct. 25. Went to church at Centenary in forenoon have a pain in my side that bothers me considerably: got twenty patients in this afternoon: went to Baptist Church in the evening and took great fancy to the new styles of the ladies: air rather cool.

Oct. 26. Pleasant day: nothing of note transpires.

Cleaned out the baggage room: wrote two letters: got two shirts I had made in lower part of town that cost me $5.00 and are entirely spoiled: got awful mad: concluded I've learned a lesson.

Cleaned yard in the forenoon, played sledge with Corp. Turner after dinner, got five games out of seven: at 2 p. m. went to Doverman's to have alterations made in shirts she is making for me: didn't find them at home and wrote a letter to her: stayed in all evening and read the Cincinnati Gazettes.

---

[38]The United States Sanitary Commission was created to improve upon sanitary and medical facilities in army camps and hospitals. They fought for – and won – reform of the Army Medical Bureau, and instituted the first hospital trains and ships. Women were prominent as nurses and as administrators in "The Sanitary."

Oct. 29. The day is beautiful. Stayed home all forenoon: went to Dottson's to get some books to read: Mary Ellen showed me her new dress which I admired and complimented her highly on her choice: I engaged her company for Saturday evening to attend a circus.

I made $2 on tobacco, sold a couple of boxes of segars [sic], I have had on hand to send to the Co. but was obliged to dispose of them on account of failing to get transportation.

Wrote a letter to B. Fowler and it is now high to seek shelter in my cot.

Nov. 1. Yesterday I was busy all day: the hospital was filled full of wounded on Friday night and everything came on our hands at once.

Went to the circus last night, had a bully time, didn't get home until 10: this afternoon I took a good nap: have been at home all day: received two letters, one from Sister Anna and the other one from Lib Taylor of Ohio: went to church at the John Street M. E. in the evening.

Nov. 2. Been busy at home all day: J. Dunn, the Ward Master, went home on furlough this a. m. which left me the duty of two to perform: had a great time with the washerwoman: was down at Headquarters on business and got treated to apples and ale: remained in the office during the evening.

Nov. 4. Forenoon foggy and damp: carried in morning reports, got men at work to clean up the house, then went after mail: got some catsup, rags for dressing wounds, apples, dried, also two barrels green apples.

I then took the washerwoman's rations to her: got a bird's eye view of Benina and thought her a little angel.

Stayed at home all afternoon: last evening spent the time at Mrs. Mann's playing euchre with Belle and Sally and listening to the notes of a piano.

Nov. 5. Weather pleasant with a beautiful breeze from the s. w.: attended to morning duty: put up some medicines and put away the clean clothes which came in last night: didn't go to bed till 11 o'clock, was employed writing letters and trying to obtain a furlough: expect it to prove a failure.

Nov. 8. Yesterday I was busy cleaning the house and yard, drawing rations, giving out cloths, etc.

I intended to go out to Dowerman's to get a shirt, also to Dotson's to take some borrowed books back but was too busy.

Weather cool but pleasant.

Today it was 11 a. m. before I got to rest a minute: wrote two letters went over to

Dotson's and had a pleasant visit: went to church with Miss E. S. in the evening. Weather chilly.

Nov. 11. Weather clear and cool but fine for the season of the year.

Commenced bookkeeping on Monday: like it remarkably but have little time to devote to it at present: was down to Headquarters and got a pail of ale for the sick.

I hardly get time to turn around for myself since Jack [J. Dunn, Ward Master] left.

Got acquainted with the Miss West's, like their appearance well; made arrangements for an oyster supper.

Nov. 14. Weather has been rainy since yesterday morning: deferred having the house cleaned on account of the mud: made out our postal return yesterday, found it very tedious: also prepared the pay rolls and had them signed and am hoping to be paid this week.

Have just finished the morning's work: it is 12 a. m.: wanted to attend church but had too much to do: am going this evening: going to see Miss Emma this evening for the purpose of procuring her company for an oyster supper.

I will now lay my journal aside and go to the kitchen and get a bite to eat as we have no dinner on Sundays.

Nov. 16. Weather rainy, health on the decline: been busy ordering rations, having the house put in order, etc.: got a pail of ale from Headquarters together with some flannel and oil cloth for stand and tablecovers: came down on a glass of blackberry cordial and some apples while at H. Q. which were very acceptable: didn't get supper till 6:30 as head cook (or kitchen maid, as he is styled) came near breaking his arm in falling out of a wagon.

It is now 8 p. m. and my lesson in bookkeeping is to be prepared for tomorrow evening before retiring so good-bye journal till a more convenient season.

Nov. 20. Weather rainy and cold.

Had orders last night to prepare for general inspection today: in consequence of which I have been busy all morning: it is now 11 and I have my forenoon duty completed.

No inspectors have arrived and it is rumored to be a big scare.

This morning's mail brought me a letter from J. Fargher.

For the last week I have been troubled with rheumatism so in my right shoulder that

I can neither rest day nor night.

Am getting along remarkably well with my bookkeeping as I have two sets finished and intend commencing a third this evening.

As I write there is a N. Y. Regiment passing down Main Street bound for Chattanooga.

A new steward was assigned to our hospital yesterday which has a tendency to change the program of things in general.

Nov. 22. Sunday – but it couldn't be proven by my conduct throughout the day for I have had to work all day: forenoon I was busy giving out clothes and policing quarters: afternoon I intended calling on Miss Dotson but had too draw dishes for the Hospital and didn't get through till 4 and then I cleaned up and went to Emma's and spent the evening till church time: paid a phillopena [sic] present[39].

I have just returned from church and Keggy and Savage are just going to bed and are having a gay time over the peculiarities of their drawers.

Nov. 24. Yesterday was a day long to be remembered by me: just as I got into the heart of the morning's work, my old friend, Johnny Fargher came upon me to my great astonishment: he had been up at Madison visiting his brother who is acting Hospital steward U. S. A. at that place.

Well, I entertained as well as I could till I got my work done and we then went to Harris' Oyster Saloon and had oysters and coffee: went by the depot and procured him free transportation through the Superintendent and by the time we got to Hosp. 1 it was time to fill up for dinner: afternoon went to the River and looked at the many curiosities on its beautiful banks: returned at 4 just in time to receive pay: after tea took another dish of oysters that I won off Campbell: started Johnny home at 8 and that ended the day.

Today the weather is cold and clear and I feel quite bad: head aches and sore eyes: did morning duty and went to P. O. with Keggie after which we undertook to put up a stove in our room black from one end to the other and gave up on account of not finding pipe to fit: took near all evening to clean up what dirt was made.

Got a pair of pants at the Depaw House [Depauw] where they had been for the purpose of being colored.

Nov. 25. In the evening of last night I went over to Miss Dottson's, stayed till 8, and returned to the Hospital found Keggie, Mastermann, and Turner, about ready to go to the Ladies's fair: was persuaded to go and we had a fat time till 11, when we returned to our old stand to dream over the merry past.

I also received an invitation to help the Old Grey Goose Thursday next (Thanksgiving Day) and it is my intention to go.

Weather clear but chilly.

---

[39]A **philopena present** is an obligatory gift. The term comes from a game played with two kernels of a nut shared by two people. If one of the players fails to meet a specified condition, he owes the other a gift.

Got up at 6:20, washed and ate breakfast at 7, detailed me for policing house and grounds, corded two cords wood. Sent half cord to w. woman, got ready to take an inventory of Gov. property in Hospital, and ate dinner.

VOLUME II

I purchased this book of Zeke Day, of this city on the 24th day of Nov., 1863, for the purpose of continuing a journal which I have been keeping for some time.

Should I be so unlucky as to lose this book, the finder will oblige by sending it to LaPorte, Indiana, in the address of Abram Hupp.

Nov. 27. Forenoon clear and pleasant. Put 18 c. of wood in cellar: in the afternoon I went downtown and got this book, a couple of collars, and some other trinkets. Went over to Stoke's in the evening and stayed only a short time: went to station at 8 and saw train come in.

B. A. Masterson bought a can of oysters and a pound of crackers, took them home and had a fine feast, after which we all went to bed.

Nov. 28. Weather rainy and cold.

I got up at 7 this morning: breakfast was nearly over when I got down to the kitchen.

Appetite poor: drank a cup of coffee and ate a piece of toast.

Took me all forenoon to arrange the clothes: afternoon had leisure and employed it writing and reading.

Nov. 29. Weather very cold, snow flakes flying all day.

I arose in the morning at 7, felt bad, had severe headache: ate breakfast at 7:30.

Got my work done at 10: dressed and attended services at Wesley Chapel: the text was "Is Jesus Merciful?"

The minister preached but half of the sermon and is to finish tonight.

After returning from service, Savage bought a basket of hickory nuts and several of us had a fine time cracking and eating them.

Went to church at the Centenary in the evening.

Nov. 30. Got up at 6:30 and almost froze making my bed. This is the coldest morning this fall.

Sent the clothes to the wash woman and tended to other duties about the hospital till 9 a. m.: then was kept busy until noon seeing to the drawing of clothes for the patients.

After dinner Frank Mastermann, H. Keggy, and myself got ready and went down to

Mr. Eckers and had our negatives taken for photographs, which are to be ready Wednesday.

Nothing worth mentioning occurred after this during the day.

Dec. 1. Weather cold but clear.

Nothing of importance today.

We sent six men to Madison this forenoon.

Last night Keggy and I passed the evening at West's and had a gay time.

This afternoon was busy drawing rations.

Dec. 2. Weather very pleasant.

I got my morning duty done by 9: Keggy and I went down to W. Green's and raked his yard which took us till 10.

We then went to Louisville: had a good time running around until 3 p. m. when we returned to N. A. very much fatigued and with a very poor opinion of Louisville.

Dec. 3. Didn't do anything worthy of note.

In the evening went to an oyster supper. Weather fair.

Dec. 4. Made sidewalk and dug hole for dirt in the forenoon: in afternoon went around to different hospitals on business.

I spent the evening at an oyster supper at Miss E. N.'s and had a lively time.

Dec. 5. Weather pleasant.

Was busy in forenoon policing quarters.

In the afternoon I wrote two letters, one to Sister Anna, the other to Miss Sweetness of LaPorte. Received one from Miss Anna S. J. Dunn and passed the evening very agreeably till 10 at Mrs. W's.

Didn't retire until 11:30.

Dec. 6. Rose at 7. Changed clothes and ate breakfast at 8.

Attended church at Centenary, heard a splendid sermon. I had no dinner but took a piece of bread and butter after coming from church.

I went with Savage and Keggy to the shipyard.

Had supper at 8 and went to the Christian Church.

Dec. 7. Rose at 7 and put my room in order before I had breakfast.

After meal, I tended to the week's washing and policing the quarters.

At 9 I started into the country with some ladies: had a pleasant time and saw some beautiful country.

Returned at 2 p. m. and went out to the Dowermann's with Keggy to see about some shirts. Keggy was riled up considerably at the distance being so great.

Stayed at home during the night.

Dec. 8. Got up at 6:30 feeling very badly but said nothing: after morning duty drew clothes for the patients after which I drew seven days rations for the Hospital, which took up the forepart of the day: ate no dinner but took a large dose of oil which made me very sick: lay abed till 3.

Stewart [steward?] came in my room for me to go down town; took a good vomit and started.

Our business transacted we returned and I laid down till 7 when I took some men to the depot who were being transferred to Miss.: returned home and retired at 10 p. m.

Dec. 9. Wednesday. Rose at 7, ate at 7:30, straightened things around in my room, then went down town with the steward, purchased some glass and putty and at 11 a. m. when we returned did some private sewing till dinner: spent the afternoon at Mrs. Miller's and became acquainted with some secret conversation that has been going on about me and went to the Christian Church in the evening.

Dec. 11. Friday. Got up at 6:30, ate at 7:20, cleared my room, did some work around the Hospital and finished my time until noon by writing: remained in house all day.

Weather rainy and chilly: nothing of importance occurred last night: spent the evening very agreeably at Miss Qualey's.

Dec. 12. Weather rainy all day: remained in Hospital and received two letters, one from Fargher and one from Sister Ann: felt very much gratified at the reception of Sister's letter: wrote a long letter to mother and sent her my photograph.[1]

This evening at 5 o'clock Mr. Willoughby died, disease unknown, and his wife being here, it was a very trying time: Mary, his wife, is staying at Mrs. Mann's for the night.

It is now 10 and as I intend to sit up, will lay aside my journal and repair to the office.

Dec. 13. Rose at 7:10, breakfast at 8: was up till midnight with Willoughby's corpse last night.

Mrs. Willoughby stayed with Mrs. Mann after 11 p. m. when I paid a visit to Dottson's: in the evening heard a sermon at Centenary: retired at 10 p. m.

Monday, Dec. 14. Ceased raining, is fast turning cold: has much the appearance of snow.

---

[1]This is the photograph of Ormond Hupp as a young man, figure 5-2, page 177.

In forenoon attended to clothes and daily duty: afternoon, remained indoors: took a dish of oysters in evening: went to bed at 10.

Tuesday, Dec. 15. Cold and cloudy until 2 p. m.: busy at one thing and another till 3 o'clock.

Examining board was around at 2 p. m. and marked a good many for discharge and the front.

Wednesday, 16. Weather rainy and disagreeable: nothing of importance took affect today except one death of typhoid fever at 8 p. m.: sick but four days.

Thursday, 17. Rose at 7: was stirring around at one thing and another all day.

Weather disagreeable, very muddy underfoot, stuck to the house as close as possible: intended going out this evening but as the other boys all left the office I was compelled to remain and take my turn on the morrow.

Friday, 18. Rose at 8: slept very poorly as Keggy and I undertook to sleep together: the bed being too narrow and the night being so cold, that a disagreeable night was spent, the effects of which are easily felt today.

Helped open a dead body for the purpose of ascertaining whether it was poisoned:

Masterman and I had the body to sew up: had quite a tedious time as it was awful cold.

Didn't feel well in the afternoon.

Sat. 19. Dec. Slept very cold last night: rose at 7:20 and found the coldest morning of the season: ice froze all over the meadows.

Had considerable work to do in forenoon about the house, afternoon Turner and I walked out to Dowerman's: had a pleasant visit and before leaving they treated us to some apples and hickory nuts.

Arrived home at dark, took supper, then B. K. Masterman and I started to church at John Street but there being no service the evening was spent at home.

I traded coats with a man in Ward 3 and wrote a letter to Aunt Eliza during the evening: didn't retire till 12.

Sunday, Dec. 20. Weather more mild than yesterday but quite cold: went to church at Centenary in morning: afternoon made a short call to Dottson's after which J. Dunn and I took a walk in the upper part of the city: remained at home in the evening and gave the other boys a chance.

Mond. 21. Rose at 7, had business which kept me confined to the hospital all day.

Weather cold and cloudy.

Tues. 22. Weather clear but cold: was running around all forenoon to get some wood: succeeded in getting one load: went to John Street Church in evening, a great revival is being held there, five converted tonight.

Wed. 23. Weather cold and cloudy: slept very cold last night in consequence of Keggie's kicking the cover off: resolved to mash him: stayed around Hosp. all day: went to revival again in the evening: accompanied Miss Dottson home retired at 11, resolved to attend church on the morrow evening.

Thurs. 24. Had a good night's rest last night: rose at 6:40 and just got my room cleaned when the breakfast bell rang: ate light breakfast, took a collection of $15 for Christmas dinner and commenced preparing for same immediately: afternoon nothing but the regular routine of business transpires: went to the John Street Church revival in the evening after which Frank, Keggie and I went to the Baptist Church where there was a splendid Christmas tree on exhibition: stayed but a short time then returned home and retired.

Friday 25. Got out of my warm nest at 6:30, put the room in order, then Keggie and I read the Bible till breakfast which was at 7:30.

I ran around town till 10 a. m. to get potatoes for dinner: after getting orders on three persons for dinner: after getting orders on three persons I succeeded.

The day being beautiful, everyone seemed to be enjoying a happy Christmas.

After my hunt for the Irishman's apples I fulfilled a request to call on Miss W. for the purpose of drinking wine and making away with cake, at which duty they will tell you, I made a full team.

Things passed off lovely till half past two when the kitchen bell announced the turkeys fit subjects for battle: the advance was made at once and owing to the great surprise of the enemy, a complete victory was gained, scarcely a bone left to tell the tale of its many comrades.

I remained in the office then until 6:30 p. m. with the rest of the boys, namely O'Leary, Masterman, Keggie, and Dunn, and the time spent by telling tales and ruminating over the past.

Having received an invitation during the afterpart of the [day?] to attend a social circle in the evening, I met the favor with promptness: the result was a general good time and I believe, entire satisfaction. Retired at 10 o'clock.

Sat. 26. Rose at 6 somewhat earlier than common, owing to Keggie's having gone home and leaving the morning's reports, which have to be carried in at 7 for me to do.

Weather much changed from yesterday, been raining all day and this evening the fog is so thick one can see but a few feet.

I have been employed this afternoon in commencing an inventory of Gov. property in the Hospital.

I have felt all day as though the bed was the proper place for me, but like a valiant soldier have braved it through.

I am remaining at home this evening the first time in a week and feel more like hearing from home than I have for sometime past, but judging from the past, it may be six months ere I receive a letter.

Sun. 27. I retired last night at 10, but for some unaccountable reason lay awake until near one: during the time I was thinking of nearly everything that has happened during my life: rose at 6:30, found the rain descending in torrents and no decrease in fog: made my bed, washed and carried reports to H. Q. before breakfast.

Since my morning duty I have been doing a little of everything: sent two small pox cases to Louisville, Brown and Caldwell.

Much excitement prevails in out Hospital in consequence of the disease.

The rain has been falling steadily all day: intended to get out this eve but it is entirely too wet.

Mon. 28. Hated to get up: felt so sleepy but managed with a little aid to get out at 7: drizzling rain fell all day: very unpleasant to venture out.

I have done nothing but what duty called me to out of the House.

In the evening went over to Mrs. Sebastion's on business and stopped but a few moments: had to go over to West's and make arrangements for an oyster supper that was to come off Wednesday evening: after which the time was spent at Mrs. W.'s playing a social game of euchre which lasted till 11, returned and went to bed immediately.

Tues. 29. Rose in good season.

After morning services was busy the remainder of the day taking an invoice: had considerable trouble to account for many things.

Accepted an invitation to attend a social gathering in the evening at Mrs. Sebastion's and had one of the gayest times imaginable: the cake, cider, and apples that were served on the occasion were a sin to little folks: broke up at 12 to meet for an oyster supper at 7 next evening.

Found pleasure in seeing Miss Qualey to her respective place of abode. Retired at half past 12.

Wed. 30. Rose at 6:30. Washed, cleaned up my room, and carried the morning reports down before breakfast. Had a little work to do around the Hospital which kept me employed till 9 a. m.: rest of the day I helped Dr. Green [Greene] put boxes around some trees in the yard: in the afternoon Frank and I both went down.

Got sadly disappointed in the oyster supper, there not being a can in the place: however the company met and had a general good time which lasted till half past 11, was the result: several came near getting tight by mixing wine with cider.

During the evening had quite a contested game of checkers with Miss Lucy West which resulted in a defeat caused probably by Mr. Turner's kidnapping two of my men.

The meeting closed to meet on Friday evening.

The weather pleasant all day, only agreeable day this week.

Thurs. 31. Rose at 6. Found it raining as I expected last night: continued raining until dusk.

Had made arrangements to go to a candy pulling but the storm prevented, so remained in all day, also in the evening.

Had a man die in Ward 4 which I had to lay out.

Jan. 1. 1864. Found it the coldest morning of the season: was employed all forenoon in helping to dissect a body: got through at 12 m., took dinner with Mrs. Warner, had chicken, turkey, wine and everything of the best and was promised a nice new year's present. I also received a basketful of goodies as a present from Mrs. Dottson.

Sat. [Jan.] **2.** Somewhat warmer than yesterday but the thermometer gives evidence of very cold weather, standing at 30 degrees below zero.

Was busy all day getting wood and other necessaries for Hospital use.

In the evening Mr. Turner and I accepted an invitation to attend a taffy pulling at Dottson's and a general good time was enjoyed: came near getting tight on blackberry cordial.

Sund. 3. Didn't get from under the covers till 8 o'clock in consequence of our not having anything to eat: was busy running after rations till 3 p. m. at which time succeeded in part in getting the rations.

Turner and I spent from 3:30 p. m. to half past four at Mrs. Sebastion's: had a pleasant time and went to church in the evening.

Mond. 4. Arose this morning at 7, after enjoying a good night's repose and found snow about 4 in. deep: was busy until 9 having the pavements cleaned.

People are improving this time by running everything in the shape of a cutter: weather clear but cold: thaws, nowhere but under the nose: put in my spare time reading a book styled "Thirty Years in the Arctic Regions,": wrote a letter to Mag Harper: received two, one from Mag, the other from Miss S.

Tues. 5. Weather very cold but clear: enjoyed a good night's rest as Keggie and I moved our beds together and doubled the clothes which kept us warm as mice: had a bother with the Commissary Clerk relative to the rations.

Turner and I went to Dowerman's and spent the evening: had a pleasant time sliding on the ice: froze one of my toes coming home.

Wed. 6. Was busy this forenoon: after tending to the morning duty, put up a stove which has proved a failure several times: in the afternoon Dowermann's people called on us and we had a very agreeable time, drank a bottle of muscat wine.

Some of the company came very near getting tight: spent the evening with Miss E. – a sociable time was spent. I got the philopena on Emma.

Thurs. 7. Weather very cold, sleighs running very frequently. 9 a. m. went to postoffice, came by Dr. Green's and left an official letter, stopped at Mrs. Warren's (our washer woman) and split her a pile of wood.

Got a letter from Sister Julia in which was enclosed a piece of silver as a token of friendship.

7 p. m. went to Mrs. Sebastions's, at her request Turner and I engaged in a game of euchre: left at 11 p. m. and soon found myself lying on a soft mattress with eight blankets over me to keep out the severe cold.

Fri. 8. Rose at 6:30, built fire and cleaned the room, then fixed for breakfast which was ready at 7:30: went down town to buy a load of wood but found it too dear: brought the clean clothes over at 10, was occupied till dinner cleaning snow off the pavements: 1 p. m. cleaned out the baggage room 4, and had a scuffle in the snow with the steward, and came near freezing my lips in the operation.

At 7 Turner and I went to the Sebastion's to a taffy pulling: had to go after the Miss Wests which was an easy pill to take: could scarcely make candy out of the syrup but succeeded from 10:30 to 12: had the gayest time pulling wax that I ever witnessed: played one game of checkers with Mrs. S. before leaving, came out best.

Sat. 9. Rose at 6:40 and owing to the neglect of getting kindling a fire wasn't built until after breakfast: enjoyed one of the best night's sleep I've had in many a month.

At 8 a. m. went to Commissary for some back rations but failed in getting them: was in Ward 1 all my spare time till dinner, helping to wait on a sick man by the name of _______ who came in from Campbell yesterday didn't think life would last until noon: at 1 p. m. went down town to see the 38th Ind. come in, who have enlisted in the veteran service and have a furlough of 30 days: found some good looking ladies that I had formerly been acquainted with and had a jolly time till 3 when I returned to the Hospital and found ______ sinking.

Got some whisky down him but didn't appear to do any good: at 4 made a call at the Dottson's, found all well: Mary had her picture done she has had on hand for six weeks: had some good candy, brought Fowler's shirt home, which she had made this week: took supper at home at 5: at 5:30 went down to Haffold's and made a trade for some kerosene oil and letter paper: spent the evening at Mrs. Warren's.

Sund. 10. Keggie and I slept together and enjoyed a good night's rest: got up in time to get the room put in order and read two or three chapters in the Bible before breakfast.

At 8 went over to the wash woman's to get clothes: at 7:30 laid out a corpse that died at 7 last night: from 11 a. m. till 2 p. m. wrote letters and done other private business that had been delayed until evening: went to St. John's Church and heard an interesting sermon (text Luke 14:18: And they all with one consent began to make excuse.)

Mond. [Jan.] **11.** Rose at 6, breakfast at 7:30, went to H. Q. at 8 for the purpose of drawing clothing for the patients and before returning made arrangements with Shrader, the undertaker, to furnish a coffin.

At 9 took two men to H. Q. to be returned to duty and before returning drawed rations for 10 days: missed dinner and had to put up with a cold snack: 2 p. m. made another visit to Commissary for the purpose of procuring extra rations, and had complete success.

At 4 took a furlough to H. Q. to be forwarded to [Gen.?] Burnside: remained in during the evening.

Tues. 12. Rose somewhat earlier than common: 9 a. m. went to post office, came home by commissary and had the rations of flour taken to the bakery: noon when I arrived home: at 2 went to washer woman's for clothing: from 3 till 5 was on the hunt of wood, failed in getting it.

At 7 Turner, Keggie, and I went to the Mite Society which met at Mrs. Montgomery's: the company was very interesting: made several new acquaintances.

The town clock [see photo in narrative] announced the hour of 12 before the assemblage dispersed.

Wed. 13. About the usual hour found me in readiness for breakfast feeling remarkably well, having enjoyed a sweet night's rest.

All I did forenoon was to make a fruitless effort to get wood: spent an hour showballing, made a general thing of it.

A great many troops passed to and from the front this morning.

Afterpart of the day I policed quarters in general: weather pleasant: snow melted so as to spoil sleighing.

Thurs. 14. Had the pleasure of enjoying a good night's repose; nothing worthy of note met my observation during the day: had general inspection at 9 a. m. by Serg. Culver and he pronounced the building in good condition.

Weather has the appearance of a storm: spent the evening at Miss M.

Q.'s: after being there sometime Lila West and Keggie came in which added much to the merriment of the evening.

Fri. 15. It being about midnight when I retired last night, concluded to rest till the first bell rang for breakfast which was 7: at 9 took some men to Head Q.'s and after doing some duty round the house read the Louisville paper till dinner.

S. M. Turner and I went down the street for the purpose of making arrangements for an oyster supper in the evening: all necessary provisions being attended to I returned and left Turner to get a partner, then read in the book called 'Habits in Good Society' (which I commenced about a week ago) till supper at 5 1/2.

Called on Miss S. E. for the purpose of procuring her co.: in the evening at 7 Turner, Keggie, and myself lit out for the purpose of having a good time, which I am happy to say we were willing to acknowledge before quitting our friend, Mrs. S. [Sebastion]

Sat. 16. 6 o'clock found me washing: considerable earlier than I am accustomed to rising, had all my morning work done till breakfast: at 8 a. m. made a fruitless reconnoiter for wood: 9-11 put things in order in the cellar and finished the forenoon by reading.

At 1 p. m. took care of bed clothing that had been lying in the yard for some time: found employment till 7 in receiving and issuing clothing for the ensuing week: 7 1/2 went down street for butter: at 8 took a bath which I have needed for some time and gave myself to slumber at 10 1/2.

Sund. 17. At 7:30 breakfasted: till 9:30 had employment around the house: at 10 took a case of measles to No. 2 Hospital: attended services at John Street at 11: 1 to 2 p. m. read the Bible: occupied some time doing a little of everything until evening service when feeling a need of grace attended service at J. St.

Mond. 18. Rose at the usual time, had the halls policed and snow shoveled from the pavements by breakfast: at 8 attended to the dirty clothes: 10 took a stroll down town for the purpose of getting some chickens: at 2 p. m. took some sick from the [Ohio R.] Ferry to the depot who are on their way home.

At 7 p. m. went to the Commissary: it being raining and snowing altogether made it very disagreeable under foot: found pleasure in finishing my book, Good Society.

Tues. [Jan.] **19.** Turned cold last night after midnight and snowed about 6 in.: was busy until 10 cleaning the pavements.

Had fifty recruits to feed that are on their way to the front: they brought so much snow in the house it took a half day to clean up.

From 11 till 12 read in Dr. Franklin's Travels in the Arctic Regions:

find it of much interest and am resolved to finish it before taking up any other reading.[2]

Spent the afternoon at Mrs. Dottson's: went to Mite Society in the evening with Keggie and Savage: formed the acquaintance [sic] of Hattie Brannon and thought her sweet as a June Bug: enjoyed a pleasant time, returned at 10 and retired at 11.

Wednes. 20. Rose at 6: after putting the room in order read the Bible till breakfast with Keggie, at 9 went to the Commmissary at No. 5.; Head Q. and returned via the post office: 11 a. m. drew rations, rested until 3 p. m., when I went to Parker's and got an order filled for butter, chickens, and eggs: at 7 went to Mrs. Sebastions's and had a gay time: went to bed at 11.

Thurs. 21. Up and had breakfast at 7: went to work at 8 to deliver orders to Nonnemaker.

Nothing of importance occurred during the day except received my furlough and made preparations to depart tomorrow.

Fri. 22. Was ready and started for home at 12 by way of Jeffersonville – had to lay over till 5 p. m.

Sat. 23. Arrived at Indianapolis at 3 a. m., took bkft. at City Hotel: lay over till 12 when I took the cars for M. City: rode with Sam Hall as far as Orr's then walked to Sister Ann's where I arrived at 3 a. m. and slept till 7. went to forenoon church at LaPorte, found many of my old friends: evening attended services at Orr's. met many whom I once associated with.

Mond. 25. Started for home at 8 where I arrived at 12 m. and took them all by surprise: after dinner had a chat with brother Otho [Arthur] and then took a horseback ride: spent the evening at home for the first time in 28 months.

Tues. 26. Rose at 6, breakfasted at 6:30: at 9 started out to see some of the folks: took dinner at Nye's, got as far as Miles's, and put up for the night, spent a couple of hours at Farger's with the sick: retired at 11.

Wed. 27. Remained at Miles's till 9 a. m., then struck out again to see who of my old acquaintances I could find and staid in LaPorte during the night.

Thurs. 28. Started home at 8 where I arrived at 12: afternoon went out with Brother Otho and did very fair half day's work: remained at home during the night.

Feb. Sund. 8. Since I last wrote in my Journal I have had the pleasure

---

[2]Sir John Franklin (1786-1847) published his account of Arctic explorations in 1828. He died in the Arctic regions of Canada while searching for the fabled "northwest passage".

of shaking hands with many of my old friends: with regret I gave them the parting hand, probably for the last time.

On Thursday I bid adieu to Father and Mother and left for N. A. where I arrived on the morning of the 7th: found everything turned upside down and at present have no permanent location: have no idea of remaining here but a short time.

Mond. 8. Slept at No. 1 with Jack, Keggie, and Horton: got very cold along toward morning: slept till 7, just got to No. 8 in time for breakfast: at 8½ went to No. 1, got my dirty clothes, took them to Mrs. Warren's for wash, stayed and wrote a letter to Miss Snyder before leaving.

At 1 p. m. went to No. 1 and wrote two letters: at 3½ Frank M. and I went to No. 5 on business: while there made a resolution to quit smoking: spent the eve at No. 1.

Tues. 9. Rose at 7. breakfasted at 8, at 8½ went to the Express Office: at 9 went to No. 1: at 11 Frank and I went to the P. O. by the way of Dr. Green's [sic] and brought up at No. 8 and took dinner: went to the P. O. and started a box of pens to C. W. Miller. then went to No. 1, wrote a letter and went to Mrs. W.'s and had a P. H. hemmed: spent the evening at Mr. S.'s.

Weather clear but cold.

Wed. 10. Weather fair cold: slept at No. 1 with J. Dunn and Horton: nothing special to date: spent most of the time in writing and reading: went to Stokes' in the evening, had a good sociable time: retired at 10½.

Thurs. 11. Wednesday was quite cold, and a great change has taken place as it is as pleasant as a summer's day: read papers forenoon and at 2 p. m. went to No. 5: went to Day's Book Store by the way of Dr. Green's [sic] office: 7 p. m. went to Miss West's, stayed till 8, then to the depot, met a couple of friends, went home with them and stayed all night.

Fri. 12. Rose at 6:40, reported at No. 8. at 7: after breakfast went to baggage room, the rest of the forenoon spent at No. 1, played checkers with Sherer, beat 3 out of 5 games: at 3 went to No. 1, returned at 4: after supper walked with F. Mast. to the upper part of the City, returned and stopped at H. Q. till 6½, at 7½ went to the depot, returned and went to bed at 9 p. m.

Sat. [Feb.] **13.** Weather clear and quite cold.

No general orders on hand and being at liberty, spent most of the day at No. 1 where the 38th Indiana are concentrating prior to their uniting with the Great Army of the Cumberland: at 2 p. m. took a walk to the river: spent the evening at No. 8.

Sund. 14. Rose at 7. After breakfast washed, put on clean clothes, and went to forenoon church at Centenary: after dinner took a walk with

Frank, Reggie, and Scott to the Soldiers burying ground via Rodger's where I left the boys and took a short walk before returning to the Hosp.: spent the evening at Mrs. D.'s. ate apples and mince pie till I was in misery: returned to No. 1 at 10, was persuaded to stay all night and retired immediately.

Mond. 12. Enjoyed a very poor night's rest as the 38th boys were on a tight and caroused around all night: when I walked I felt more like a broken down army horse than a human being.

Spent the forenoon at Mrs. W.'s: afternoon commenced nursing at No. 9 Hospital in Ward B: not well pleased with the arrangement of things but hope to have some things differently arranged: am not discouraged.

After supper did up work, wrote a letter and then went to the depot to meet a friend.

Tues. 16. Weather changed last night and is so cold today it will freeze very good rot gut.

Rose at 6, did a part of morning work before breakfast: was busy until 10½ in the Ward: took a walk to the Post Office, returned too late for dinner, got a cold snack which answered till supper: spent the afternoon in the ward reading and writing: set up with Franks till 2 o'clock: eat a tin of sugar during the time.

Wed. 17. Being up so late last night caused me to sleep till breakfast.

The Board of Examiners having sent word to keep all in the Hosp., a guard of invalids was placed around the building and I found myself caged for the day, but as the weather is cold, it displeased me but little.

Have some fears of being stuck in the Invalid Corps but have made up my mind to shun it if possible.

10 p. m. and the Board has passed and I am all right: don't intend to pass another Board while here: passed the evening at Warren's.

Thurs. 18. Weather cold snow flying all day: have a lame ankle, can scarcely get around: spent most of the day in the ward: wrote a letter home, hobbled to Stokes's and spent a pleasant evening.

Fri. 19. Rose at 6:25: had but 3 hrs. sleep, was up with a wounded man; during the night eat a half tin of sugar syrup which has a bad effect.

The day is rather cold: remained in most of the time until evening which I spent at the Depaw House.

Sat. 20. Had a good night's rest and feel much revived from yesterday, dreampt of home in this night, thought Sister Julia got married.

Was employed in the Hosp. till dinner: went to No. 1 via Dr. Green's [sic]: at 4 returned via the P. O.. got LaPorte paper but was disappointed in letters: spent the evening at Mrs. Warren's.

Sun. 21. Rose at 7, as I was allowed to lay without interruption: was till 10 a. m. doing morning duty, after which occupied time till dinner by writing a letter: at 1 p. m. took a walk with Frank to No. 1.

Had a long chat with Jack and Mr. Sebastion.

The 38th left this a. m. and such another house as they left human eye never beheld.

Went to John St. Church in the evening in co. with some friends: from there went to the depot and saw Keggie off, returned to church in time to see marriage, after which saw the fair sex to their abodes and returned and sat up until 2.

Mond. 22. Weather pleasant: done morning duty which took till 2 a. m.: took a walk around lawn till dinner: at 1 went to No. 1, returned at 2: stayed in the ward till supper, then went to No. 11 via Head Q. and No. 1 and got some glycerin for Frank.

Tues. 23. Was out at 6: busy in the house till 3 p. m.: O'Leary was ordered here from No. 1 to act as steward and he's having a general tear up: I am ordered to act as Commissary: concluded to do so while I stay.

Weather pleasant till evening when we had quite a storm.

Tried to trade pens with Eugene Shere but after 2 hrs. gave it up and went to bed – was waked up in the night by a dutchman: had a gay time getting him straightened out.

Wed. [Feb.] **24.** Pleasant weather, has much the appearance of spring: breakfast: policed the commissary: at 9 a. m. started out on the hunt of soft soap: didn't succeed: ordered some hooks to hang up meat on the way home.

Remained in the Com. till after dinner: at 2 p. m. went up to No. 1, found Jack and took a walk up to Vincennes St.: came back via Mr. Johnson's Grocery where I found Mr. Turner and agreed to meet him at Mrs. Sebastion's tomorrow at 7 p. m.

Spent the evening with Miss M. E. D. [Mary Ellen Dottson] at her request, on leaving I promised to spend Sunday afternoon with her.

They are all well, but down on the Emancipation Proclamation.[3]

T. H. 25 Nothing more than the regular routine of business until evening, when according to promise I went to Sebastion's and had a general good time: got very much interested in the welfare of one Miss Fowler.

Weather clear and warm with heavy wind in afterpart of the day.

---

[3]Lincoln issued the Emancipation Proclamation on 22 Sept. 1862 to take effect 1 Jan. 1863. It freed the slaves in all parts of the nation still in rebellion (but not in Union-loyal areas). Many in the North failed to appreciate this shift in war objectives from saving the Union to freeing slaves. Apparently the Dottson family was still voicing reservations 17 months after the proclamation was issued.

Fri. 26. At work clearing up the Commissary room all forenoon and now its no cleaner than a hog's nest should be.

Got a letter from Fowler of Ill.

Weather clear and quite pleasant: spent most of the afterpart of the day in writing: attended ch. at Centenary in evening.

Sat. 27. Till 9 a. m. had employment in the Commissary, then wrote a letter and finished up the forenoon by reading: 2 p. m. went to No. 1 with Frank, returned via H. Q. where we spent an hour in social chat with Mac and Dick: was employed writing for the steward from 4 till 5½: spent the evening with Turner at No. 4.

Sund. 28. It has been raining quite hard all day - a more dreary time I've not spent in a long while: had promised to spend the afternoon with Miss M. E. Dottson, but deferred going on acct. of rain till another day, and to add to the wearisome day, Frank Mastermann, a particular friend, left for his Reg.

I spent the day writing and reading.

Mond. [Feb.] **29.** The weather turned cold and sleeted considerable the later part of the night: quite disagreeable.

My employment has been of various kinds: 11 a. m. we were mustered for pay: 1 p. m. took knives to the machine shop and ground them: at 4 issued the meat: at 5 expressed F. M.s trunk home: stayed in. wrote a letter to A. Wing.

March, Tues. 1. Snow this morning to the depth of 4 in. cloudy and disagreeable from 8 a. m. to 3 p. m., employed in drawing rations: came near having a fuss with the C. S. relative to candles.

Got a pleasing letter from Keggie: went to Centenary Church where they are holding a grand revival: there were several converts, didn't break till 10:30: Turner and I went home with the West girls where we stayed till 11:30: I then made my way home.

Wed. 2. Cleared off beautiful and is a pleasant day. had head ache in forenoon, go through with the usual routine of business: afternoon put a window in commissary. got some boards for cupboard at No. 1: had oyster soup for supper: at 7 fixed a collar on and went to Stokes' where I spent one of the most pleasant evenings I ever passed in the place: promised to meet at Sebastion's Fri. eve, returned at 11.

Thurs. 3. Owing to my being up so late I didn't get out till 7: by the time I got ready breakfast was ready and waiting: 8 a. m. went to P. O. and was fixing Com.'s till dinner: 1 p. m. went to H. Q. for nails, failed in getting them, bought 2 lbs. and worked putting up a cupboard in order to lock up preserves, milk, butter, and many other articles which are tempting to a soldier.

Got two letters, also a pair of boots: felt very tired and concluded to spend the eve in the Hosp.

Fri. 4. Felt sick before getting up but after stirring around a while felt much better: after receiving and issuing morning rations we undertook to make a bin for coffee and sugar: was obliged to leave it unfinished on account of being disappointed in getting nails.

Nothing of great note transpired during the day: 2 p. m. Turner and I took a stroll down to the Day Gal. and saw some good looking women: got my old boots half soled, cost 50c, (15c more than it was worth;) at 6 went to No. 4 had a chat with the boys, found R. Wilson down with erysipelas [infectious streptococcus].

Turner and I then struck out for all it was raining so hard, to fulfill an engagement at Mrs. S.'s: there being few of us we had more than a gay time, broke up at 11:30.

Sat. [Mar.] **5.** All quiet on the Potomac and as I want to write a letter will lay my journal aside for that purpose.

Weather dark, cloudy and cold.

Sund. 6. We have had another fine day, every body is fixed up and on the go: after I got morning duty done felt myself tired and seated myself at the window fronting the street and took items till dinner: I believe there have been more people on the street than I've seen unless on a special occasion.

Intended to go to Dottson's after dinner but the steward kept me all afternoon helping to make out monthly reports. Went to Centenary church in the eve, heard an interesting discourse after which was a prayer meeting: five were converted: had the pleasure of conducting Miss Emma and Mrs. S. home.

On arriving at the Hosp. found it 11 o'clock and retired.

Mond. 7. Feel fine today: had my morning's work done at 9, wrote letter to Sister Julia which occupied my time till noon: 2 p. m. went in the Commissary and was there till supper, putting things in order and issuing rations: Mr. Turner and I took a walk after supper along the river, talked over all our confidential talk and as the evening was very pleasant enjoyed it much: stayed in the Hosp. during the evening.

Tues. 8. Rained last night, considerable, but cleared off at 9 this a. m. and has been a pleasant day: my employment has been of various kinds today: rec'd a letter from L. S. which kept me in good spirits: met at Mrs. Sebastion's with Miss E. S. and Emma Fowler and there being two boys to four of the opposite sex. I complied with Mrs. S.'s request and went for J. T. D.: we had a jolly time till 11½ and retired to our respective abodes.

I made a promise before leaving to call on Friday evening.

Wed. 9. Owing to my resting very poorly last night I have felt miserable, more like being in bed than on duty, as has been the case: retire at an early hour, have severe headache and a jerking pain in one eye.

Thurs. 10. Rained all night, cloudy till 10 a. m. when the sky became apparent and the ensuing part of the day was beautiful: was kept busy drawing and arranging rations till 3 p. m.

Owing to a severe cold which I caught yesterday, I feel quite dumpish: it appears to be settling in one of my eyes. If I should get the sore eyes it will be a pretty how-de-do just as I am to leave for the front.[4]

Fri. 11. Slept but very little last night, suffered with my eye, very badly inflamed and muscle inflamed, resolved to take the thing cool, barely doing my duty and spending the rest of the day in bed.

As I promised to meet at Mrs. S.'s in the evening and not wishing to forfeit my promise, got ready and went: as Miss Maggie Watson was there without co. it fell to me to see her home.

Sat 12. Find I have to content myself in the ward as a patient for some time: this forenoon I suffered much pain, got some sugar lead and commenced applying at noon and soon felt relieved, but it is about the same this evening.

Sun 13. Rested very poorly last night, my right eye is becoming affected: have given up work and taken up my abode in wd. as a patient: my determination is to be as patient as possible till I get better: sent a note by the politeness of Mr. Turner to Miss E. excusing myself from service this evening: find no satisfaction in anything I get at.

Mond. Owing to the condition of my eyes I'll not attempt to do any writing. I'm confined to the ward and a more disagreeable time I never witnessed.

Thurs. 16. Since I wrote the above I have not been out of the house: this morning I changed the medicine and feel easier this afternoon but I have but little confidence in doctoring eyes with any strong medicine.

This is the last I shall write till I can see better.

Sund. 19. Have not been out of the house since my last writing: think my eyes are improving: I am having one of the lonliest times ever experienced outside of Libby[5]: by good care I expect to get out by next week.

There has been considerable interest transpired the past week but it would be doing an injustice to use my eyes.

---

[4]This is the first solid indication that the gay life of New Albany is soon to be forsaken for the rigors of the front.

[5]This mysterious reference may refer to "Libby Prison" in Richmond, VA, a prisoner of war camp for Union officers. Of course, this is only conjecture.

April. Sat. 2 Yesterday it rained all day without ceasing: didn't do anything but cook and eat till evening when I went out to Stokes' and had a pleasant time till 11. It has ceased to rain today but is still cloudy: didn't get up till 9, by the time breakfast was over it was 10½: had nothing to do but box a few blankets.

Thurs. Mar. 31. This is the first I've been able to write since the 20th and to do my eyes justice I would refrain but get so tired sitting around doing nothing I can't content myself.

The past week I've been improving rapidly, suffer but little pain unless I expose myself in windy weather.

Nothing has transpired lately: been to see my Duck twice since I was taken sick.

The weather has been very changeable: have had considerable rain.

The 13th Mich. are in town raising thunder: they are about two thirds drunk and cause more excitement than has been here for weeks.

April 7. Made up my mind last evening to join the Co. busy till 2 p. m. at which hour left N. A., reported at Louisville and expect to stay over tomorrow as I was too late for transportation for tomorrow.[6]

Fri. 8. Passed a disagreeable night, there being about 200 in the building (or prison, as it is styled by the boys) a great many were tight and such a hullabaloo as was kept up, I never heard.

Was disappointed in getting off this morning, however I'll make the best of it: as it is raining and is like to all day, I don't care anything particular about going out in town: I don't feel spited to any extent.

The change from a good bed to the hard floor goes rather tough, but all I ask is health.

Louisville is lined with officers and troops, passing and repassing, with a majority for the front.

Sat. 9. Hustled out and breakfasted at 4. 5½ got orders to leave for Nashville, 7 left the depot, had a very agreeable ride, landed at Nashville depot at 7 p. m.

Took lodging at the Johnnie Officers' Prison to await further transportation: there was no want for attendants, but they were too much mixed with the Gray Backs to be desirable.

Supper, coffee, and a slice of bread went rather tough, but hoping for a better day am contented, wishing nothing but speedy transportation to my destiny.

Sund. 10. Gloomy enough in the old dungeon this a. m., owing to my partner playing a little chicanery with the blankets last night, I slept

---

[6]This passage marks the end of Pvt. Hupp's 17 month stay in New Albany, Indiana.

miserable cold and feel more like a condemned mule than anything else: it is now 8: there are some hopes of us leaving at 10: if so all right.

Providence lent a helping hand and started us at 5 a. m. Nothing occurred of note till the train reached Tullahoma [TN], when in getting off to get a pie I lost my revolver: it was found by Perles and I had the fortune to recover it.

Mond. 11. Reached Stevenson at 6 this a. m., took breakfast at Soldier's Home.

Since I left this place a year and a half ago many changes have taken place: then there were many citizens in the vicinity: at present there is scarcely one to be found.

There are two regiments of Inf. and a Bat. of Art. stationed as a guard with about 100 negroes which are kept to do the drudgery.[7]

5 p. m. and no train to Chattanooga which has been due since 3: a telegram says she won't be in before 8: if so we have another night's ride tonight and it is impossible for one to enjoy any rest: could I have found a clean spot out of the sun I might have slept some today, but that was impossible.

The staple production of the place is negroes and Gray Backs, of the latter I think it excels any port I ever was in.

Tues. 12. Left Stevenson at 9 last evening, arrived at Chattanooga 2 this a. m.. stopped Soldier's Home till 7 when the train left for Laudon and I had the luck to get aboard: reached my destination (Cleveland [TN]) 1 p. m. wasn't certain whether any of the Battery was here or not, but about 15 min. told the story, I found the center section camped about 1 m. from town on the most beautiful camp ground I ever was in: they had anticipated I would remain in [New] Albany until my term of service expired.

After having a general chat with my comrads, C. W. Miller and I took a long walk and had a talk over things which had origin since last we met: felt very lonely at night as is natural in consequence of being taken from such an interesting society of the opposite sex.

Wed. 13. Was excused from roll call and slept till breakfast: spent the forenoon in and around camp: afterpart of the day done some washing and made addition to the bunk which had been accustomed to accommodating but two.

Thurs. [Apr.] **14.** Nothing particular today to record in my journal:

---

[7]By this time in the war many black regiments had been formed, some engaging in combat. By the end of the war some 300,000 Negroes serving in 166 regiments fought on the Union side. The black laborers at Fort Stevenson were, no doubt, local former slaves - not soldiers. Their treatment by Northern forces here apparently differed little from what they were used to as slaves.

Miller and I got a permit and visited the famous city (Cleveland) after dinner: it has every appearance of having been a beautiful place before the horrors of war had reached it: there are but few of the higher class remaining here. they have left the place and joined their Southern brethren.

Before coming back we went to the Hosp. where J. Egner is confined: he gave me a jacket which I left in the Co. when leaving: had no idea of ever seeing it again: left it in city to be repaired and aim to have it on the morrow.

Fri. 15. Nothing of importance today: what spare time I had was devoted to letter writing: on guard from 7 to 11.

Sund. 17. On account of moving to the Battery at Blue Springs, had no time to devote for myself: at 2 p. m. we reached the boys: was busy till dark fixing quarters: slept very disagreeable last night, was out grazing horses all forenoon, at 4 went on grand review.

I am very much dissatisfied with the situation of our camp: we are to move tomorrow and it is hopeful it will be for the better.

We are now stationed 4 m. from Cleveland on the Knoxville and Dalton R. R. 88 m. from the former and 22 from Dalton: country is rolling, nothing but the valleys can be farmed: but few farms are harmed and are in as good farming condition as before the war: had the horses not been taken by the rebels a good crop would be put out the present season, but as it is they are dependent on the Gov. for support.

April 25. Since my last writing the weather has been pleasant with cold nights, but as my partners and I have 5 blankets between us we manage to sleep very comfortable.

Yesterday (Sunday) we were out a mile from camp on grand review: the reviewing officer (Gen. Whittaker)[8] had got about half through when the heavens started a cold bath on His Majesty which caused him to retreat in good order and his troops ditto: today we were on battalion drill all forenoon and grazing horses the afterpart of the day: the boys scarcely get time to eat their meals, let alone doing their washing and other necessary work.

Had a gay time last night on guard, the 2nd time since my return.

Sat. 30. The weather until yesterday has been clear and quite warm: last night it rained near night which has been of great benefit, not only to

---

[8]Gen. Walter C. Whitaker (1823-1887) was a veteran of Shilo and Stones River, and later led troops at the division level at Lookout Mtn., Chattanooga, the Atlanta Campaign, and the battle of Nashville. As a Kentucky state senator in 1861 he proposed the resolution that kept Kentucky in the Union after the invasion by Confederate troops.

the citizens in this vicinity but also the Army: having to graze horses it has started the grass afresh which will add much to the recruiting of the horses preparatory to the marches we are about to make: the forest trees present the appearance of summer.

There has been no diversion in military matters the past week any further than making preparations to move: have had battalion drill twice in Monday and Thursday.

I have had the pleasure of receiving two letters and have mailed 8.

May, Mon. 2. Yesterday the battery was ordered on review at 8 a. m. but owing to the wet and disagreeable morning an order came delaying same till 2 p. m., but not till we were harnessed and ready to move out, the forepart of the day was spent grazing horses: at 2 moved out to be gazed upon by Gen. Stanley[9], Brig. Gen. Whittaker, and staff (the Brigadiers are now consolidated which gives them the appearance of our old division.)

At present our brigade numbers 8000: since the war commenced I have yet to witness a more perfect appearance of soldiery.

After the Brigade formed a hollow square with the battery in one corner which position was kept while 2 deserters were drummed out of service: one had his head shaved and they presented a pitiable sight.

It was some time after sundown when we arrived at Camp: I have been out on a battalion drill all forenoon.

We had a balky horse in the team which caused considerable trouble and just as we reached camp it commenced raining and has finished up the day to perfection in so doing.

Tues. [May] **3.** Last night we had a heavy frost and the coldest morning since my return: the day is beautiful.

Camp is all in a bustle preparing to march between now and tomorrow morning: supply train has moved up to Cleveland to load with orders to be at Red Clay (8 mi. from Dalton) tomorrow noon.

Done my washing this forenoon and packed my clothes in the evening.

We marched with 5 das. rations: the general supposition is that our destination is Dalton.

---

[9]Gen. David Sloan Stanley (1828-1902) was a veteran of numerous campaigns in the far west, including Kansas, Missouri, and Mississippi (Corinth). As Chief of Cavalry of the Army of the Cumberland he was at Franklin, Nolansville, and Stones River. When Hupp saw him, he was leading the 1st Division, IV Corps, Cumberland. He eventually took part in numerous battles in Georgia (incl. Atlanta) and became commander of the IV Corps. He won the Medal of Honor in 1893 for his actions at Franklin, remaining in the Army until retirement in 1892.

Marched at 12 m., reached Red Clay at 7: camp in the woods close to a beautiful run: on guard first relief: got no sleep.

Wed. 4. Reveille at 3: our brigade moved at 5 a. m. moving very slowly as our advance had the country to scout and more or less skirmishing.

At 2 p. m. went in Camp on the Kingold [Ringgold] and Dalton Road 12 mi. from the latter place.

Here the enemy was found to be drawn up in line 1½ [miles] ahead.[10]

Infantry worked till dark on breastworks: our batt. is in position on the yard of a bitter secessionist: the [artillery] piece I belong to is within 10 feet of the door and as they have one of the fairs I propose to take my headquarters under the roof.

The country is very broken and rough: Tiger Creek runs to the east of us about ½ mile: it is a beautiful running stream about 10 rods wide.

There is very little land under cultivation: timber principally oak with much underbrush.

People more ignorant than any part in Africa: they can't tell their ages and know nothing of places 3 and 5 miles around them, and the negroes can't tell east from west.

At 5 got supper which I relished, you bet: at 8 Charley and I made our pallet and lay down under an oak tree in the yard probably to be routed in ½ hour.

Thurs. 5. Enjoyed a good night's repose: pickets did considerable firing which was unheard after 9: nothing exciting along the line: changes are being made by moving the line further (or extending rather) to the west: at 5 p. m. our brigade moved half mile: no more indications of advancing than this morning: at 6 o'clock we are in a new position within 20 rds. of the famous Catoosa Springs, which, if we don't move before tomorrow, I intend to visit and take note of their different names.

The position our line now holds can defeat 200,000 men.

At 7 eat supper, sat around till 8, made our pallets and got to rest for the night.

Fri. 10. No disturbance during the night: tended stable call at ½ past 4: breakfast at 6.

Water call at 8: after which Charley and I visited the Springs of which there are 22 in number styled as follows:

---

[10]This passage marks the prelude to the Battle of Rocky Face Ridge (May 5- 11) centered around Dalton, GA. It marked the opening battle of the Atlanta Campaign conceived by Gen. William Tecumseh Sherman, Commander of the Military Division of the Mississippi. Hupp's unit was now part of Gen. George Thomas' Army of the Cumberland (some 61,000 strong) charged with the task of a frontal attack on entrenched Confederate positions.

White sulphur, Blue, Red, Green, Black, Yellow, Healing, Red-Sweet, Sweet-Beet, Emetic, Chootmobasgo, Chaly Beat, Congress, Free Stone, Buffalo, Coffee, Magnesia, Alkali, Epsom, White Clover, Lee, Sulphur-White Excelsior.

This place is said to have been a grand resort for pleasure seekers during the months of August and September, also for invalids: for convenience the grounds are ornamented in grand style, with various houses for amusement there are two bowling alleys, several bowery houses, a daguerreotype gallery, two battling houses and several other buildings of minor importance: the main building is of brick three stories high with balconies on either side of the 2nd story running the entire length: there is also a building 200 ft. long, 1 story high, about 15 ft. wide with a porch on both sides divided off into rooms for the convenience of families: attached to the premises there was said to have been one of the finest livery stables ever known in the south: the whole is in an enclosure of about 5 acres, the ground just rolling enough to present a beautiful picture: picturesque scenery.

The most singular characteristic connected with the great Georgia watering depot is that the springs, all of which are within a half acre of ground, neither affording the same kind of water.

It is now 12 m. if at leisure this afternoon I'll give a description of camp.

No time to take notes this evening: prepared to advance in the morning: received orders at 6 p. m. that no man should fall out of the ranks to assist the wounded from the field until after the battle is decided.

Charley and I lay down at 9 but it was high 11 before my eyes closed in sleep.

Sat. [May] **7.** Reveille at 2½ a. m., all in readiness: our brigade (the 2d command by Whittaker) moves off in advance in the Tunnel Hill Road: 6 a. m. have halted a mile from camp: can distinctly hear skirmishing on the left: halt 15 min.: line of battle formed, move forward, advance ½ m.: meet with many obstructions which hinder us but little: advance to the top of Buzzard Roost Ridge.

Halt 15 min., fire five rounds at about 3000 Cavalry, when they skedaddled and at once our line marched on Tunnel Hill without opposition, where I now write.

The enemy are falling back on Dalton, such is the supposition at least.

1 p. m. have advanced this part of the line ½ m. took a position, fired 5 rounds which caused the enemy to fall back.

The ground which we now occupy was covered with rebel troops to the no. of 10,000 so stated by citizens.

The land is very rolling and before its occupation by the C. S. was heavily timbered, but is covered with rifle pits and log houses.

3 p. m. have not yet moved: pickets are being thrown out which indicates our staying over night, doubtless for the purpose of giving the flanks time to advance.

6 fire rounds at a squad of Cavalry.

Sund. 8. Troops coming on different parts of our line all night: Reveille at 4: have lain in line of battle all night without advancing.

6 a. m. eat breakfast, having procured a good supply of meat and crackers when leaving Catoosa Springs: I have yet a plenty for 2 days: as our rations ran out tonight, I'll not be apt to suffer if we fail in getting rations which will doubtless be the case as it is unsafe for wagons in the front.

8 a. m. The signal Eng. fired for the line to advance: at once the Army threw out the skirmish line and started down the valley which lay in our front: the ground which has been gained up to 4 p. m. has been hotly contested for: skirmishing commenced within 40 rods from where they started: up till 4 p. m. our 2 pieces which have been in front from the start, held their position taken yesterday, occasionally firing a shot at Buzzard's Roost: 5 p. m., move out to the skirmish line where firing and musketry is going on quite brisk, both to the right and left: I know not the object in taking this position, but suppose it is for the purpose of opening an old Rebel Fort about a mile in front.

We are waiting the coming of two more pieces when I suppose the dance is to commence: I have spoken for a partner in the first set.

Our line is but a mile in advance this morning: it has not been the intention to bring on a general engagement on Sunday but the general impression is the grand docia [?] will come off tomorrow unless the enemy retreat: weather yesterday and today has been as hot as I ever witnessed.

½ past four 2 batteries are in the above named position (the 7th Penn. and ours) open fire on an important point on the right of the Gap: keep it up ½ hour: it is then taken by the Infantry: heavy firing is heard on the right: supposed to be McPherson's[11] forces, which part of the line we are now waiting for: heavy skirmishing is now being constantly kept up in our Brigade but as yet I have heard of none being killed or wounded.

---

[11]Gen. James B. McPherson (1828-1864) commanded the Army of the Tennessee and was considered by Sherman to be one of the North's most promising generals. On July 22, 1864 during the Battle of Atlanta he moved to the front to rally his men, but advanced too far and stumbled into Confederate skirmishers. Ordered to surrender, he turned his horse and ran but was promptly shot from the saddle. He was 35 years old. Upon seeing his body, Gen. Sherman wept.

Mond. 9. Reveille at half past 3: are ready to move out at 5: musketry firing was kept up along the entire line of pickets all night, which is about ¼ of a mile in advance of our section.

Mond. 16. Since my last writing our battery has been engaged with the enemy every day: yesterday and the day before we had hot work:[12] Saturday evening were charged by Stevenson's Rebel Div.[13]

Fri. 20. Was compelled to lay aside writing to move forward: now that we have a day of rest (the first since the 3rd) I have seated myself and hope not to be disturbed for at least a ½ hr.

Well, to continue with Saturday evening's proceedings, the Infantry which supported us gave way and became perfectly demoralized, but not so with the battery which kept up a galling fire of double charge canister for a ½ hr. at which time old Joe Hooker[14] double quicked a brigade of his boys in and we were safe: the enemy retreated, leaving over 200 dead in the field and the wounded were carried off as they fell back.

Since the 16th we have been pressing the enemy closer (as they are retreating toward Atlanta) than has ever been the case before.

Yesterday [May 19th][15] the battery was in the immediate advance: fighting commenced at 7, pressed them until 10 when they were found to be drawn up in line of battle (and as we supposed were going to fight) but it proved to be a mere demonstration.

Our lines were formed at once and at 1 p. m. we advanced driving them 1½ miles with considerable opposition: but no general engagement: darkness closed the scene and gave way to the ambulances which scattered themselves over the field picking up the wounded and dead.

It is hard to name any accurate no. we have lost so far: probably 400 would be too low an estimate.

---

[12]With this brief passage (and following sentence) Hupp relates his experiences in the battle of Resaca, GA July 13-16, 1864. One of a string of battles leading to Atlanta, it ultimately resulted in the withdrawal of Joseph E. Johnston's Confederate force to Allatoona pass near Dallas, GA, site of the next battle.

[13]Carter Littlepage Stevenson (1817-1888) served under John Bell Hood during the Atlanta campaign. He distinguished himself at Resaca and Kenesaw Mtn. Later he fought at Nashville and Bentonville in the Carolinas. After the war he was a civil and mining engineer.

[14]"Fighting Joe" Hooker (1814-1879) commanded XX Corps of the Army of the Cumberland during this campaign. He had once commanded the Army of the Potomac but was relieved by Meade (victor at Gettysburg) after Hooker's defeat at Chancellorsville.

[15]These passages describe skirmishing at Cassville. The Confederates had laid a trap here for the divided Union forces but fell back with only minor skirmishing after erroneously overestimating troop strength on the Union left (their first target).

It is generaliy believed the great battle will come off a few miles in advance of this place, as their men are getting tired of running.

Sund. [May] **22.** Our Corps [IV Corps; Oliver O. Howard] with the 20th [Hooker] and 14th [John McAuley Palmer] is still at or near Kingston: the enemy is reported to have left our front but where they have gone is not yet ascertained: it may be Atlanta, but the general impression is contrary.

The right wing of the Army is moving around which accounts for our lying still.

1 p. m. have just received orders to send to the rear all baggage except 1 blanket, 1 shirt, 1 pr. drawers and 1 pr. socks: march at 4 in the morning.

The weather has been extremely hot from 9 a. m. till 4 p. m. for 10 days past.

I have seen finer country since leaving Dalton than I have seen in the south: the farms are all well improved with large orchards, good buildings, and everything that can give comfort to life, but the Army has greatly altered its appearance: fences are mostly destroyed, many of the houses laid in ruins by the flames and the coming crops will amount to nothing notwithstanding the prospects were never better than before the Yankee invasion: the land generally speaking, this side of Dalton is well watered both for stock and family purposes: timber consists mostly of oak, very little chestnut, with now and then a lonely pine.

The inhabitants (what few remain) are of a more enterprising character (especially among the farmers) than we've been privileged to meet this side of Nashville: Kingston has been a beautiful little village of about 1000 inhabitants, with two churches and several schoolhouses: at present it is desolate enough, having been riddled by our boys.

Mond. 23. 10 a. m. I have but a few moments to write troops have been moving to the right since 2 o'clock – our corps is to march at 12 m.

Nothing new today, weather exceedingly warm.

Tues. 24. Since 2 p. m. yesterday we (or the 4th corps) have marched 10 mi.: owing to other troops in advance we have had to march very slow: 5 mi. from Kingston we crossed the Etawa River, a beautiful stream about 20 rods in width: the country remains level with good improvements, but scarcely any remain at home to take charge of the large crops of corn and wheat which have the most promising appearance of anything I've ever seen in the south.

Sund. 29. The enemy has made a stand: the 20th corps (Hooker's) engaged the enemy on the 25: had a brisk fight and lost heavy as the enemy had great advantages.[16]

Our corps was got in position at 11 p. m., next morning the battery was taken along the lines to the left 1½ mi. where we went in position which we held 2 hrs., at which time were relieved by Bridges' Batt. Our Howitzers were then sent to reserve: our section then moved ½ mi. farther to the left in Gross's brigade where a cross fire was opened on us, compelling us to keep silent, the sharp shooters kept a continual pecking at us until darkness closed the scene of action.

We were then marched back to the Batt.: on the following day, the Co. was ordered to a close support at 8 a. m., but owing to the sharpshooters' fire were soon taken back out of their range as we were not wanted on the line: in the afternoon of the same day Cap. took the cannoniers to a point on the line but a short distance from the enemy's works for the purpose of fortifying for the guns: before 2 hrs. had passed had 1, Jake Kertz [Kurtz] shot dead and 1 wounded both with the same ball.

Having completed a temporary protection for the cannoniers [sic] against sharpshooters, the guns were taken out at 6 p. m. and opened fire at once which was doubly returned by sharpshooters which lasted till darkness prevailed: our loss was 1, Gabe Suhart, shot dead and 1 horse: 8 withdrew 4 guns, leaving two howitzers in possession.

Great addition was made to our work by the Pioneers [military engineers] who worked diligently all night: next day (Sunday 29th) the 2 guns remained in possession without opening fire, the other 4 laying off the line about 40 rds.

Heavy skirmishing all along the line, our forces paying dearly for the little advance made in the line.

Mond. p. m. our section went into position: had just laid down for a few hours sleep when the enemy made a 11 o'clock charge: the brasia lasted but ½ hr., finding they could make nothing, retreated to their holes and quiet prevailed the remainder of the night.

The battery held their position without opening fire during the day, heavy skirmishing in our front caused us to lay close to our hole: in the evening after firing ceased our section withdrew, being ordered to King-

---

[16]This is the battle of Dallas, GA (also known as New Hope Church, Pumpkin Vine Creek, Allatoona Hills, Burned Hickory). The Confederate commander, Jos. E. Johnston held Allatoona pass, a formidable defensive position. Sherman decided to skirt him by a flanking movement to the west toward Dallas, a move that was countered by Johnston. Frustrated, Sherman's forces returned to the east toward the main rail line, a move also countered by Johnston. A series of actions followed leading up to the Federal repulse at Kenesaw Mountain, near Atlanta.

ston with Cruft's Brigade as a guard to the Corps Trains. moved off at 9½ reached the Pea Vine Creek 4 mi. from the line, at which point we lay the remainder of the night.

All the Army trains are kept on the north side of said creek and are only taken up to the line as they are needed and never during the day unless it be for ammunition.

Well, our train began to pull out at 3: as the guard were ordered in the rear it was 8 a. m. before we started.

There has been no rain since the 24th which has caused it to be worse than dusty: never marched in a more disagreeable time: moved unmolested.

June Wed. 2. Moved out at 7 a. m. crossed the Etawa River 4 miles from Kingston at 9. At this point Gen. McPherson had a sharp engagement with the enemy on the 25th of May: the contest was for the bridge, our fire being too hot caused them to abandon the scene.[17]

12 m. reached Kingston where the whistle of a locomotive announced the Cracker line: all eight went in camp about 40 rds. east of town, were all about played out, but from the afternoon's rest which we got, our spirits were revived and if necessary, could have pulled out for the scene of action.

7 p. m. Had a good supper, having drawn full rations for 4 days during the afternoon.

Thurs. 3. Lay silent till 5 o'clock for the first time in 4 wks.: after breakfast the Lieutenant, having learned we would not be likely to leave today owing to the lack of forage to load the train, let the boys strike off for the stream to do their washing.

Charley and I got ours done by 9 a. m., spent the remainder the forenoon in clearing up my things and writing up the Journal: 1 p. m. and has commenced raining.

Sat. [Fri.] **4.** Have not left Kingston yet, owing to the lack of forage, expect to leave tomorrow: been showery all day: occupied most of the forenoon writing letters: after part of the day read the escape of John Morgan and Capt. Hines from the Ohio Peniteniary [sic], and grazed horses.

Nothing of importance heard from the Army troop stationed at this point: are busily fortifying for the defense of Rebel Cavalry which is liable to dash in any hr.

---

[17]This is a clear reference to the hostilities near Dallas (May 25-27), but Hupp may have gotten his generals mixed up here. Gen. Geary (2nd Div. of Hooker's XX Corps, Cumberland) made a daring dash across the burning bridge over Pumpkin Vine Creek at Owens Mill on the 25th. Possibly the action involving McPherson centered around some other bridge.

Wed. [Tues.] **8.** We left Kingston on Sund., rained all day, marched to ______: went into camp for the night: roads very bad: put up the tarpaulin and had a good night's rest: pulled out at 7 Monday morning: still continues raining: roads getting worse.

Reached _____, camped for the night: Tuesday very little rain: cross the Pumpkin Vine Mts., camp at _____, the heaviest day's march on the road.

Wednesday, train[18] commenced moving at daylight, we being ordered with the rear guard didn't move till 9 a. m. ceased raining, roads getting better, reached the battery at 9 p. m.: boys very tired and were soon in their bunks and almost as soon asleep.

Found our Corps 8 miles to the left of where we left them: the casualties in the battery since our leaving has been 1 wounded.

Rebels retreated Saturday night, our force occupies their works and are preparing for an advance which will take place within a few days.

The [rail] cars ran through to Etawa on Tuesday: the place was occupied by McPherson on Monday.

The battery is in good fighting condition: forage has been rather scarce for the past wk. as well as rations, but the heavy trains which arrived yesterday will furnish ample supplies for some time and as the cars are up with the army there will be no danger of our starving: weather still continues lowery with now and then a shower.

Charley and I have been busy all forenoon fighting Gray Backs: came off victorious and hope to remain masters of the field during the remainder of the campaign.

The first mail for 8 days reached us today: I was favored with 2 letters, one of which was from home: nothing could be more acceptable: also got a couple copies of the LaPorte Union which were welcome messengers among the boys of that Co.

Thurs. [May] **9.** Army still living in Camp: expected to march this morning but were happily disappointed.

Are under marching orders and expect to march at early noon tomorrow: weather fair and quite warm: am on guard, have spent my spare time letter writing.

Our camp is situated 4 mi. from Ocolona Station in a dense forest of oak: we are furnished with water but a few rods from camp, by a beautiful spring, good as any water we've had on the campaign.

---

[18] The term "train" can refer to a railroad train, or to a train of wagons, artillery pieces, marching soldiers, etc. Although troops were sometimes moved by rail, in this case Hupp is referring to the other kind of train; the kind that moved over muddy (or dusty) unpaved roads.

Ocolona is a small station on the Atlanta R. R. 30 mi. from Kingston.

Fri. 15. The 10th our Corps took the advance, moved out 2 mi. from the line toward _____ where we encountered the enemy drawn up in line of battle and have been whittling away ever since last night: it rained almost constantly and it is now almost impossible to move troops: today the weather presents a fair prospect for the better.

Since our coming here we have done very little firing, probably 100 rounds will cover all.

Our section is apart from the rest of the battery, they being to the left of the line about a mile.

Last evening we moved the section ¼ mi. to the right and have not yet opened fire in our new position but expect to before the day closes: our works are very good but will stand cannonading but a short time: there has been cannonading on the left since yesterday: it is rumored our forces are attempting to turn the enemy's right.

16. Enemy fallen back from our immediate front, caused by movements on the left. 11 a. m. have advanced about a mile, fighting more or less along the entire line with what result I am unable to say.

Enemy gradually falling back: strong apprehension of a heavy battle before many days.

The second volley fired from our section yesterday is said to have killed L. G. Polk[19]: no casualties in the batt. lately: health good, plenty of rations, and consequently but little grumbling.

We are now on a place which has been hotly contested for 3 days past: it affords the best view of the surrounding country I ever beheld: the range of the Altoona [Allatoona] can first be seen, and even the famous Lookout and Mission [Missionary] Ridge can be distinguished towering above all the others in the distance.

Received a very welcome letter this morning containing several photographs

Mond. [May] **20.** Have not taken opportunity to write in my journal for several days: since the 17th a great amount of rain has fallen: enemy has fallen back to within 1¼ miles of Marietta, but not without considerable stubbornness yesterday and the day before: our corps (the 4th) lost many in killed and wounded on the 17th: Capt. Simmons [Simonson] was

---

[19]Leonidas Polk (1806-1864) was an Episcopal Bishop related to President James Polk. Although a West Point graduate, he accepted a commission from his friend, Jefferson Davis, and was appointed Maj. General in June 1861. At Perryville he was second in command to Bragg and was promoted to Lt. Gen. after that battle. He was killed by a rifled cannon shell on June 14 (not the 15th as in Hupp's account) at Pine Hill (Pine Top, Pine Mountain). At least three batteries have been credited with this kill; most reports lay the "honor" on the 5th Indiana.

killed with a musket ball while on the skirmish line overseeing works that were being constructed for our battery: his loss is greatly felt with us boys as he has been to us as a father since we enlisted.[20]

The battery has had but little fighting to do for 2 days: Gen. Stanley, our new Comd. giving us a little rest although we remain in reach of the enemies musketry: no harm done to us since last report but are all feeling bad caused mostly by the rain.

Rations of hard tack short: have none for noon and don't draw till this evening.

While writing am seated behind oak about a foot through: enemy have cross fire and its hardly safe: was rejoiced to hear from Sister Lib [Anelizabeth] last night.

8 a. m. have not taken position yet: boys are scattered around through the batt. mostly sheltered behind some object to turn the bullets: before us lies a large mountain covered with Rebels and Reb. Art, which it is thought will be tried today: if it should, the loss of life will undoubtedly be great.

Hasn't rained any since last evening but has much the appearance of renewing the contest soon.

Am very anxious to write a couple of letters, doubtful whether I get the chance soon.

Thurs. 23. Since the 20th there has been a great amount of fighting all along the line: at times, where we have been stationed, the line being farther advanced than any portion of the line, the enemy had a raking cross fire on us which did a vast deal of damage: we were very fortunate, lost 1 man killed with a solid shot: held the line with hard struggling: last night moved about 3 mi. to the right where our forces appear to be concentrating.

Enemy from all appearances is bound to fight the decisive battle at this point: it is reported Ewell has taken com'd of their Army where we now are.[21]

---

[20]Capt. Peter Simonson (not Simmons) was leader of the 5th Indiana since its muster in. He was killed on June 15 during one of the various battles leading up to Kenesaw Mtn. Official Records show only one officer lost in this battery during its three years of continuous service.

[21]Gen. Richard S. Ewell (1817-1872) saw service at 1st Bull Run, Seven Days Battles, Cedar Mountain, 2nd Bull Run and Groveton (where he lost a leg). He also led forces at Gettysburg, Kelly's Ford (wounded), the Wilderness, and Spotsylvania. A fall from his horse at "Bloody Angle" in the latter campaign (May 1864) rendered him unfit for further field service. Thus, "Dick" Ewell was not commanding any troops facing Hupp's unit at this time – the prelude to the battle of Kenesaw Mountain.

The enemy attacked our lines 7 days and got repulsed and we are now expecting another attack today.

Sat. 25. The line as far as I could hear yesterday, was more quiet than for many days, very little cannonading going on and that on the left: have not changed positions since the 23rd.

Weather extremely hot.

As we are posted near a fine spring and have had but little to do, the days have cleaned themselves up, which together with the rest we are having we feel just like new.

We are at loss to account for the stillness, but better at present that it be known to the one only, time will reveal all.

Yesterday my idle time was occupied in washing my clothes and writing letters, which was the case throughout the Com'y.

11 a. m. cannonading commenced about an hour ago, about 3 mi. to our left and has increased to a continual roll with scarcely any cessation: it is supposed to have commenced from the enemy for the purpose of an attack on some other point: should it be here, we are ready, but I think it will come off, if at all to the right.

[NOTE: The following ten paragraphs concern the battle of Kenesaw Mountain, June 27-29]

Tues. 28. When I last wrote we were quietly lying in line of battle: Sunday all was quiet in our front, some cannonading was heard both to the right and left, but it proved to be nothing serious.

Yesterday (Monday) at 8 a. m. a heavy charge was commenced: the parties engaged were parts of the 4th, 14th, and 15th Corps: a murderous cannonading was kept up ½ hr. and then the Infantry went for the Johnnies [divisions of Smith (2,XV), Newton (2,IV), and Davis (2, XIV)].

The result was not as satisfactory as desired: failing to dislodge them from their works, they fell back but a short distance from the same and fortified [Davis' 2nd Div., XIV Corp]: which position has since been held and is now so well fortified that no fears are entertained of the result in case of a charge.

Our loss in this bloody affair was large, probably 2000 in killed and wounded [1,999 to be exact!]: the great difficulty in the charge was the extreme heat: by the time the charging column reached the point where their strength was most needed, most of them were given out, which of course would have proven disastrous: while cool weather might have crowned us with victory. We lay under a heavy artillery fire the greater part of the day – our loss was nothing.

Today our 4 Napoleons have been firing at intervals all day: Johnnies have been playing artillery on us in return, but owing to the strength of our works, there have been no casualties.

Reports are afloat that the 4th, 12th, and 20th Corps are to move on the extreme right of the line tonight, which in all probability is the case: this move (if not a disastrous one) will send the enemy south of the Chattahooche.[22]

We are all well, in good spirits, anxious to see the termination of the campaign, but don't expect it under a month.

Crackers short, meat and coffee does very well: received a letter from home of much interest.

Thurs. 30. Yesterday afternoon we took our 2 Rodman Guns to Big Shanty and turned them over, they being unfit for further use until repaired: in their stead we got 2 guns from Spencer Batt. M. 1st Ill.[23]

Being late when we arrived at the station, stayed all night and returned this a. m.: found the line as it was yesterday: a severe brashia was made between the hours of 12 & 2 by the Johnnies, which lasted an hr.: resulted in a repulse with considerable loss: weather has much the appearance of rain: all quiet along the line as far as I can hear except the peck-peck of the skirmishing which is constantly kept up both day and night.

Sat. July 2, 1864. Since Thursday there has been but little fighting: I have heard of no changes being made on either side: last night there was considerable maneuvering of transports, all but one Div. of the 14th Corps moved to the right [see footnote 22]: where they will turn up I am at a loss to say, probably to the extreme right with the intention of making an early attack on that point.

The day was extremely hot: having but little to do our boys hugged the shade which we have constructed close to our fortifications, which is a safe resort against the bullets and very often shell which the Johnnies send over the line at all hours of the day, musketry being much worse at night than by day: scarcely a night passes but what we have one or more brasias: this 3 a. m. heavy cannonading commenced about 2 mi. to the left: kept getting nearer and nearer and at 5 the batteries in our Corps were paying their usual respects to the Rebs, this being the extent of the line that was ordered to fire: firing kept up till 7 when the sound of artillery ceased,

---

[22]On the night of July 1 Sherman sent McPherson to the extreme right in an enveloping movement around Johnston's forces (a tactic he had used previously). Subsequently Johnston retreated to a line along the north bank of the Chattahooche River, about 7 miles northwest of Atlanta.

[23]A gun of this type reportedly killed Gen. Polk at Pine Mountain. The term "Rodman" was used for the 3 inch ordinance rifle, a very accurate, long range cannon.

save an occasional shot on the extreme left: what this feint was for we boys are at a loss to know: some are of the impression it was calculated to draw the enemy's attention from our right, they are supposed to be massing their force.

Up to noon it has been hot enough for one to wish for an ice house to crawl in: 6 p. m. had a nice shower: remains cloudy the remainder of the day: air much cooler.

Skirmishers pecking away quite brisk but no danger of bringing on a general thing as either party is too saving of life to venture out the other's works.

Co. drew a small quantity of clothing today: was anxious to get a shirt and blouse but was baffled in the attempt: have the promise of a blouse the next draw that's made but expect to come out as today there being so many in want.

Wed. 6. On the night of the 2nd the enemy fell back, being so compelled by movements on the right which left the great Kenesaw with several other prominent mountains in our possession, along which their strong line was formed a line which has been stronger contested for than any other point since the campaign.

[Note: What follows are events leading up to – and including – the battle of the Chattahoochee River (see footnote 24)]

We followed close in pursuit on the morning of the 3rd: McPherson, during the course of the night, moved to the right with the 15th and 16th Corps which brought us in on the extreme left with the exception of a brigade of Cav. – thus we moved forward until 4 in the afternoon: 9 a. m. took possession of Marietta which lies on the south side of the Kenesaw, a beautifully located place, of about 1500 inhabitants in times of peace – but very few are left and most of them women and children since the Rebel's retreat.

During the course of the day a number of prisoners were taken - how many I am unable to say, reports say 3000.

Wed. [July] **7.** Having moved forward 4 mi. the enemy were found in their gopher holes and fortifications to give us battle: our Steel pieces and 2 of the 14th Corps', which was to our right, took position and made it so hot for Mr. Johnny that they were obliged to abandon dirt throwing, which they were busy at and hug the earth for protection: sharp shooters were playing a full hand with our boys but didn't succeed in getting a game as none were injured by their balls.

On the night of the 3rd, we fired with our 2 pieces all night at intervals of 5 min.: at 6 on the morning of the 4th the 2 Batts. of our Div.

were got in position and at once opened a murderous fire on the Johnnys' gopher holes: it happened that just at this time they were changing skirmishers thus compelling them all to hug the ground: kept up fire till near 9 then quieted down till there was but a couple of pieces firing an occasional shot.

10 a. m. orders came that an attempt would be made to carry their rifle pits: after three batteries for ½ hr., doing them much damage, the charge took affect by Col. Gross' Brigade, which proved successful, taking a number of prisoners.

The first line of battle was immediately thrown forward under cover of a hill where they soon had a line of works that gave them protection to the dangerous position – as soon as the line of battle advanced the enemy opened artillery and kept it up all day – our two batts. kept still as it was unsafe to fire over our lines, consequently we laid low, which hindered them from gaining our range, although shell were exploding all around us doing no damage: during the forenoon fighting we lost 2 wounded (1 mortally) also 6 horses.

Built works in a new position all night, found the enemy had gone in the morning and all our labors lost.

As we had the advantage on the last day's march Morton's Div. took it today – throwing us in the rear: the distance was 6 mi. to the river, had no fighting but heavy skirmishing until it was reached.

Our line represents a horse shoe in shape: the 2 wings resting on the river: a great number of prisoners were taken during the day: they report if Johnny had 50 miles further to retreat his army would be destroyed.

We took position at Div. Hd. Q. on a high mountain about ¼ mi. from the river with our section only: at 6 last evening the other 4 guns were planted near the river bank – our position affords us a fine view of the country south of the river: the smoke from the machine shops in Atlanta can be seen distinctly and by climbing an oak the city is plainly to be seen, the distance being about 4 mi.

It has been discovered today that most of the enemy's force has crossed the river: they still have the R. R. bridge without having shown any signs of destroying it: scarcely any fighting has been done on this part of the line - what is going on on the right I am unable to say: there has been considerable cannonading in that direction but I don't anticipate further movements until a supply of rations reaches the army.

It is reported our corps is to remain here 5 or 6 days: since we left the Kenesaw I have never experienced hotter weather: notwithstanding the extreme heat and the heavy duty our boys have had to endure since we left

Marietta, good health prevails, are all in good spirits - better than 2 wks. ago.

Crackers shorter than I like to see them and owing to Charley having his stolen on the night of the 4th we are having to pick up every scrap without regard to dirt and making use of it. This will only last till tomorrow as we will then draw for three days.

I have been employed washing my clothes and making an effort to rid myself of the "army pets" which has been the general employment of our section.

The other 4 guns have done some little firing across the river at a fort

Fri. 8. Have been quiet since taking this position: a demonstration was made for some purpose at 8 p. m. last evening: cannonading continued ½ hr.: our Napoleons playing a prominent part: the general supposition is that we are to remain in camp till we are paid: the 14th Corps as well as ours are ordered to clean up camp which is as good a proof for the same as could be asked.

The weather is extremely hot as usual: blackberries are just beginning to ripen: was out this a. m. grazing horses with the intention of gathering enough for a taste but couldn't find a half dozen – came to the conclusion I would not undertake climbing over the mountain again for all the berries in the C. S. A.

We were told when we left the Altoona [sic] Mts. we would find level country all the way to Altoona but experience traveling thus far has taught us different, for the country is nothing but ridge after ridge of hills and mts. the entire line: it may be the people don't know anything about level country, if not, they are excusable.

All is quiet along the line as far as can be heard: the damages to the R. R. being repaired up to these points last night cars were but a short time in making their appearance.

All is well in the battery: boys having done up their washing are laying around in the shade: many improve the time by writing to the dear ones in the rear – Joe Allen wishes me to mention that he advanced in force on the Gray Backs for the first time during the Campaign and succeeded in driving in the skirmishers only.

Monday [July] **11.** On the 9th we remained quiet in camp without firing a shot: Sunday at 8 a. m. our Brigade moved off to the left: we had got good works in progress and supposed we were to remain some time but it is nothing strange these times.

Well, we moved down (or up the river rather) about 5 mi. joined Schofield [Army of the Ohio] on the right and quietly went in camp: on the march the troops declared they never experienced such heat and but few were to be found in the ranks when we halted: we were blessed with a shower along in the afternoon which cooled the atmosphere and was a great help to the wearied boys.

11 a. m. and we are still in the position taken yesterday - are fixing up camp as though we intended staying some time but it is only good proof for pulling up soon: troops of the 23rd Corps are moving today, as part of it went over the river yesterday the supposition is that they are also moving in that direction.

Weather clear but a trifle cooler than before the shower: Charley and I have a full supply of rations for the coming three days and if we lay here we anticipate an easy time.

Wed. 13. Wednesday, I'm told, whether it be or not is a hard matter to prove in this Co.

7 a. m. our division in motion: at 9 we were crossing the river on a canvass pontoon at the same point where Schofield effected his most brilliant crossing on the 8th: his line we found formed a mile from the river on as good a position as I have seen lately: passing him we moved 1½ miles to the front (or toward Atlanta) forming a new line on another ridge: went into camp: there is said to be no force of the enemy within 3 mi. of us: the other 2 Div. of our Corps came up last evening and formed on our left: we have good works to protect against assault but there appears to be no fears of an attack: more than likely we'll move forward tomorrow.[24]

Weather very hot: too much so to enjoy life: spent the day laying in the shade when off duty.

Fri. 15. Yesterday was a noted day with us boys: 7 in the morning we were told there would be a general inspection at 9: the appointed time found us ready to receive the benediction which occupied till 11½: it was the first inspection we ever passed under a regular officer: 4 of our boys went to Marietta after horses, returned at 8 with 8 only.

A shower came blundering along about 8 last evening which came near drowning all out: wet Charley's and my blankets so that we spent a sweet night: this morning is cloudy and has much the appearance of renewing the contest.

---

[24]After being nearly enveloped by McPherson on July 1, J. E. Johnston retreated to Smyrna and from there to a position north of the Chattahootchee River (July 4). While Thomas (Cumberland) kept his center invested, McPherson (Tenn.) threatened to cross the river downstreamwhile Schofield (Ohio) prepared a surprise crossing upstream at the mouth of Soap Creek on pontoon boats. These same boats (linked as a bridge) were later crossed by Hupp's unit. Fearing encirclement, Johnston again retreated toward Atlanta on July 9. It would be September, however, before Atlanta finally fell (dramatized in the book/movie *Gone With the Wind* by Margaret Mitchell).

Sat. [July] **16**. Had reveille at 4: done up morning duty, by which time Charley had the meat fried and gravy made and John Walton (who cooks for us) having coffee ready we sat down under a small grub oak and partook of our plentiful repast: our officers concluded pastures were too poor to graze, consequently the boys employed most of the day in writing letters, thinking they were to march tomorrow – weather a degree or so cooler than many days past but too hot for comfort: I wrote two letters in the forenoon and did some mending in the afterpart of the day.

Mond. 18. Yesterday all within our camp was quiet, though constant skirmishing was going on to our front and left all day which was caused by a reconnaissance [sic] by Wood's Division of our Corps: the 14th Corps effected a crossing while it was going on.

Last night we drew a day's rations which gave us 3 days from this morning and it was evident a movement was to commence in the morning: we were accordingly woke up at 2 a. m., infantry commenced moving out at daybreak: 6 o'clock arrived before our brigade left the camp: as we were in the rear we had no fighting: moved in a south easterly direction a distance of 7 miles – brought to a halt at 5 p. m. – formed a line of battle to remain over night: this point is 7 miles from Atlanta to the north and east.

The boys had a better country to forage in today than I've seen since the campaign: as I am driving a team of course there was no chance for me to get any eatables – but my partner, C. Miller brought in a mess of potatoes and some fine blackberries which served as a fine supper – made our bed down in a log stable with the expectation of having a good night's rest.

Wed. 19. Were permitted to rest till daybreak – after breakfast harnessed and hitched up – expected to move out immediately, but not so – in the course of ½ hr. unhitched and grazed: while out I picked up a quart of berries which Charley put up with some apples he got of Sabe, making a dish for dinner which was much relished: not knowing when we would have to leave ate at 10½: there has been considerable cannonading to our right during the day: but as yet it has been very quiet on this part of the line - they have just blown "pack up" [bugle signal] at 3rd Brigade Head Q. and no doubt our section will be called out, if not the battery.

Weather much cooler than last wk. – health of boys good: I was very unwell all day yesterday but am allright [sic] today.

Thurs. 21. On the evening of the 19th our battery moved out on the line and fired a few rounds when darkness closed the scene for the evening: the morning of the 20th pursued the enemy at 8 a. m. our Div.

being in advance on this road it was nothing strange for our section to be with the skirmishers: forced our way about 3 mi. when the enemy were found to be in works and striving hard to play on this part of the line for a season: skirmished all afterpart of the day: here our battery all went into position and fired at intervals until dark – about 3 p. m. a general engagement could be distinctly heard to our right both with infantry and artillery: it proved to be with Hooker and [Gen. John] Newton who were attacked 3 times and as many times repulsed the enemy: the loss to the enemy is said to be 4000 in K. & W. [killed and wounded]: the night of the 20th was employed in constructing works for the guns about 40 rods in front: we lost 1 killed and 1 wounded in this operation: done by sharpshooters before 9 o'clock: by 5 on the morning of the 21st our guns were ready to do their duty in works which afforded protection against musketry provided one did not get in range of the embrasures [gun opening]: the boys were employed in this day strengthening the works and working the guns: our two Rodmans set their missiles for the first time in pursuit of Atlanta: the time fired by them was 30 min. - with all the elevation they would bear as the range of the place was not exactly known and couldn't be found from this point – it is hard to say whether our firing did any damage.[25]

About 2 p. m. on the morning of the 22nd we were apprised of the enemy having fallen back by the unresisted forward movement of our skirmishers: about 3 they occupied their works which were about 40 rods from our front at daybreak: this part of the time was again in motion - moved forward about 1½ mile as near as I can tell when we reached the top of a high eminence - here a few rounds from our Rodmans gave us to understand the enemy were only waiting for us in the outer works of the city which could plainly be seen with the naked eye: after firing a few rounds it was deemed prudent to keep still as they commenced playing on us while we were in a poor position and without works: at 2 p. m. we moved ½ mi. to the left where we found the remainder of the battery ready to take position – a heavy cannonading was kept up along this part of the line the remainder of the day.

---

[25]The foregoing long paragraph describes the battle of Peach Tree Creek, July 20, 1864. After Sherman succeeded in turning J. E. Johnston's defense at Chattahoochee River (July 4-9), Johnston was succeed by Gen. John Bell Hood on the 17th. On the morning of the 20th, Thomas' Army of the Cumberland had secured a bridgehead across Peach Tree Creek, less than 5 miles north of Atlanta. Schofield and McPherson were busy enveloping Atlanta on the east. Hood ordered an attack against Thomas' forces at 1 p.m. but a delay in troop deployment put off the attack until 3 p.m., exactly as reported by Pvt. Hupp. Federals lost about 1,600; Confederates about 2,500 killed or wounded, much less than the 4,000 related by Hupp (Sherman estimated 4,796 Rebel casualties).

We learned this evening McPherson had a brisk engagement in the morning: was driven quite a distance and lost one Batt. [Battery 'H', 1st Ill. under DeGress]: also that he and his staff were viewing some point away from his lines a short distance, when they were encountered by a small body of Cavalry, who fired into them, killing the Gen. instantly: the same has since been confirmed.

His troops attacked the enemy and drove them beyond the line they held this morning, taking all the guns lost in the morning [Mersy's Brigade, XVI Corps], with one additional Batt. - the fighting could be distinctly heard from this point and proved to be the bloodiest of the campaign.[26]

Sat. [July] **23.** Nothing of note transpired today that I've heard of: considerable cannonading at different parts of the line all day to which the enemy replied with promptness: their fire does scarcely any damage.

Mon. 25. Yesterday was spent as the day before in regard to fighting: 9 a. m. we rec'd orders to prepare a camp and strengthen our works[27], in consequence of which we done but little firing – by nightfall our works were strong enough to be held by a very weak force, which will be the case in order that the flanks can have the main army for further operation: today we've been discharging our 2 Rodmans throughout the day – we hear considerable cannonading all along the line – a flank movement is in operation but is not perfected so as to give a person not acquainted with the same any idea of it.

Weather cooler than usual – have had no rain for several days – have been employed in reading and letter writing my spare time during the day.

Thurs. 28. Are in the same position as when I last wrote – have done more or less firing every day – 11 a. m. yesterday the Johnnys opened a battery on us for the first time since we came here – they threw a few shells and then quieted down.

---

[26]The past 3 paragraphs describe events of the battle of Atlanta (Hood's Second Sortie), July 22. After falling back from Peach Tree Creek, Hood assumed a position within the defensive works on the northern outskirts of Atlanta. Troop deployment was similar to Peach Tree Creek but the Federals were closing in toward Atlanta. Gen. McPherson was killed that day in a battle that CSA Gen. Hardee described as "one of the most desperate and bloody of the war". Compare this to Hupp's assessment in the last sentence. Federal losses were estimated at 3,722; Confederate losses about 8,000.

[27]"Works" (breastworks) refers to trenches commonly reinforced with timbers, and with some covered areas for added protection. Works on both sides were sometimes protected in front by crossed sharpened poles *(chevaux-de-frise)* and log palisades to discourage infantry assaults. These semi-permanent emplacements were adopted during the latter stages of the war, particularly at Atlanta and later at Petersburg and Richmond. They presaged the trench warfare of WWI.

Our line assumed a different front on our left night before last, the 15th, 16th, 17th having moved to the right: Schofield (who joins us on the left) has formed his line in a half moon, commencing at our left and running to our rear, in order to prevent a flank movement: let the enemy approach us from either direction they will find a front: our Cav. started on an expedition at 1 a. m. on the 27th: their supposed destination is Macon, Americus, and Andersonville: the 2 latter places hold between 20 and 30 thousand of our men who have been taken prisoners during the past year.[28]

A detail from the battery was out after forage yesterday and done very well – got a load of wheat, 1 of corn stalks, several bu. apples and a very fair quantity of potatoes.

All is apparently quiet in this part of the line – now and then a cannon shot exchanged and considerable skirmishing is constantly kept up, which has become a military necessity it appears: had a fine refreshing shower last evening, this morning the air is cool – goodbye, Mr. Diary, for the present.

Sat. 30. The fighting on the right on the 28th was desperate – the enemy charged our works 4 times and each time met with a repulse[29] when the Blue Coats went for them and captured 2 lines of works with 15

---

[28]The foregoing few paragraphs were written during events leading up to the battle of Ezra Church (Hood's Third Sortie; July 26-28), and the last sentence refers to Sherman's simultaneous cavalry raids on rail lines south of Atlanta. Sherman sent Oliver 0. Howard's (McPhersons's replacement) Army of the Tennessee around the west of Atlanta with the purpose of disrupting rail lines leading into the city. Hood sent Gen. Stephen Lee (distant relative of R. E. Lee) to cut off the Federals at the crossroads of Ezra Church but found the Union troops well entrenched there. Subsequent Confederate assaults were a failure and resulted in over 800 casualties.

The cavalry expedition involved troopers under George Stoneman, Edward McCook, and Kenner Garrard. The objectives of this ambitious raid were to disrupt rail lines south of Atlanta and to free Federal prisoners at Macon and Andersonville (the latter was Stoneman's idea). In existence from Feb. 1864 to Apr. 1865 Andersonville Prison was the most notorious of the war; some 13,000 men (or more) died there of disease and starvation. Stoneman's raid was ultimately unsuccessful in freeing Federal prisoners, and was otherwise considered a miserable failure resulting in around 50 percent casualties. Only limited track was destroyed near Lovejoy's Station at the expense of high casualties among Union Cavalrymen.

[29]Battle of Ezra Church, west of Atlanta: the first attack was by Gen. James C. Brown's division, Lee's Corps, against Giles Smith's division of Howard's Army of the Tennessee. Brown's Confederates took terrible casualties from the well-entrenched Federals, but then gathered up reserves and attacked again. This attack was also unsuccessful. The third charge was by Gen. H. D. Clayton's division against the left side of the Federal right flank, also repulsed. The fourth assault (over the same ground covered by Brown) by Gen. E. C. Walthall's division of A. P. Stewart's Corps resulted in a bloody rout. These futile assaults proved a costly Confederate blunder, with over 5,000 casualties compared to about 600 for Union forces.

stands of colors: the battle as officially reported from Gen. Howard, foots up as follows: Rebel loss, 10,000, Federal, 2,000: on the same day of the battle they opened a 32 lbs. on us firing at intervals of 15 min. during the day, but as yet it has effected no damage: considerable cannonading has been kept up on this part of the line for several days – the line remains about the same. About midnight last night the enemy's skirmishers commenced a hearty fire which was kept up till 6 this a. m. when our Art. cooled them down.

At present the lines are apparently quiet: on the night of the 28th our 2 Rodmans shelled the city [Atlanta] all night.

An old friend, B. F. Mastermann of the 5th Ind. Cav. came to see me night before last – had a good old chat – he stated a Cav. expedition of all that could be mounted in the Army started on a raid under Stoneman the night previous, their destination supposed to be Macon and Americus, for the purpose of releasing our prisoners and cutting railroad communications in the enemy's rear: should they be successful it will be a grand move [see footnote 28].

Weather clear and cool today: yesterday 'twas very hot and cooling shower in the evening was the result.

Aug. Tues. 2. Nothing since my last writing occurred till last night, there being no change of lines since the movement from the left to the right: at dusk the 23rd Corps which lay to our left and rear moved to the extreme right: our corps (the 4th) strengthening the works and stretching their line so as to be able to hold the line of the moving Co. This morning found us fronting the rear, a mile back of our position before the city and as near as I can judge, 2 mi. to the right: today we are busily employed putting up works for the guns: should the enemy attack this part of the line desperate fighting will be the result for in another day we will have good works and will be able to fight a heavy battle with our weak forces: fighting is anticipated on the right, as it is over in that direction the Army is massing for the purpose of destroying the enemy's communications: yesterday afternoon the enemy opened their big camp kettle on one Battery and fired 8 or ten shells, 2 or 3 of which struck our works but done no damage: the batteries along our line all opened fire which called his attention in another direction.

Fri. 5. Wednesday our section was ordered on the line where we remained from 11 a. m. until 9 p. m. A heavy demonstration was made at the point where we are at – still farther to the right considerable fighting took place, our lines advanced, took the gopher holes where our line of battle now rests: the 2 lines at this point are but a short distance apart which will oblige the enemy to keep a strong force on this part of the line whether any fighting takes place or not.

Thursday (yesterday) our Sec. and right lay in camp – the teams went after forage, got a good supply of corn stalks but nothing more: Johnson and I were on guard: as the day was pleasant it was no task: between the hrs. of 12 and 2 done my washing in the company with Charley Miller: between 8 and 10 in the evening I heard very heavy and irregular cannonading far to the right, have no idea what caused it or which party commenced to fuss.

2 p. m. I have heard since morning that the enemy attacked the 23rd Corps and met with a heavy repulse: last night the 23rd A. C. is said to command the Macon Road – 3 p. m. Charley and I have just returned from the creek where we have been making a scatterment among the Army pets[30]: a heavy demonstration is just being made in our immediate front: the roar of the Inft. and Art. is terrific – but if it be nothing more than a demonstration, it will last but a short time. News reached us yesterday that Grant had taken Petersburg with 10,000 prisoners and Stoneman occupied Macon, but little confidence is put in the report.[31]

Wed. 10. On Friday night we abandoned the line facing the rear and have been in front of Atlanta about 1 mi. to the left of our first position where we have been since: there's been nothing going on since we came here,but a couple of demonstrations together with heavy skirmishing at different times: Sunday there was scarcely any firing to be heard: Monday we did a little shelling at the city with the Rodmans: yesterday afternoon (Tues.) the artillery along the entire line opened fire at 11 a. m. and continued until 4 p. m. which was all directed to Atlanta: the supposition was the enemy was evacuating, which has since proved false. This morning there is heavy cannonading on the right, a general engagement is supposed to be in progress – Sunday there was great excitement in camp, caused by two spies dressed in officer's clothes which were caught (or said to have been caught), we've heard nothing of the matter since.

---

[30]"Army pets" refers to various vermin that infested soldier's bodies while on campaign. These consisted of lice, fleas, and in the south, chiggers. These are the larvae of certain red mites whose bite causes severe itching.

[31]Not only did Gen. Stoneman's cavalry not occupy Macon, he was captured, along with most of his men, by Confederate Gen. Alfred Iverson while moving north from an unsuccessful assault on Macon. He was released in a few months and later commanded the Dept. of the Ohio.

Grant did not take Petersburg until April 2, 1865. Richmond fell the next day. This set the stage for Robert E. Lee's surrender to Grant at Appomattox Courthouse, April 9, 1865. Joseph E. Johnston surrendered to Sherman in North Carolina on April 26. The last Confederate forces (Kirby Smith to Canby) surrendered on the 26th of May, 1865, effectively ending the Civil War.

Fri. [Aug.] **12.** Last night we received a dispatch announcing the fall of Mobile: about the same amount of confidence is put in the report as the one received from Petersburg a few days since[32]: the roar of art. on the right since day before yesterday has been kept up with scarcely any cessation either night or day: we have heavy guns working in that direction, but what calibre I can't say [30 pound Parrotts and other siege guns brought by rail from Chattanooga]: last night the shell from one (which fired every five minutes all night) could be plainly seen to burst in the city: we haven't fired a shot since the 11th: are in our position taken on the 6th: the Johnnys became interested to know whether we still occupy this point: every now and then, after treating us to a few shells they drop it and all is quiet then on this part of the line except the pecking of the skirmishers, which at present are about ½ mi. to our front: details are made every day for the purpose of erecting a shade over our horses, which will doubtless be evacuated before half completed: for several days the weather has been hot and showery – no complaint of sickness, but since the 8th the boys have been pulling every way but aright owing to the non-issuing of pork for 10 days – it goes hard enough to have no other meat but lean cow – good thing we're old soldiers, got so we can live on anything the Gov. issues – one great consolation, 'twon't cost as much when we get home to sustain life as 'twould otherwise – but I have written enough for this time.

Sund. 14. Yesterday we remained quiet in camp till 9 p. m. when orders came to open fire with the 2 steel pieces [Rodmans]: the cannoniers were summoned to their posts and firing at once commenced – the fire directed at Hardies' [sic: Gen. Hardee's] ammunition trains and must have had good effect, for but a few rounds were fired before a Rebel battery commenced replying very furiously for the purpose of drawing the fire, which they gave up in about 1½ hrs. as we didn't notice them although they had an enfilading fire on our lines: the firing was kept up till 4 this morning - during the time we fired 360 rounds: their shells killed 2 and wounded 1: the fire was general on our part all along the entire line: today everything is quiet on this part of the line: far to the right cannonading has been kept up all day.

Boys are feeling remarkably well considering the scanty rations of cow.

Wed. 17. Mond. Nothing new, more than Cavalry to our left started off in a great hurry after Forrest (it is thought) who is said to be playing

---

[32]Mobile, AL was held by 10,000 Confederate troops and 300 guns under Gen. D. H. Maury. He evacuated in the evening of April 11, 1865; Union Gen. E. R. S. Canby then occupied Mobile on the 12th.

havoc in our rear[33]: yesterday our part of the line was very quiet: 2 very handsome Atlanta ladies came in about noon: there was one came in on Monday[34]. Last night the Inft. of our Corps moved far enough to the left to occupy that part of the line vacated by the Cav.: cannonading still continues on the right without cessation: those who came into our lines yesterday and today report our shells killing a great many women and children: on Sat. last a shell exploded in the dining room of a dwelling during a meal, killing 4 and wounding others: weather very warm: I took the cholera morbus night before last and it came near using me up, have not been able for duty since, am as weak as a kitten today and have a severe headache.

Sund. 20. This part of the line is unchanged since the 17th: we have been engaged in demonstrating for the purpose of drawing a force from the enemy's left. I never, since I came in service, have heard such cannonading as was kept up between the hrs. of 2 and 4 Friday a. m. last: the whole earth appeared to be atremble and the explosion of shell almost illuminated the city: weather rainy all day.[35]

Sept. 17. Not having convenient time for writing it has been laid aside for some time: on the 20th of Aug. we pulled off the line before

---

[33]Gen. Nathan Bedford Forrest (1821-1877) was one of the south's most capable leaders. His task was to use his cavalry to disrupt rail lines and other lines of communication in Sherman's rear, in Tennessee. His success is mirrored in Sherman's statements that "there never will be peace in Tennessee till Forrest is dead" and "'That devil Forrest' . . . must be 'hunted down and killed if it costs ten thousand lives and bankrupts the Federal treasury.'"

Sherman's immediate cavalry nemesis, however, was Gen. Joseph Wheeler (1836-1906). Hood ordered him to Sherman's rear to cut rail lines and create havoc in the Union supply lines. Unfortunately for the Confederate cause this tactic had little effect, and left Hood without the "eyes and ears" of his cavalry (cavalry was commonly used to gather intelligence). For this reason, Sherman nominally ignored Wheeler's raids, feeling that Hood's lack of Cavalry at the front gave him (Sherman) an advantage.

[34]The war in east Tennessee and northwest Georgia had taken its toll on foodstuffs for southern civilians as well as soldiers. Sherman's siege of Atlanta caused shortages for the civilian population of Atlanta, which may explain the activities of these southern ladies behind Union lines. They may have been begging for food – and possibly, for the shelling to stop.

[35]The brevity of the events summarized from here to the end of Hupp's diary attest to intense activity culminating in the taking and holding of the city of Atlanta. Hupp notes that his army (Cumberland) moved out from their entrenchments on the 20th; official accounts place this movement on the 25th. This was part of a grand flanking scheme (left wheel) devised by Sherman to turn the Confederate left (s.w. of Atlanta) and to cut rail communications south of the city. Leaving the XX Corps (Cumberland) to guard supplies at the Chattahoochee River, he sent the Army of the

Atlanta: where our destination was no one could surmise: on the 27th we lay in line of battle near the West Point R. R. [Atlantic and West R.R.; 6 mi. s.w. of Eastpoint]: moved forward till the 31st with but little opposition: Howard on our right had a hard fight on this day and repulsed the enemy on the 1st of Sept. (it having been ascertained that the enemy had thrown his force on Howard)[36] by a rapid movement the 23rd and 4th Corps cut the Macon road near Rough and Ready Station thus dividing the enemy's forces and placing us between them and the force at Atlanta: on the 2nd we (the 4th C.) moved up the R. R. toward Jonesborough [sic] the 2nd C. to our left moved slowly, making a complete junction within ½ mi. of the town.

The lines of the 14th C. were formed on our arrival (or nearly so) ours were formed on double quick and from 4 till after dark there was heavy fighting: the 14th sustained the heaviest loss: that night the enemy fell back badly whipped: our Army followed 5 mi., when it was ascertained that Atlanta had been evacuated and was held by the 20th C. On the night of the 2nd we were tearing down a building to fortify with: 2 of the boys, J. Allen and Sable were cooking their suppers in the fire place when it fell down injuring them seriously. J. Allen it is feared, will never recover. On the night of the 5th, the Army commenced falling back in as hard a rain as I ever saw, and dark was no name for it: on the 7th we reached the long contested city: our battery passed through a small portion of it: the houses were badly shot to pieces, the destruction of cars, locomotives, Art. S. [small] arms, art. ammunition and machine shops is beyond description: we went in camp near Decatur R. R. where we left – and where we have been since.

At present we are preparing to turn over the Batt.: this morning everything went but the horses and camp equipage, we are to be relieved of the H______ this p. m. and by the first of the week it is said we are to start for Indianapolis.

Since we came back the weather has been pleasant, with cool nights:

Ohio (Schofield) to Rough-and-Ready, Cumberland (Thomas) to a point half way between the latter station and Jonesboro, and Tennessee (Howard) to Jonesboro. The tactic was ultimately successful; Hood evacuated Atlanta from 5:00 to 1:00 p.m. on September 1, blowing up and burning supplies to elude enemy capture. The XX Corps, Army of the Cumberland, took possession the next morning.

[36]This is the battle of Jonesboro, a town about 15 miles south of Atlanta on the Macon and Western R.R. Howard's entrenched Army of the Tennessee was attacked by Confederate forces under Hardee, with two Corps directed by Gens. Cleburne and Lee. The Confederate assault resulted in numerous casualties and failed to repulse the Federals who stood fast by the Flint River.

for the past week I have been unable for duty, but am getting all right again.

HOME AGAIN!

The Narrative

A Biographical and Historical Perspective

by

John L. Berkley

Chapter 1
Introduction

Ormond Hupp was an American of the nineteenth century. To say he was typical of his times would be only marginally true, and mostly false. In his unquenchable desire to join the Union army and quell the Southern rebellion, he stood with many others who, in the opening days of the Civil War, lusted for a chance to fight. He was atypical in the sheer intensity of his determination to join the fray, in spite of a physical deformity that would have easily excused him from such duty. After being hospitalized for a severe battle wound, he returned to the front and again put his life in harm's way. Strength of conviction or foolhardiness? Wherever one seeks an explanation for his youthful exuberance, one thing is certain. Ormond Hupp was no ordinary youth, and as time would tell, he was to become a rather extraordinary man.

Hupp's diary stands on its own as a valuable historical morsel, revealing the rigors, pleasures, pastimes, and pain of a common soldier in the Union army. Its value to historians is multiplied by the fact that it deals with campaigns in the western theater of the Civil War, whereas journals and letters from the eastern theater (Antietam, Gettysburg, etc.) are more common and better publicized. In addition, the time period covered is extensive, running from nearly the very beginning of the war to near its end. His particular company, the Fifth Indiana Light Artillery Battery, was involved in many major campaigns in Kentucky, Tennessee, Alabama, and finally, the assault on Atlanta with Sherman. This was not a unit that spent the war in garrison duty or polishing canons in an armory; they were either preparing for, marching to, or engaged in battle for most of the war.

Pvt. Hupp was absent from his unit for about a year and a half, missing all of the Tennessee campaigns (Stones River, Tullahoma, Chickamauga, Chattanooga), and herein lies something of a bonus for historians. Wounded in the Battle of Perryville (Kentucky), he spent considerable time in Army hospitals in New Albany, Indiana, later becoming a nurse after recovering from his wounds. This interlude from front-line duty was a time of considerable socializing by this Indiana farm boy, particularly with members of the "delicate sex." Thus, in addition to insights into military hospital life, we are also given a tantalizing glimpse of social life in a fairly typical Union town during the height of the Civil War. Ormond was no shrinking violet when it came to entertaining the ladies. In fact, he could more properly be described as a Lothario. His affections were showered on many more than one New Albany belle at any given time, but in keeping with the times and discretion, Hupp's journal leaves the reader to imagine what may have ultimately transpired beyond card playing, "philopena" games, and sampling cobblers and homemade wine.

Hupp later abandoned his lady friends and rejoined his battery, participating in the Atlanta campaign, which dominates the final sections of the diary. From the time he volunteered for Mr. Lincoln's Union army in September of 1861 to his mustering out in November of 1864, his diary makes it clear that his wartime experiences were of a nature that most men would consider quite enough excitement for a lifetime. But Ormond Hupp's life did not end with the war (as happened to over 600,000 others), nor was it entirely uneventful before the war.

Ormond was not an ordinary man, and the fact that he was a lowly private during the war should not be taken as evidence for mediocrity. He had attended a year of college at Notre Dame (his family were confirmed Baptists!) before answering the call to preserve the Union, a cause for which he expressed strong sentiments. I suspect that had he been older in 1861, he may have joined as at least a non-commissioned officer, for he certainly had the brains for leadership. This assessment is based on his post-war life in which, by shrewd wheeling, dealing, and efficient farming, he became one of the wealthiest men in his county.

The following chapters, therefore, consider the whole life of Ormond Hupp, not just the very important war years. Luckily, his early life, particularly his very unlucky childhood, was preserved in still-existing genealogical records. Similar accounts along with records in the Hupp family Bible, National Archives records, family letters, and even eyewitness reports were used to reconstruct his later life. Although no Civil War veteran remains alive (the last died in 1956), at this writing, many living people still hold memories of veterans. I have relied on the childhood memories of my mother (one of Hupp's granddaughters) and some of her cousins for anecdotes about Ormond Hupp in his elder days.

These stories reveal a man of wit and humor, who above anything else, enjoyed a good practical joke. This veteran of our nation's bloodiest war was also a devoted family man who could be stern, but was always fair; a man who kept a tight hand on his finances, but could be generous almost to a fault.

One purpose of this exercise is to show that the soldier in war was first and last, a civilian: one who could risk life itself for the promise of something better after the guns fell silent. In the case of Ormond Hupp, life did indeed take an upturn after the war, which could be taken as some personal compensation or justification for the sacrifice. He prospered despite the general declining economic prospects of the "Gilded Age" in which he lived out his maturity. His good fortune is reflected still in his many modern descendants, some of whom yet till the Missouri soil of his spacious and bountiful farms. This story is especially for them, for none of us would be here now had Ormond not been so skillful at dodging Minie "balls" and artillery shells.

Chapter 2
Origins

I shall go out with the chariots to counsel and command, for that is the privelege of the old; the young must fight in the ranks.

Homer, Iliad IV

In his diary, Ormond Hupp commonly refers to inhabitants of various regions as "American" in origin. This designation no doubt refers to people whose ancestral roots included one or more generations of native born stock. On the other hand, recently arrived Irish, Germans, or other ethnic groups would qualify as immigrants, whose claim to "American" status would have to await the test of time.

Hupp unquestionably thought of himself as "American," and so he was. His paternal ancestors, including the first to step foot in the New World, were German. But their blood lines were soon diluted by marriage to women who, like most white Americans at the time, already sported bloodlines that mostly included English, Scottish, Irish, and German origins. In fact, the bulk of all fighting men in the Civil War were of British, Irish, or German extraction.

The name "Hupp" can also be spelled Hup and even Hoop. The first immigrant of that name (or some variation) landed in America in the mid 1700's, although his exact name or other pertinent information about his life and death are largely speculative (see Appendix I). His name may have been Philip or, possibly, John. What is certain about him is that he was from Germany and he settled in the Shenandoah Valley of Virginia. He married a woman by the name of Elizabeth, and together this almost mythological pair launched the Hupp family in America.

Philip and Elizabeth settled in the northern Shenandoah valley near the town of Winchester. Their sons, at least six in number, were noted for their heroics as Indian fighters.

In 1775, the Hupps built a fort eighteen miles south of Winchester that still stands today. It was used to protect the family homestead from Indian attacks, which took their toll on several of the brothers. Five of these original Hupp brothers (no information exists on possible sisters) eventually migrated to Pennsylvania and at least one to Ohio. The brother who remained in the Shenandoah was Balser, great-grandfather to Ormond Hupp.

In 1776, Balser bought an 89 acre tract of land on the north fork of the Shenandoah River about one mile north of New Market, Virginia. This farm (expanded later by additional purchases) lies at the northern boundary of the New Market Battlefield Park. This boundary was expanded in 1984 to included much of the old Hupp homestead. Not much is known about Balser except that he was a farmer, presumably a good one. He married twice, once to a woman named Mary, and then, after her death, to Barbara. Mary is Ormond Hupp's great-grandmother.

Balser died in 1829, 35 years before the Civil War Battle of New Market was played out in the hills just south of his property. This battle pitted Union General Franz Sigel against a Confederate force under John C. Breckinridge. The battle is remembered primarily for the fact that it involved youngsters from the Virginia Military Institute (VMI) who were ordered into battle to bolster the Confederate forces. According to legend, these military cadets, aged 14 to 20, charged and captured a battery and took close to 100 prisoners. In fact, at a cost of 57 casualties, they managed to capture a single artillery piece from Capt. Alfred von Kleiser's 30th New York battery, but that needn't detract from their honored place in Condeferate history. The Cadets' determined charge did drive the battery from the field, inflicting severe casualties on horses and men in the process. In the end, Sigel's Union army retreated with considerably greater losses compared to his outnumbered enemy – and a superior degree of embarrassment.

Abraham Hupp, Ormond's grandfather, was born some time in the 1760's to Balser and Mary. One of at least seven children, he married Elizabeth Knopp on April 19, 1802. She lived to the ripe old age of 90 but Abraham was not so lucky. He died in 1829, the same year as his father.

Abraham was primarily a farmer, but served a stint during the War of 1812 as an ensign in the Navy. The couple had six children, one of whom was Abram, Ormond Hupp's father (see preamble to Part II of the diary). Two years after Abraham's death, his widow moved the youngest sons (Abram, Jacob, and Michael) to Mad River Township, Champaign County, Ohio, to be near the eldest son, John, who had married in 1822 before moving to Ohio. Abram's two other older brothers, Samuel and Isaac, remained in the Shenandoah valley.

The Ohio homestead where Abram lived as a youth was just east of the actual "Mad River," so named for its habit of flooding more often than most folks deemed convenient. Perhaps to escape the floods or just to search for fertile ground of their own, the three brothers, including Abram, moved to northern Indiana in 1836. Abram settled in Center Township near LaPorte and the next year married Ormond's mother, Elizabeth Gardner, late of Cincinnati, Ohio.

La Porte (French for door or gateway) was founded in 1830 by French settlers in an area of northern Indiana once explored by LaSalle. Its name derives from its position as gateway to the rich lands to the north and west, including the shores of nearby Lake Michigan. It was incorporated as a town only one year before Abram's arrival (1835), and as a city in 1852.

The economy of the area has always been centered on agriculture, but modern LaPorte also sports an industrial base that includes the manufacture of farm machinery, clothing, plastic and rubber products, furniture, and other goods. Until just two years before Ormond's birth, it had been home to the Potawatomi Indian tribe who had lived in harmony with the white settlers for many years. Their forced removal to lands west of the Missouri River was a source of sorrow for both local whites and Indians.

While occupied as a farmer in the LaPorte area, Abram was elected doorkeeper of the Indiana legislature from 1845 to 1846. Politically he was a Whig, and later a Republican, which goes far to explain his son's very pro-Union sympathies. The Whigs pushed for policies that presaged today's free market capitalism. They stressed the value of wage-earning laborers working at diverse jobs in factory-scale manufacturing endeavors over the former system of individual artisans and journeymen. The Whigs championed the managers, entrepreneurs, and financiers as generating the economic growth that would elevate all – including manual laborers – to new levels of prosperity. They also advocated massive government-sponsored public works programs (virtually unknown in the early 19th century), and generally supported the idea that a strong federal government was beneficial to business.

The Whigs, and later the Republicans (who attracted many supporters from the ranks of the defunct Whig party), were also sympathetic to the aspirations of blacks, and their strength grew along with the abolitionist movement. On the other hand, the Democrats, both north and south, were blatantly racist, and promoted the idea of states' rights that was later to become a watchword of secessionist passion. I mention these things because they bear on Ormond's strong desire to fight for the Union cause in the Civil War. Politically most Union supporters were also Republicans, the party of Lincoln.

Abram Hupp was a member of the Masons (inducted 1839), and lifelong parishioner in the Baptist church, as was his son, Ormond – a tradition that extends to many of his modern descendants. During Ormond's recuperation in New Albany (after his wounding at Perryville), he experimented with many denominations, but his clear choice was the First Baptist church. One wonders whether or not his parents would have condoned his dabbling with other churches (including Roman Catholic). Regardless, his spiritual wanderings were very short lived. As was true of his father before him, Ormond Hupp lived and died a very confirmed Baptist.

Ormond was the second child of Abram and Elizabeth. He was preceded in birth by his beloved sister, Anelizabeth (also known as "Lib," Ann, and Elizabeth) with whom he corresponded during the war, and who visited him in New Albany. Eight other children joined the family in time (Appendix I), including Julia, the fourth child, and another favorite of Ormond's. He describes sending some of his miliary pay to Julia, as well as to his father.

In the year Ormond was born (September 10, 1840), Thomas Nast, the cartoonist; Pierre Renoir, the painter; and Peter Ilich Tchaikovsky, the composer also made their earthly debuts. Frederick William IV ascended the throne of Prussia, and Queen Victoria of Great Britain married Prince Albert. The Mexican-American war, where many Civil War era commanders on both sides were to hone their skills, was only six years away.

When he died eighty-six years later, World War I was six years in the past, and the Nazis were already making nasty noises in Germany.

Ormond had his own battles to fight as a young child – with ill-health and misfortune.

At three years of age he was stricken by a "fever" with symptoms and effects that resemble polio. This was bad enough, but during recovery he suffered a paralytic stroke that affected the whole left side of his frail body. Although he recovered fairly rapidly from this condition, the development of his left foot was permanently delayed, leaving him with more of a stump than a fully formed foot. This malady would have easily sufficed in later times to exempt anyone from military service, but Ormond was not to be denied. He stuffed his club foot into his boot using socks tamped into the toe as padding, and enlisted in the grand Union army. Apparently the pre-induction medical exams of the time were not so thorough as to require the removal of boots. If his walking gait betrayed a limp, no one noticed, or cared.

As if the ravages of polio were not sufficient punishment, at age five, while placing wood in the fireplace, Ormond's apron caught fire and he

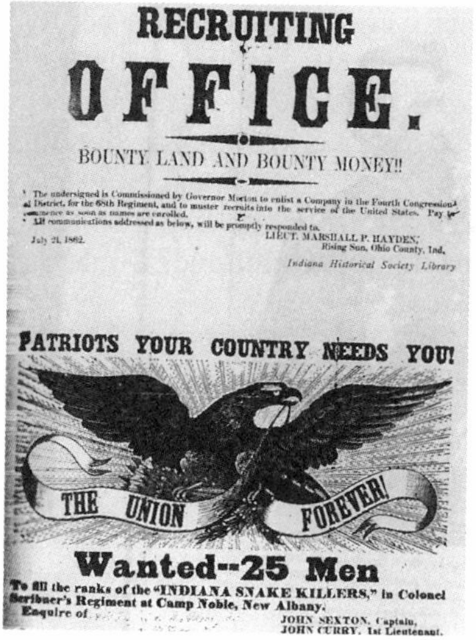

Figure 2-1a

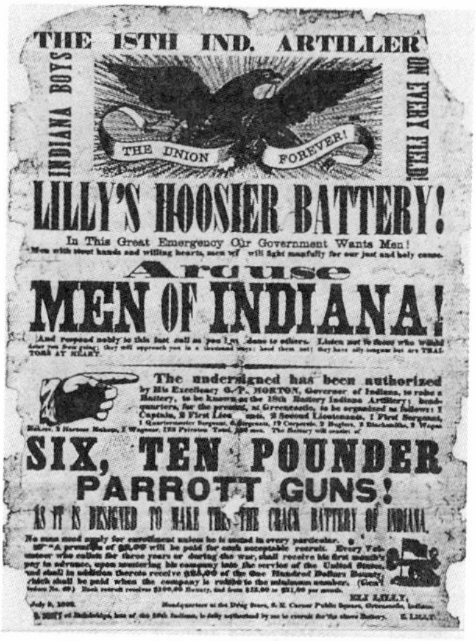

Figure 2-1b

Figure 2-1(a & b) – Recruiting posters soliciting Indiana volunteers early in the war. Hupp was very likely influenced by such posters to join the Union army. (a) Ad for Benjamin Scribner's regiment ("Indiana Snake Killers") from New Albany, where Pvt. Hupp would eventually land in a military hospital. (b) Poster for Eli Lilly's (of pharmaceutical fame) Hoosier Battery (Lib. of Congress).

was severely burned over much of his body. This was an experience that would be reprised at Perryville, where the exploding shell that ripped gashes in his arms, also tore off his clothes and badly burned his body. For six months, little Ormond clung to life, suffering intense pain. Without the benefit of a modern burn unit, that he did not die from shock or infection (here, or in New Albany after Perryville) approaches the miraculous.

But Ormond's brushes with death did not stop after his burns healed. While following behind his father who was cutting Burdock with a cradle scythe, Abram accidently struck his son in the shoulder, the blade penetrating to the bone. The wound nearly killed him, although Ormond eventually recovered. Some years later, he was nearly trampled by a runaway horse-drawn wagon. By luck or fortitude, he managed to cheat fate or Providence to survive his precarious childhood, a major accomplishment!

In 1861, at age 21, Ormond Hupp again placed himself in bodily jeopardy by signing up as a volunteer in service to the Union Army. He signed up in September and was officially mustered in for a three year enlistment in November. He left the plowing, planting, and cultivating to his father and brothers (all of the latter were either not born yet, or too young to fight) and set off for training in the state capital, Indianapolis.

Ormond's diary made clear that he harbored no regrets about his decision to join (or if he did, he did not express them), nor did he question the cause for which he fought. The Union must be preserved, and it would take more than a chronically lame foot to keep him down on the farm. He had eluded death so many times in childhood. Could war be so much worse?

Chapter 3
Answering the Call: Indianapolis to Huntsville

The palavery kind of Southerners; all that slushy gush on the surface, and no sensibilities whatever – a race without consonants and without delicacy.

Willa Cather (a Virginian): My Mortal Enemy II.i

In the fall of 1860, Abraham Lincoln defeated Stephen A. Douglas for the presidency. Actually, four candidates were vying for the job: three Democrats and Lincoln, the lone Republican. Had his opponents united behind a single candidate, Douglas being the logical contender, they would have beaten Lincoln by almost a million popular votes. Lincoln did not carry one southern state, and split New Jersey with Douglas, yet still won the electoral vote contest and the presidency. If any one event can be said to have directly precipitated the soon-to-erupt Civil War, it was the election of this western, small town lawyer to lead a country already seriously divided over the contentious issues of slavery and states' rights.

On December 20, South Carolina led the way to secession. It was followed on January 9 by Mississippi, Florida on the 10th, and Alabama on the 11th. Ten days later, the senior senator from Mississippi, Jefferson Davis, bid farewell to his Senate colleagues and tearfully left to lead the new Confederacy of southern states that now also included Georgia.

By the time Davis was inaugurated President of the new Confederate States of America on February 18, Louisiana and Texas had joined the rebellion. North Carolina, Virginia, Tennessee, and Arkansas eventually pledged their fates to the Southern cause.

At 4:30 on the afternoon of April 12, a lanyard line was pulled that fired a canon shot on Fort Sumter in Charleston Harbor and secession became more than just angry words. That shot and the many others to follow resonated across the nation, with reverberations heard around the world. However, we are interested in how the news played in northern Indiana; Center Township, LaPorte County, to be exact.

Ormond Hupp was not yet 21 years old when Fort Sumter surrendered to the South Carolina Militia, but the news of its capture had its affect. Recruitment posters soon appeared in the northern states announcing the call to arms to quell the southern rebellion. On May 3, Lincoln issued a call for 42,000 three-year volunteers, and Ormond needed no prodding to join the crusade.

Hupp stood 5 feet, 7 inches tall with dark brown hair and hazel eyes. For a year he was enrolled as a college student at Notre Dame, and may have intended to return. However, "Father Abraham's" call to arms changed his plans forever. His determination to join the ranks compelled him to hide the fact of his deformed foot from the recruitment officers. With the aid of specially constructed orthopedic boots, whatever limp he may have displayed was hardly noticeable. Besides, military physicals in those days required that a soldier could breath, was in possession of all limbs, was capable of unassisted locomotion, and was free of obvious chronic ailments. Ormond qualified on all counts – more or less. His journal notes that he enlisted on September 16, 1861, in his hometown of LaPorte, the very first day that the 5th Indiana Battery was authorized for recruitment. We can assume that his motives to join were purely patriotic (with an element of adventure-seeking?), there being no draft law at the time to compel anyone to join. Conscription was not instituted in the north until Congress passed the "Enrollment Act" on March 3, 1863.

Northern military units were made up of regular army (or navy, etc.) personnel, state and local militias and home guards, and volunteer units like the one Ormond joined. Enlisted volunteers served for a specified period, usually from one to three years. Ormond enlisted for three years.

Officers either belonged to the regular Army, in which case they most likely received their training at West Point, or they were commissioned in the volunteer corps (some held dual commissions). Many of the latter officers were political appointees, some of whom, but certainly not all, evolved into competent leaders as the war progressed. Captain Peter Simonson, leader of the 5th Battery, was a volunteer officer, and a very good one as it turns out. He was genuinely concerned for the welfare of his men, and Ormond's journal makes it clear that they, in turn, regarded him highly. He was also a competent field officer who never panicked under attack, but who was also skilled in tactical withdrawals when prudence or orders so dictated.

The full name of Pvt. Hupp's regiment was the 5th Indiana Independent Light Artillery Battery (in the first muster record "light" is replaced

Figs. 3-1 – Bat. A, 2nd U.S. Artillery at Fair Oaks, VA; the 5th Indiana Battery had a similar appearance. Note that in the artillery, everyone rides. (from A Photographic History of the Civil War in Ten Volumes, *vol. 5, p. 33.)*

by "mounted" artillery). He never bothers to mention the name of his unit in his journal, to describe his uniform, personal arms (he mentions only a revolver), or his regimental flag. These aspects of his military experience were too familiar and commonplace to bother describing to his intended audience, mostly relatives and other contemporaries. His youth may have also contributed to the oversight.

This was an Indiana volunteer unit raised under the auspices of the great Civil War governor of Indiana, Oliver P. Morton (1823-1877). In those days, allegiance to one's state was, by and large, paramount compared to devotion to country. State volunteer units, in particular, although fighting for the Union, were doing so as proud representatives of their states, whose legislatures funded and equipped them. Governor Morton was especially effective at raising large numbers of men for the Union cause, at one point personally borrowing over one million dollars to underwrite the state's troops when the Indiana legislature balked at the heavy price tag. One result of the Civil War was to imprint a national identity on a people who had previously considered themselves first and foremost, residents of individual states.

The 5th Battery was recruited from Whitly, Noble, and Allen Counties, in addition to LaPorte County. Things moved fast for the recruits after enlisting in their home counties. On September 17 (Hupp diary: 18th), they rendezvoused in Indianapolis to begin the training (mostly drill and more drill) that would mold them into a capable fighting unit. They were officially mustered into service on November 22, 1861, with Peter Simonson as captain. Initially, the battery's armaments consisted of two 12-pounder howitzers, two six-pounder rifles, and two six-pounder smooth-bore cannons (see Appendix IV). The 5th Battery was considered a "light" artillery unit because its cannons were all relatively small and light weight for great speed and maneuverability in the field. This contrasts with siege, garrison, or seacoast weapons which were larger and heavier pieces, designed for more stationary assignments. Light artillery units like the 5th Indiana Battery were designed to support infantry and cavalry units in the field.

Ormond Hupp's first military muster record (forms that recorded payroll and attendance) dated November 22, 1861, notes that he was officially mustered in on September 22 by Lt. Col. Thomas J. Wood. Students of the Battle of Chickamauga near Chattanooga, Tennessee (Sept. 19-20, 1863) will immediately recognize his name for his crucial role in the Union rout there that nearly destroyed the Army of the Cumberland. We will revisit him in Chapter 6.

On the 27th of November (Hupp diary: 25th) the "boys" of the 5th Battery boarded a train for Camp Gilbert, near Louisville. They arrived on the 29th and probably drilled some more before shipping out to camp at Bacon Creek, Kentucky, near the village of Jonesville. Bacon Creek at this point flows only about 10 miles north of Munfordville on the Green River, the principal stream in the Mammoth Cave region. The troops arrived there on December 20 (Hupp diary: 8th) after receiving orders to join Brig. General Ormsby M. Mitchel's Third Division of General Don Carlos Buell's Army of the Ohio. Mitchel was a noted astronomer before the war, and had helped found the Naval and Harvard Observatories. Before that, he had graduated from West Point (1829) and had taught mathematics there until he resigned in 1832. He then taught astronomy at Cincinnati College. Pvt. Hupp and his friends would be under the command of this astronomer-general as Buell's army moved southward into the very heart of the Confederacy.

While General Buell's Army of the Ohio was in winter headquarters at Bacon Creek, the strategic situation for Union armies in the western theater was fairly stable, with opportunities for concerted jabs into the Confederate interior in the spring. Union forces in early 1862 were in firm control of most of the border state, Kentucky, although a large

Confederate force under General William J. Hardee occupied the southern city and rail center of Bowling Green.

General Leonidas Polk, the cleric general who was also Episcopal Bishop of Louisiana, had occupied the Mississippi River town of Columbus, Kentucky, since September of the previous year, violating Kentucky neutrality and upsetting many of the natives. His force of about 12,000 countered General Ulysses S. Grant's 20,000 men in southern Illinois. Grant operated within the Department of Missouri under the overall command of General Henry W. Halleck based in St. Louis. Confederate General Albert Sidney Johnston held the center of the Rebel line with about 43,000 troops at Columbia, Tennessee.

The Union plan of action in the west was relatively simple. The two major armies under Grant and Buell would move south, cross into Tennessee converging toward one another like the jaws of a giant pincer. Whatever Confederate units stood in the way would be crushed or pushed aside as Union forces forced their way toward the vital rail line of the Memphis and Charleston railroad which linked Memphis, Chattanooga, Knoxville, and Charleston, South Carolina. Union control of this supply line would be nearly as devastating to the South as their taking possession of the Mississippi waterway, another eventual Northern objective. Once in control of the "Memphis and Charleston" in northern Alabama, Buell could use it as a troop transport and supply line to move either east or west. While in Kentucky, Buell had promised Lincoln that he would move on Chattanooga in eastern Tennessee as soon as he gained control of northern Alabama and its prized rail line. Aiding the Union loyalists in eastern Tennessee was one of Lincoln's pet obsessions.

What does Ormond Hupp's diary have to say about any of this part of the campaign?

The answer is, "not much." Ormond rewrote this part of his diary after the original was lost at the Battle of Perryville, so his recollection of dates and events was not perfect. But his seemingly inexplicable brevity in describing his actions from Bacon Creek to Bowling Green, Nashville, and finally to Huntsville, Alabama, results from events that had occurred previously to the west. Simply put, his passage through these former Confederate strongholds resulted in little of substance to record. This enigmatic lack of action on the road to Huntsville is attributable to a Union victory so momentous that it changed the course of the war (at least, temporarily), and catapulted the victorious commanding general – Ulysses S. Grant – to instant national fame. This event was the taking of Fort Henry on the Tennessee River, followed by nearby Fort Donelson on the Cumberland River a week later.

Forts Henry and Donelson were strategically important "stop valves" on their respective rivers, both of which were important commercial and military arteries for the South. The Tennessee, for instance, links the important cities of Knoxville and Chattanooga in the east, eventually flowing across northern Alabama and nearly straight north across Tennessee to flow into the Ohio at Paducah, Kentucky. The Cumberland flows through Nashville and parallels the Tennessee River as they cut across Kentucky to the Ohio. The two forts were situated where their respective rivers closed together (present Lake Barkley and Kentucky Lake) on the Tennessee-Kentucky border so to guard this important water access to the southern heartland. Grant and Halleck knew that control of these forts would be necessary if they were to ever establish dominion over the Mississippi valley and other parts of the Confederate interior.

Fort Henry was taken rather easily on February 6 by an assault of Federal river boats specially constructed for such campaigns by Flag Officer Andrew H. Foote. Grant's forces were bogged down by mud so never really took part in the fort's Surrender by Confederate General Tilghman.

Donelson proved more tenacious. Foote's gunboats were repulsed and Foote was seriously wounded. Grant's raw troops, reinforced by a contingent under General Lew Wallace (author of "Ben Hur") from Buell, eventually gained the upper hand and forced most of the Rebel troops to flee to the south and east. The fort's commander, General Floyd (President Buchanan's Sec. of War), and second in command, General Pillow, escaped after passing command to General Simon B. Buckner. Buckner's request for surrender was met by Grant's message that nothing less than "unconditional surrender" was acceptable. The fort was in Union hands by February 15. Ironically, another group to escape capture at Donelson was General Nathan Bedford Forrest and his cavalry. They would act as a major source of misery and consternation for General Buell in future campaigns.

With the taking of Fort Henry by the "bluecoats," Albert Sidney Johnston's Confederates were feeling hard pressed. Conferring with General Beauregard, hero of Sumter and First Manassas, Johnston decided that a hasty, albeit orderly retreat south might be prudent. Kentucky would have to be abandoned.

Meanwhile, Ormond Hupp and the rest of the Third Division were slogging their way toward Bowling Green in the mud and cold. They arrived there on the 9th of February (Hupp Diary states that he left Bacon Creek on 11th and arrived on 14th) to find that Hardee had already evacuated. This was a difficult trek for the soldiers because of the

Fig. 3-2

Fig. 3-3

Fig. 3-2 – Confederate calvary raider, General Nathan Bedford Forrest. Forrest's horsemen raised havoc for Buell's army by attacking supply trains, destroying bridges, and otherwise disrupting communications (from A Photographic History of the Civil War in Ten Volumes, *vol. 10, p. 21.*

Fig. 3-3 – General Ormsby M. Mitchel, X Corps, Army of the Ohio. Mitchel commanded Union forces occupying Hunstville (from A Photographic History of the Civil War in Ten Volumes, *vol. 10, p. 187.)*

miserable conditions of the roads and foul weather. Whereas before they had ridden in relative comfort on railroad trains, they now had to walk (as an artillery driver, Hupp rode a horse). Hupp noted that in Bowling Green ". . . our first soldiering commenced."

Hardee was on his way to Nashville to rendezvous with Johnston. On the 15th as news of Donelson's fall reached Nashville; church bells tolled in sorrow and panic struck the populace who feared that Grant, with Foote's gunboats, or Buell, would appear at the city gates at any moment. Nashville was particularly vulnerable because the confident citizens, sure that the winds of war would never blow their way, had neglected to erect even minor fortifications. Eventually, Hardee and Johnston evacuated the city toward Murfreesboro, leaving General Floyd, the fugitive from Donelson, in charge of keeping civil order and securing as many supplies as possible before the arrival of the Federals.

As he had lost Donelson, Floyd also lost order in Nashville. Rebellious mobs claimed part of the Confederate military rations for themselves. N. B. Forrest eventually arrived to restore order, and shipped vast quantities of badly needed supplies to the safety of Atlanta before slipping out of town. He left in response to reports of bluecoats arriving on the north shore of the Cumberland.

Arriving Sunday the 23rd, these advance cavalry soldiers from Buell's main force were met by the mayor of Nashville who rowed across the Cumberland to present them with the keys to the city. He had promised his constituents that he would convince the blue soldiers not to fire their artillery into the city or otherwise attack. Nashville surrendered without a single shot fired.

Buell did not actually enter the city until Wednesday the 26th, although the city was firmly in Union hands by the previous day. He had been delayed by muddy roads and washed out railroad bridges which had to be repaired for his supply trains.

Hupp's dates for arrival in Nashville correspond well with official records; he stated that he left Bowling Green on the 22nd and arrived in Nashville on the 25th (Tuesday). What he and his fellow soldiers found was a virtually deserted city, stores closed, houses abandoned; all because Grant had taken Forts Henry and Donelson, gatekeepers of the Cumberland and the Tennessee. Hupp reports being encamped in Nashville for a full month (to March 25) without recounting a single detail. The retreat of the Confederates, along with many of Nashville's civilians, guaranteed a relatively pleasant, if uneventful, interlude for Hupp and the boys in Tennessee's capitol city.

In late March, the 5th Battery moved out of Nashville toward Murfreesboro, eventually passing through Shelbyville and Fayetteville, Tennessee, before crossing the state line into Alabama. There being no rail lines along this route, they marched the over 100 miles on foot.

Advance units, including the 5th Indiana Battery, arrived on the outskirts of Huntsville on Friday, April 11. Surprised by the intruding Union troops, Confederate garrison troops attempted to flee on railroad trains, leaving east and west of the town. It was here that the 5th Battery opened up their field pieces in their first real military action. With a few well placed artillery shells, they succeeded in stopping all the fleeing trains except one. Interestingly, this account, retrieved from a regimental history, is not mentioned at all in Ormond Hupp's diary. Instead, he delivers the wry understatement, "we arrived to the great astonishment of the citizens." Indeed. Alabama, underbelly of the Confederacy, and its Memphis and Charleston Railroad had been invaded and partially occupied by Yankees nearly one year to the day after the surrender of Fort Sumter.

The reaction of the Huntsville ladies to the blue clad intruders from

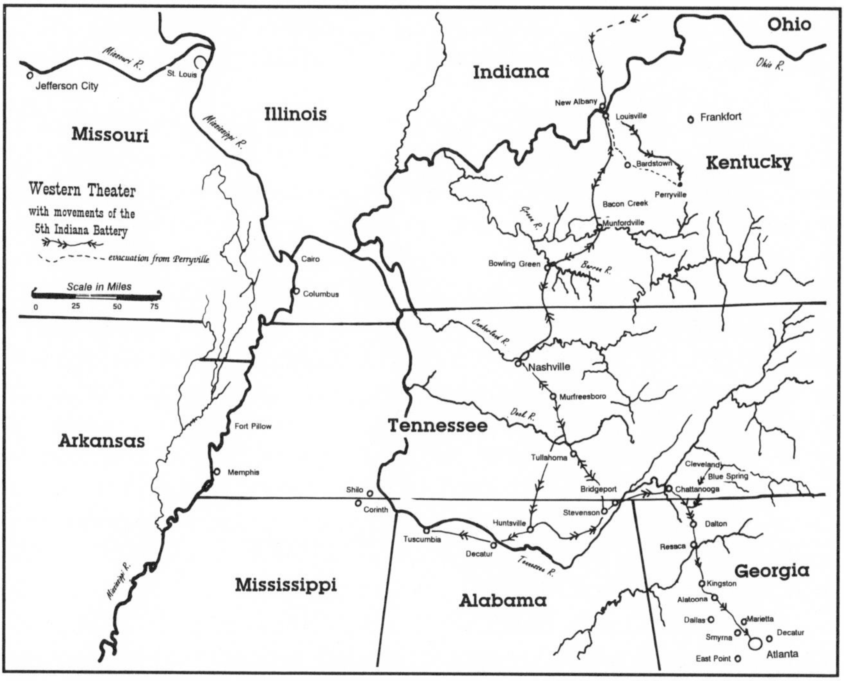

the north contrasts sharply with how occupation troops under General Benjamin Butler were treated in New Orleans. Following Admiral Farragut's successful assault on the lower Mississippi forts, St. Philip and Jackson, Butler occupied the city on May 1, not long after Hupp and the boys entered Huntsville. To show their disdain for the "foreign invaders," the ladies of New Orleans showed such disrespect, particularly for Union officers, that Butler soon issued his famous "Woman Order," in which he proclaimed that any Southern woman who insulted or assaulted a Union soldier would be arrested as a prostitute. Such measures were not employed by Ormsby Mitchel in Huntsville, for as noted by Pvt. Hupp, at least some of the Huntsville ladies eventually warmed up nicely to their young conquerors.

Many a Huntsville family, however, decided not to trust the generosity of the invaders and quit the town altogether, leaving homes and possessions to the fates – and scavenging – of Union enlisted men. For example, Elizabeth Sheffy, widow of prominent physician, Dr. Lawrence Sheffy, "...ran, at first, with the refugees, to Mr. George Steele's place to hide in the wine cellars. All of her silver was hid in the garden. When they became used to the sound of firing they came home again." One of Mrs. Sheffy's slaves, Douglas, was later enlisted as General Mitchel's body guard. His loyalty to his white "family", however, was so strong that he daily "requisitioned" food stores from the General's pantry to be secreted off to the Sheffy home.

With his troops in firm control of the city, Ormsby Mitchel settled in as occupation commander of occupied Huntsville. General Buell and the bulk of his army never made it to Huntsville, but had turned west to help reinforce Grant at what was to be known as the Battle of Shilo (Union victory, April 7).

Certainly one could do worse than to pick Huntsville as a place to spend some time, even if you were not entirely welcome. Located a few miles north of the Tennessee River in the foothills of the western reach of the Cumberland Plateau, it presented a graceful picture of the antebellum South. An Agrarian community in form and spirit, it nevertheless sported many elegant mansions, including the home of Reuban Chapman, a former Congressman and Alabama governor, who at the time of the Union occupation was the Confederate emissary to France. Another fine home belonging to the Calhoun family had a deep dungeon where the family silver was stored. It is said that Harriet Beecher Stowe obtained the idea of the dungeon in Uncle Tom's Cabin after a visit to the Calhoun place.

Huntsville is crossed in the east by a prominent, wooded north-south trending ridge called Monte Sano. Maple Hill Cemetery, situated at the foot of the west side of Monte Sano, is no doubt the cemetery described by Hupp in his journal. His encampment, where he spent most of his time after the raids on western Alabama (see below), was located on top of a lower ridge to the west of Monte Sano, in "Old Town." It was a rectangular parcel of land roughly bordered by Eustis Avenue, Lincoln Street, Echols Avenue, and McClung Street. Near the old city center is a park containing the Big Spring issuing from a limestone cavern, once an important source of water for the city as it was when Hupp described it in 1862.

Hupp was not impressed by what he regarded as the pathetic state of agriculture in the area in 1862. Nevertheless, Huntsville and environs was, and still is, a major producer of cotton and corn, with fruit orchards also contributing to the local economy. Industry suffered in Huntsville up to the late 19th century because of its relative isolation from southern markets. For years, the Tennessee River acted as a geographic and economic barrier, and trade with northern markets suffered for lack of a major northern rail line. This situation began to change in the 1890's with the construction of a new cotton mill, and accelerated after the World War II as Huntsville became a center for aerospace research and development. The place whose agricultural practices Ormond Hupp disparaged in 1862 as being "fifty years behind those of Indiana," is now the home of the Army Redstone Missile Arsenal, NASA's Marshall Space Flight Center, and the Alabama Space and Rocket Center.

On the day they arrived in Huntsville, the 5th Battery was ordered to mount two of their field cannons on flatcars pushed ahead by two different locomotives, one headed east and the other west on the Memphis and Charleston line. Hupp rode on the westbound train headed for Decatur, across the Tennessee River. As he describes it, within four miles of Decatur the train veered off the tracks, wrecked by Confederate saboteurs. The northerners retreated back to Huntsville under fire, abandoning a spiked (made inoperable) cannon in their haste. The next day a heavier force succeeded in storming and taking Decatur after dousing a fire set by the fleeing Confederates on the Tennessee River bridge. They camped for three days before setting out by rail for Tuscumbia, a small town in northwest Alabama near the famous Muscle Shoals (rapids; now a lake) of the Tennessee River. It would become the birthplace of Helen Keller in 1880.

The Union brigade arrived by rail in Tuscumbia on April 15, by Hupp's recollection, where they camped on a plantation with "75 slaves." His account of the "boys" pilfering Confederate Aid-de-Camp Nelson's Mansion in the Tuscumbia area shows that General Buell's official constraints on any depradations against civilian property, including that of Southern sympathizers, were not enforced very well outside Buell's main army contingent, at the time, on its way to Shilo to reinforce Grant. Nevertheless, Pvt. Hupp's ill-gotten booty, consisting of three books and no less than 5 gallons of wine, is revealing. We know from his diary and from eyewitness accounts of his later years, that Ormond was an avid reader, and enjoyed an occasional sip of the vintor's art.

On the 20th of April, things got hot for the Union brigade in Tuscumbia. They were attacked in force by rebel guerrillas, so decided to "skedaddle" east, back down the rail line toward Decatur. About half way to Decatur, at Courtland, they were again attacked with the loss of 20 men captured, although they inflicted untold casualties on the enemy. On the 23rd, they reached Decatur and fired the Tennessee River bridge behind them as they pressed on to Huntsville. Ormond Hupp expressed sympathy for the bridge, but it was repaired soon after by Buell's forces returning east from Shilo.

The "reconnaissance" mission to Tuscumbia had not resulted in locking up northern Alabama or winning friends for the North, but it was useful in showing the resolve of southern guerrilla and regular CSA units to throw out the northern hordes. After a month away from their Huntsville "home", the Union raiders returned on the 25th of April to begin their peaceful month of encampment in Huntsville. Below, in the wide valley that stretched to the horizon, slaves worked in the corn fields.

As Pvt. Hupp went about his business on his hilltop encampment – and his consortium with Adelaide and Josephine off the hill (see journal) – General Mitchel's troops, on the east side of town, were engaged in more daring exploits. As on the west, trains with mounted cannons roamed between Huntsville and Stevenson, gauging Confederate strength in the area and generally trying to make things thick for the Rebels.

The most famous raid of all – perhaps of the entire war – was waged by 22 volunteers under the command of a civilian, James J. Andrews. Later known as "The Great Locomotive Chase," these men were charged with the task of disrupting the vital rail line (Georgia Central) between Marietta, Georgia, and Chattanooga, Tennessee. It served as a vital supply line between these important southern cities; its disruption could have served as a prelude to an all out campaign against Chattanooga, and later, Atlanta.

On the evening of April 12, just one day after Huntsville was occupied, these men boarded a train for Kenesaw, Georgia, just north of Marietta (now a suburb of Atlanta). When the train stopped for breakfast at the station, the raiders, dressed as civilians (thus subject to arrest as spies), slipped off the train on the opposite side of the tracks. They then climbed into the engine *General*, fired up the boiler and took off north for Chattanooga, later pursued by Confederates in the engine *Texas*. The raiders stopped once to cut telegraph lines and pile ties across the rails, but never succeeded in permanently damaging the road as planned. The *General* finally ran out of fuel about 90 miles down the line at Graysville. The men fled into the woods but were captured and tried in Atlanta. James Andrews and seven others were executed as spies. Fourteen of the men were imprisoned but a year later eight of the men overpowered their guards and escaped. Later, the other six were paroled and became the first ever recipients of the Medal of Honor.

On June 9, during the closing hours of the Union victory at Corinth, Mississippi (just south of Shilo), General Buell received orders from Halleck to move his army east. Earlier, Memphis, western terminus of the Memphis and Charleston line, fell to Union troops. Buell was sent east with the ultimate goal of joining up with Ormsby Mitchel and moving on Chattanooga. Success there might also allow a venture up the East Tennessee and Georgia rail line to attempt the capture of Knoxville, a favorite target of the President's. Atlanta was another tempting plum to the southeast.

Heady with the recent success of Union armies from Roanoke Island, Virginia, (Feb. 8) to New Orleans, Memphis, and now Corinth, Halleck was persuaded, principally by Ormsby Mitchel, that an eastward plunge into the Cumberlands and beyond was not only feasible, but that success was nearly certain. Mitchel was convinced that control of the Tennessee River between his vantage place at Huntsville and Chattanooga was crucial to the operation.

When his request for gunboats was refused by Washington, he constructed his own and named her *Tennessee*. This craft, a converted horse ferry armored with cotton bales, was armed with a single 10 pounder Parrot rifle (rifled cannon) and was supposed to provided support for Buell's troops during the planned assault of Chattanooga. Although she never realized her full potential, the odd looking make-shift craft did intimidate Confederate forces who tried to cross to the north side of the river, and caused many a river town to lower their Confederate flags.

In support of Buell's eastward migration, the middle section of Hupp's Battery was sent northeast on foot, attached to the 19th Illinois Infantry to Winchester, Tennessee. Their orders were to protect rail lines from Murfreesboro to Shelbyville against Cavalry raids, specifically by John Scott and his men.

Buell was having his own troubles with Confederate cavalry, almost as soon as he moved out of Corinth. Nathan Bedford Forrest and John Hunt Morgan made sure that Buell's trip was less than a pleasure cruise.

The Union Commander of the Army of the Ohio was constantly having to repair tracks and bridges on the Memphis and Charleston, and had to post guard contingents at many bridges forward of his position. Hupp's group was supposed to keep the rail lines clear north of the main line of assault in Alabama. They were soon ordered back to the Memphis and Charleston, however, and arrived at Paint Rock, a small village about 15 miles east of Huntsville. From Paint Rock they were to make tracks for Stevenson and the Union-held fort there. As noted in Hupp's journal, they were harassed by Confederate guerrilla cavalry but suffered few losses. Their advance cavalry units also did some harassing of their own, capturing four guerrillas with their horses and arms.

Retribution for guerrilla attacks was swift and merciless. Hupp casually noted that ". . . all that is worth mentioning in this days march is the burning of eight houses owned by guerrillas". He then described what is probably one of the most poignant moments in his entire diary; a guerrilla's wife, her house and all she owned in flames, her children by her side, begging not to be killed. The soldiers marched on, leaving her to her misery, a cogent reminder that war is only glamorous in the movies.

On July 1, the Battery was temporarily placed under General George Thomas (later to be known as "The Rock of Chickamauga") and marched to the town of Bridgeport on the Tennessee River about 10 miles northeast of Stevenson. Here the 5th Battery was attached to the 9th Brigade under Col. Leonard Harris, which consisted of the 10th Wisconsin, 38th Indiana, and the 3rd and 33rd Ohio regiments, in addition to the 5th Indiana Battery. They spent a full two months there within sight of Confederate pickets, while their main force remained four miles to the southwest at Battle Creek.

Meanwhile, Buell remained in Huntsville planning the grand assault on Chattanooga. Ormsby Mitchel was eventually transferred to Beauford, South Carolina, (where he died soon after of yellow fever), and Buell assumed direct control of Hupp's unit. At this point, Hupp complained bitterly of being put on half rations, and further accused the commanding general of profiteering by the sale of flour to civilians. This was probably an unsubstantiated charge but well reflects the nearly mutinous feelings of many enlisted men under Buell's command, here and later on.

On the 24th of August (Hupp diary: 15th) the troops at Bridgeport were ordered back to Stevenson to join the 13th Michigan in preparing the fort for evacuation. Bridgeport was the closest the Union army came to Chattanooga at that point in time. Federal troops finally did occupy Chattanooga on September 9th of the following year, but this time the Confederate high command had other plans. Braxton Bragg of North Carolina had taken control of the Confederate Army of the Mississippi from Beauregard on June 27. He had a plan to divert the Federals from their eastward plunge, a bold surge back into Kentucky, all the way to the Ohio River!

All the while they were at the fort in Stevenson, the Union troops were expecting an attack. Nevertheless, they kept up a lively conversation with Confederate pickets on the southern river bank, even exchanging provisions (coffee, sugar, tobacco, etc.) with them. These acts of fraternization with the enemy were fairly common throughout the war, but generally discouraged by officers.

Some of the locals, especially suspected guerrilla supporters, did not benefit much from the Union soldiers' chivalry. Hupp notes that even those citizens who professed solid Union allegiance, "were only watching for a favorable opportunity to kill you." Here at Stevenson – as at other posts in Alabama – the troops continued to burn down the homes of suspected guerrillas, and stole "secesh" beef to slaughter. They also purchased fruit pies from some of the local ladies, whose political sympathies could be neglected in consideration of the favor.

On August 31, the 5th Battery engaged in a heated battle with Confederate Cavalry as Fort Stevenson was in the process of evacuation. They continued as rear guard as men and materials were moved northward to counter Bragg's move into Tennessee, the capture of Kentucky for the Confederacy as his ultimate goal. In the east, General George B. McClellan was about to meet General Robert E. Lee at a town in Maryland called Sharpsburg, and a creek called Antietam. The South was moving north on two fronts, and things were about to get very interesting for Ormond Hupp and the 5th Battery.

Chapter 4
The Road to Perryville

Glittering dimly, toiling under the sun – the dust-cover'd men,
In columns rise and fall to the undulations of the ground,
With the artillery interspers'd – the wheels rumble, the horses sweat,
As the army corps advances.
Walt Whitman: from An Army Corps on the March *(1865)*

I think to lose Kentucky is nearly the same as to lose the whole game . . .

Abraham Lincoln

The evacuation of Fort Stevenson in July of 1862 was precipitated by larger events that took place about three months previously. After suffering multiple defeats at Shilo (April 6-7) and General Halleck's advance on Corinth, Mississippi, (April 29-June 10) the Southern leadership under President Jefferson Davis was in a quandary. After initial Confederate victories at Sumter, Manassas (First Bull Run), Wilson's Creek, and Ball's Bluff in the summer and fall of 1861, the South, in early 1862, suddenly found itself impaled in its midsection by Grant and Buell's bold thrusts.

In the western theater, Union troops occupied much of Tennessee, and the northern counties of Mississippi and Alabama (Hupp's location). The battles of Pea Ridge, Arkansas, (March 7-8) and New Madrid, Missouri, (March 10) both Union victories, had effectively ended Confederate hopes of driving Union forces from the "Trans-Mississippi" region (area west of the Mississippi River).

On the eastern front, "Little Mac" (General George McClellan) began his "Peninsula Campaign" on March 17th which, before it was turned back by Robert E. Lee's troops, came to within the sound of church bells in the Confederate capital of Richmond, Virginia.

Figure 4-1

Figure 4-2

Figure 4-1 – C.S.A. General Braxton Bragg, commander of the Army of Mississippi (from A Photographic History of the Civil War in Ten Volumes, *vol. 10, p. 243).*

Figure 4-2 – Union Major General Don Carlos Buell, commander of the Army of the Ohio (from A Photographic History of the Civil War in Ten Volumes, *vol. 10, p. 173).*

Obvious to Jefferson Davis and his staff was the need for fresh and dynamic leadership to save their fledgling nation from an early demise. The Union armies in the west were under the direct command of "Old Brains," General Henry Halleck, who had taken control of Grant's forces after Shilo.

After General Pierre Beauregard's loss of western Tennessee and northern Mississippi to Halleck, the need for a replacement who could reverse the Union juggernaut was deemed an imperative. The job was eventually handed to General Braxton Bragg, a native of North Carolina. Bragg had earlier commanded coastal defenses at Pensacola and Mobile before requesting transfer to Kentucky. He was sent instead to northern Mississippi to help Albert Sidney Johnston's reorganization of Confederate forces at Corinth. He commanded the Confederate right at Shilo, and helped to temporarily stave off Halleck during his slow advance on Corinth. Now, on June 27, 1862, he was handed the reigns of the Army of Mississippi with orders to drive the enemy out of Dixie. Consolidating the beaten Confederate armies at Tupello, Mississippi, he was on his way to do just that as Pvt. Hupp and the 5th Indiana Battery were fighting a rear guard action against Confederate cavalry forces harassing their retreat from Fort Stevenson.

Only three days after Bragg gained control of the largest Confederate army west of the Alleghenies, Don Carlos Buell finally made his way to Huntsville, repairing damaged tracks and bridges – some damage done by his own forces in their retreat from Tuscumbia – as he went. His passage was also hindered by the constant harassment of his supply line to the north – the Nashville and Louisville Railroad – by cavalry under John Hunt Morgan and Nathan Bedford Forrest. Buell's goal was Chattanooga, and from there, Atlanta, Knoxville, or both. Bragg was determined to beat him to Chattanooga and sent his forces northeast in a desperate scramble to prevent what, to the Confederates, would have represented a near fatal debacle.

The loss of Atlanta, in particular, would open the gates to Georgia and the eastern seaboard, later secured by the predations of Sherman during

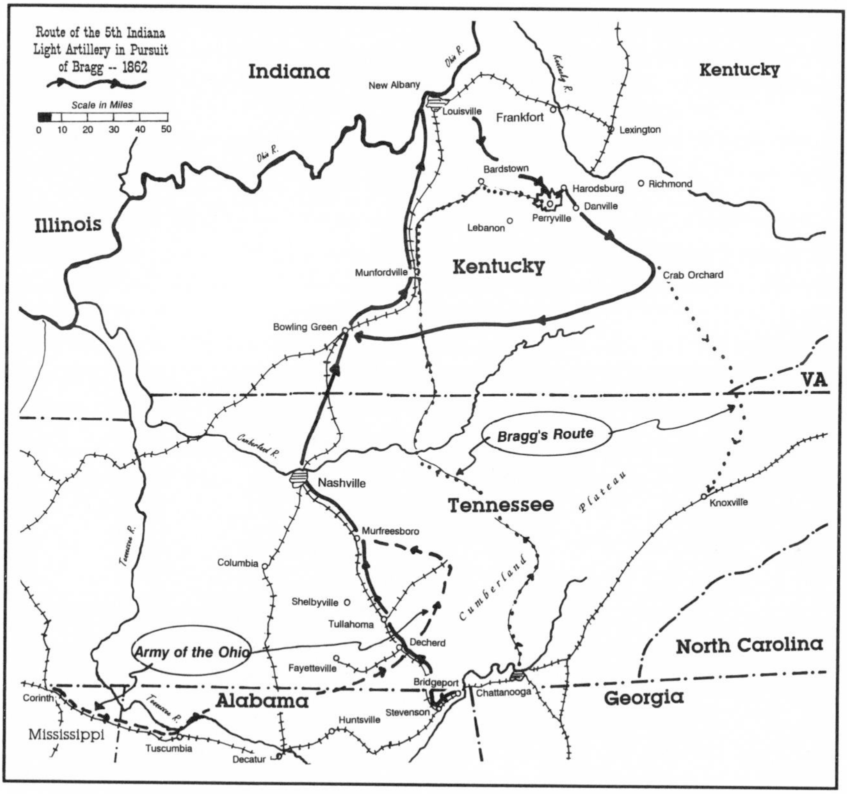

Figure 4-3

Figure 4-4

Figure 4-3 – C.S.A. General Edmund Kirby Smith, commander of the Army of Kentucky in the Lexington-Frankfort area (from A Photographic History of the Civil War in Ten Volumes, *vol. 10, p. 243).*

Figure 4-4 – C.S.A. Major General Leonidas Polk (shown in bishop's vestments), commanded Right Wing at Perryville (from A Photographic History of the Civil War in Ten Volumes, *vol. 10, p. 143).*

---

his Atlanta Campaign and notorious "March to the Sea." This event, however, was forestalled for the moment as the ever lethargic Buell was beaten to Chattanooga by Braxton Bragg. It was around this time that Hupp and the boys hurriedly departed from northern Alabama. Anticipating a move on Nashville by Bragg, Buell was moving his troops north into middle Tennessee.

In his diary, Ormond Hupp correctly stated that Bragg was attempting to obtain Buell's rear at Nashville. Bragg's original plan was to cut off Buell's Louisville and Nashville Railroad supply line south of Nashville, then to combine forces with General Kirby Smith, commander of the District of East Tennessee, and defeat Buell's forces in Tennessee. The combined Confederate armies would then move into Kentucky, hopefully "encouraging" that state's citizens to join the southern cause.

With Buell's retreat northward, however, Bragg and Smith realized that their plan to gain Buell's rear was untenable. Bragg now gave marching orders for their new target, Kentucky. He and Buell would eventually meet in mortal battle a few months hence in the Blue Grass state – near a little village called Perryville.

Pvt. Hupp noted that on September 2nd their column reached the foot of the Cumberland Mountains in Tennessee. His recollection of the freed slaves that followed the troops from Alabama is noteworthy, if not a bit embarrassing for modern descendants. He wrote, ". . . fully 500 Negroes followed us from Stevenson, men, women, and children, and a more disgusting sight I never saw in the Union Army."

Racism of this sort was common among northern soldiers, most of whom would have balked at risking their lives for the benefit of what were, to them, "disgusting" and inferior beings. Part of Lincoln's reluctance to issue the Emancipation Proclamation was fear of causing disaffection or even mutiny among the ranks of enlisted men. Ormond Hupp's comment here in the Cumberlands made it clear that freeing slaves was not uppermost on his list of wartime priorities.

In Chattanooga, Bragg organized his army into two wings, the right, under Major General Leonidas Polk (called "the Bishop", he was the Episcopal Bishop of Louisiana), and the left, under Major General William Hardee. This army struck their tents and crossed the Tennessee River headed north from Chattanooga on August 27th. Kirby Smith, in the meantime, was on his way to Lexington, Kentucky, later joined in Kentucky by a 3,000-man force under General Humphry Marshall arriving from southwestern Virginia. Thus began the strange race north for the two competing armies, Buell in the west, and Bragg and his allies on the east.

Pvt. Hupp's stay in Tullahoma in southern Tennessee, in fact, was cut short by word that Kirby Smith had crossed into Kentucky and Bragg was also rushing north. Buell ordered his troops to fall back to Murfreesboro, where Hupp arrived on September 5th. Buell now sensed that Bragg was after bigger fish than simply a confrontation with his army, and feared that Louisville on the Ohio River might be Bragg's ultimate objective. After again falling back to Nashville (where Hupp notes that his battery was reinforced by men and material newly arrived by rail), Buell called on the governors of the adjoining northern states, Illinois, Indiana, and Ohio, to issue a new call for troops to defend Louisville, an all important manufacturing city and river crossing to the north. The governors heeded the call and fresh troops began to pour into Louisville, organized by General "Bull" Nelson sent to Louisville for that purpose by Buell. Cincinnati, up-river from Louisville, was also put on alert.

Neither Pvt. Hupp nor the rest of Buell's troops in Nashville knew that General Bragg, now encamped at Sparta to the east, was being urged by the governor of Tennessee to attack Buell and retake the Tennessee capital for the Confederacy. Buell, for his part, was being urged by Washington to move swiftly to engage Bragg and cut off the threatened invasion of Kentucky.

As was his way, Buell demurred, preferring the more conservative approach of watching and waiting. Buell's infamous plodding manner was now getting him in hot water with the President and with Henry Halleck, who in July had gone to Washington as the President's chief war adviser. Buell was advised that if he did not make haste to engage Bragg in battle that he would soon lose his job. Lincoln noted that "a McClellan in the army was lamentable, but a combination of McClellan and Buell was deplorable."

General George McClellan of the Army of the Potomac also had a well-deserved reputation for his conservative approach to warfare. Like McClellan, Buell constantly complained of supply and transportation problems (in his case, mostly true) and otherwise moved his army deliberately and with great care – meaning, slowly. His failure to engage Bragg in Tennessee also arose from his over-estimating his rival's troop strength, a fault also shared by McClellan. Bragg had over 27,000 troops in Tennessee; Buell's Army of the Ohio, now in Nashville, totaled over 60,000 men. In fact, Bragg decided to ignore the urgings of Tennessee officials to attack Buell at Nashville precisely because he knew he was badly outnumbered, and that Buell enjoyed the advantage of entrenchments.

Buell eventually decided to evacuate his army from Nashville and move north toward Bowling Green. Here the dates in Hupp's diary do not quite correspond to official records (remember that he was recalling events from a hospital bed, nearly 6 months later). He notes that the troops arrived in Bowling Green on the 11th (September), although Buell actually crossed the Kentucky line on the 12th and entered Bowling Green on the 13th.

About this time, Polk had reached Glasgow to the east of Bowling Green and issued orders to Generals J. K. Duncan and James Chalmers to occupy Proctor's Station and Cave City, respectively, and to disrupt Buell's communications along the L&N rail line. Cavalry under John Scott was sent even farther north to capture the Green River Bridge at Munfordville. It is these operations to which Hupp refers when he says that Bragg had cut Buell's communications on the 15th at Green River. The communications were cut so efficiently, in fact, that Washington lost touch with Buell and for some days had no idea where he was operating.

Readers familiar with southern Kentucky will recognize that the area involved here is near to the present-day Mammoth Cave region. The Green River passes within Mammoth Cave National Park and farther east has carved a fairly deep valley near Munfordville. The L&N railroad bridge crossing the river here was the prime target of Cavalryman John Scott, who found the bridge defended by a garrison of about 2,000 Union troops led by Colonel John Wilder. Wilder was a lawyer and industrialist from Indiana with little real military experience, but he was determined not to surrender the very important Munfordville bridge.

Figure 4-5 – C.S.A. Colonel Joseph "Fighting Joe" Wheeler, 2nd Cavalry Brigade (from A Photographic History of the Civil War in Ten Volumes, *vol. 10, p. 249).*

Scott asked for help from General Chalmers who sent most of his troops up from Cave City on the night of the 13th. On the next day, the Confederate attack was successfully repulsed by Wilder's brave band, and the bridge saved for another day. It did not matter much, however, because Scott busied his men tearing up track north of Munfordville, further destroying Buell's links with Louisville and the rest of the world. It is these operations that caused Hupp to anticipate a full scale battle with Bragg's forces at Munfordville.

By the 16th (the day Hupp says they were ordered forward), Bragg had surrounded the garrison at Munfordville, demanding Wilder's surrender. Wilder's legendary response was to go to General Simon B. Buckner's Headquarters (3rd Division under Hardee) and ask for advice as to how to handle the situation. Buckner declined to oblige this request, but allowed his guest to review his troop strength and artillery pieces. Convinced of the superior odds against him, Wilder surrendered and marched his paroled troops (now numbering over 4,000 with recent reinforcements) toward Bowling Green on the afternoon of the 17th.

As Ormond Hupp observed , Buell failed to take advantage of an opportunity to give battle to Bragg, the results of which may have thwarted Bragg's northward migration then and there. His inaction, however, stemmed not from cowardice or lethargy, but from miscalculation; he was sure that Bragg would not move in a direction that would put him squarely in Buell's path.

Hupp noted, ". . . here he [Buell] lay three days within eight miles of Bragg, with a third more men, only for him to get out of the way and such a dissatisfaction among the men never prevailed in any army."

It was not the first, nor would this be the last time Buell's men were dissatisfied with his performance. Their lack of confidence in their leader ran deep, and included officers as well as enlisted men. This group psychology was to have an affect on future actions involving the armies of the Ohio and Mississippi.

Finally informed of Bragg's presence at the Green River, Buell decided to move against him on the 18th (Hupp's date agrees fairly closely here). He did so in spite of a report from Wilder (now safe behind Union lines) and the suspicions of his staff that Bragg fielded a numerically superior force to his own. Buell decided to move because he suspected (and Wilder confirmed) that Bragg's forces faced serious food shortages and would, thus, be weakened.

Bragg, on the other hand, ultimately brushed off those of his staff who wanted to force Buell into a fight at Munfordville, and gave orders to move east to Bardstown. He realized that Kirby Smith, now operating in the Blue Grass region around Lexington, would not be able to resupply his starving men with badly needed provisions. After sending Buckner's Third Division (under Gen. William J. Hardee) out to test the Federal resolve for a fight, Bragg made the decision to evacuate Munfordville when it became clear that Buell was not interested in pressing the issue.

Bragg's army was on the road to Bardstown (via Nolan and Hodgenville, near Lincoln's birthplace) by the afternoon of the 20th, leaving "Fighting Joe" Wheeler's cavalry behind as a rear guard. After a spirited fight with Wheeler's mounted defenders, Buell's troops marched into Munfordville shortly after the last of Bragg's men had departed. They pursued Bragg for a while, but seeing that his intentions were to head east for the food-rich central Blue Grass region – and not Louisville – Buell called off the pursuit. Hupp states that Bragg turned toward Bardstown at Elizabethtown, but his actual turning point was Nolan. There was a direct road from Elizabethtown to Bardstown, the Bardstown Pike, but Bragg had turned east far to the south of that point. Buell wired ahead to Louisville to have food waiting for his hungry troops and marched on toward Elizabethtown where the troops then headed nearly due north to West Point on the Ohio and Salt Rivers.

Hupp noted that the nearly half-starved soldiers were given food supplied by boats arriving from Louisville. From West Point, they marched to Louisville to obtain food, rest, and, for many, new shoes and uniforms (but no back pay! Hupp had last been paid on Sept. 1).

Hupp reported that they marched into Louisville and encamped in a city park on the 26th of September, after marching nearly continuously, night and day, for a month. Their camp, located on Broadway near the train station, was probably near the present Union Station, still located on Broadway. To the dust-caked and weary Indiana soldiers, the sight of their native state across the Ohio must have been as blessed as the respite they were about to receive from pursuing Bragg across Kentucky. Their rest would be brief, however, for the real chase was soon to begin in ernest.

Bragg's thrust into central Kentucky was part of a two pronged Confederate offensive designed to turn the fortunes of war toward the South. As Bragg invaded Kentucky in the west, Lee crossed the Potomac into Maryland (Sept. 4) hoping to enlist the people of that border state to the Southern cause, and to bring the war home to the North. He was eventually confronted by McClellan at Sharpsburg, Maryland, in one of the bloodiest battles of the war, Antietam (named for the local creek). This battle culminated at about the time Wilder was surrendering his Green River fort to Bragg (Sept. 17), and resulted in Lee's retreat back to Virginia. Typical of many major Civil War battles, no clear winner emerged after the smoke cleared, but Lee's greatly depleted and exhausted forces were in no shape to continue the battle another day.

In the west, it was Bragg's turn to bring the war to the North, and to many a citizen in states bordering the Ohio River, he was succeeding admirably. Cincinnati, protected by a garrison of Federal troops, was under martial law and the able bodied were impressed to build entrenchments around the city. Louisville was in a similar panic, with extensive entrenchments erected south and east of the city, and pontoon bridges constructed across the river to New Albany, Indiana, to evacuate any civilians who wished to go. Many did not hesitate to pack up their valuables and stream across the river to the Hoosier state.

With the addition of new recruits delivered up by the northern Ohio River states, Buell's Army of the Ohio numbered over 81,000 in late September. These governors were only too glad to send whatever reinforcements would be needed to keep Bragg and Smith's Confederate forces on the south side of the Ohio, the farther south the better. Buell divided the army into three corps: First Corps under Major General

Alexander McCook, Second Corps under Major General Thomas Crittenden, and Third Corps under Major General William "Bull" Nelson.

The 5th Indiana Battery was in McCook's I Corps (hereafter corps are designated by Roman numerals), assigned to the 3rd Division under Brig. General Lovell Harrison Rousseau, and 9th Brigade under Colonel Leonard A. Harris. Their brigade included the 38th Indiana, 2nd, 33rd, and 94th Ohio, and 10th Wisconsin infantry regiments. Alexander McDowell McCook (1831-1903), commander of I Corps, was one of the seventeen "Fighting McCooks" of Ohio. He had been with Buell since before the capture of Nashville, had served at Shilo and Corinth, and was now about to embark on one of his most important commands. He had started his military career as a three month volunteer at First Bull Run, but was made a Brigadier General of volunteers after that battle and sent to Kentucky.

With his army rested and fed, Buell decided it was time to go after Bragg whose two wings were holed up in Bardstown. However, before he could get started, two events occurred that considerably changed the complexion of his war designs. First, Washington (Lincoln and Halleck) was fed up with Buell's apparent reluctance to take on his enemy and issued an order relieving Buell of Command of the Army of the Ohio. Plans for this change were actually in the works before Buell ever stepped foot into Louisville, and now his command was formally given to General George Henry Thomas, until then, second in command of the Army of the Ohio. Thomas was embarrassed by this turn of events and declined to take over from the man who had just devised the plan for Bragg's demise. Reluctantly, Washington relented and restored Buell to command, but the communication doing so made clear that he was on probation and his actions would be carefully monitored. Thus admonished, Buell would ironically become even more cautious and less daring than he had been before, fearing that any wrong move could destroy his already faltering career permanently.

The second event was no less than the murder of one of the three corps commanders, General William Nelson. He was shot dead in a Louisville hotel by Brig. General Jefferson C. Davis who had been given the task of organizing citizen self-defense companies in the city. Reacting to a perceived insult from General Nelson (Nelson had days earlier accused Davis of being an ineffective organizer), Davis fatally shot Nelson in the heart on September 29th in the Galt House.

The loss of the irascible but highly competent Nelson was to prove a crucial blow to the Union effort against Bragg. His replacement, Charles C. Gilbert, a brigadier general and Buell's Inspector, was no match for Nelson as a tactician and leader. Normally only major generals lead army corps, and Gilbert as commander of III Corps was to prove that he was not up to the task. As will be shown later, the aggressive Nelson would likely have better managed his corps at Perryville with more favorable results for the Federals. But for now, Nelson was dead and Gilbert was Buell's only logical choice for his replacement. Ormsby Mitchel would have been much better, but he had asked to be transferred from Buell's command while still in northern Alabama (he was frustrated by Buell's slow advance toward Chattanooga).

As for Nelson's curiously named murderer, because of the emergency conditions prevalent at the time, Davis was never tried for his cold blooded crime. Due to the influence of his personal friend, Gov. Morton of Indiana (present at Nelson's slaying), he was later given a new command and served at Stones River, Chickamauga, Atlanta, and other campaigns, achieving the eventual role of corps commander. He died of natural causes in 1879, still a commissioned officer in the U. S. Army.

On September 30th, Buell made final plans to move against Bragg. His three corps would leave Louisville along three separate routes, but would reunite before doing battle with Bragg around Bardstown. Crittenden's II Corps would leave on the Bardstown road, Gilbert's III Corps would travel the Shepherdsville Road, and McCook's I Corps (including Hupp's 5th Indiana Battery) would leave on the Taylorsville Road. All of these roads trended in a southeasterly direction and converged on Bardstown.

As a diversion to keep Kirby Smith occupied, he sent Brig. Gen Joshua Sill's division of I Corps and Ebenezer Dumont's unattached division (nearly 20,000 men in all) along the Shelbyville-Lexington Road. This nearly east-west route led to the Lexington-Frankfurt area where Smith's forces were based. Buell was hoping to drive Bragg out of Bardstown toward Kirby Smith. His army, which outnumbered Bragg's forces two to one, would then sweep up from the south while Sill, Dumont, and the Union forces at Cincinnati pinched in from the west and north. It was a terrific plan, if all the pieces fell properly into line.

On October 1st, the three corps plus the Sill-Dumont feint force moved out of Louisville. Pvt. Hupp complained that no commissary wagons accompanied the troops ". . . and many of the boys suffered in consequence of it." The I Corps made 16 miles the first day and camped on the farm of a Confederate sympathizer where the troops were encouraged to burn all the fence rails they wanted in their fires. "The General [McCook] remarked that he had no mercy for the D. S. [damned secesh] and their rails but would not burn those of Union men."

By the second day of marching, mostly without food, they reached

Taylorsville and slept without shelter in the pouring rain. A commissary wagon finally arrived at around midnight with food (raw bacon and "crackers" [hardtack]). Such treatment was not likely to endear Buell to the troops, who already soundly resented having to march all the way back to Louisville under less-than-ideal conditions in pursuit of an enemy that many believed could have been cornered and defeated much earlier. This sentiment was shared by Lincoln and his staff. Among the ranks it was even rumored that Buell and Bragg were brothers-in-law and would never fight one another. Buell, in their view, was a traitor.

Hupp's corps encountered some cavalry units attached to General Wharton just beyond Jeffersontown (now a southeastern suburb of Louisville) but easily fought them off. At Taylorsville, they also encountered cavalry, but chased them southeast to Bloomfield, where Hupp and the boys arrived on the morning of the 4th.

By October 6, I Corps was camped on the Goose River (a tributary of the Chaplin River), and by the 7th had marched into Mackville, ". . . an enterprising little place of about 400, mostly Secesh." Here they slaughtered a beef and roasted it for their supper and next days rations. Hupp was lucky enough to find some "crackers" in the dirt which he promptly consumed with relish. The October weather had been extremely hot and dry, and water was very scarce. Hupp's description of the soldiers' efforts to make coffee from the available stagnant pools is instructive:

> It was a hard matter to find water in this vicinity and what our coffee was made of had a green scum over the top a whole inch thick, but it was all there was and of course we would use it in preference to our going without. The way we managed it was to boil it and keep the scum off for some time before putting in the coffee: it would in this way do very well.

What had become of the other two Union army corps by this time? Like I Corps, they had continued to inch their way toward Bardstown, being probed all the while by Confederate cavalry under John A. Wharton (the force harassing Hupp's column) and Joseph Wheeler. Finally appreciating the threat of these Union movements toward his base at Bardstown, Bragg instructed Polk to ready the army for evacuation on the 3rd. In response to intelligence that Bragg had evacuated Bardstown (completed on the 4th), Buell determined to change the direction of his forces to counter the Confederate retreat eastward toward Harrodsburg (Hardee) and Danville (Polk). Consequently, he ordered McCook's I Corps to head toward Perryville via Mackville, which is how Ormond Hupp found himself bivouacked there on the evening of the 7th.

As his troops were making a hasty retreat from Bardstown and heading east, Braxton Bragg was not with his troops but was participating in a pet project of his (some would say, an obsession), the inauguration of a Confederate Governor of Kentucky in the capital city of Frankfort. The lucky governor designee was Richard C. Hawes, who held the post in Frankfort for a total of less than eight hours. He wisely followed Bragg out of the city as Union forces under Sill pushed back Scott's cavalry on the western outskirts and began lobbing artillery shells into the suburbs. Hawes actually continued in the largely meaningless capacity as leader of the Confederate provisional government of Kentucky until the end of the war, and was elected to a judgeship in 1866.

On the 6th of October, Sill's forces brushed aside Scott's cavalry, crossed the Kentucky river and retook Frankfort for the Union, this time for good. Shortly before this occurred, Bragg became fully aware that his time would better be spent with his beleaguered army rather than fiddling with politics in Frankfort. He had supposed that Sill's forces represented the main Federal advance, but later intelligence showed him to be in error. Bragg was caught in a double quandary. Buell, with his uncharacteristic bold thrust from Louisville, now threatened his southern escape route in the Danville-Perryville area, but Sill's forces also threatened Frankfort. He knew that, to stop Buell, he needed to concentrate his forces with Kirby Smith's men who had lately occupied Frankfort and Lexington. He ultimately decided to concentrate all Confederate forces in the Harrodsburg area, half way between Frankfort and Perryville. The loss of Frankfort on the 6th, however, was a severe blow to Bragg's plans to secure Kentucky for the south. Not only did he lose the seat of the state government, but he also lost the valuable stores of food and supplies that had been gathered there by Kirby Smith. Whatever hopes he had after the fall of Frankfort to force Kentucky into the Confederate fold (he had originally hoped that friendly persuasion would suffice), now lay in meeting Buell in battle and defeating him soundly. By more chance than design, the battle for Kentucky would be fought on the gentle hills and valleys around the tiny village of Perryville on the Chaplin River.

By early morning of October 7th, Hardee had already deployed General Simon Buckner's division in a defensive mode around Perryville, as Union troops in three separate columns closed in. Although historians point to October 8, 1862, as the date of the Battle of Perryville (also called Chaplin Hills), skirmishing became conspicuously heavy on the 7th, featuring a late afternoon artillery duel involving Gilbert's III Corps on the

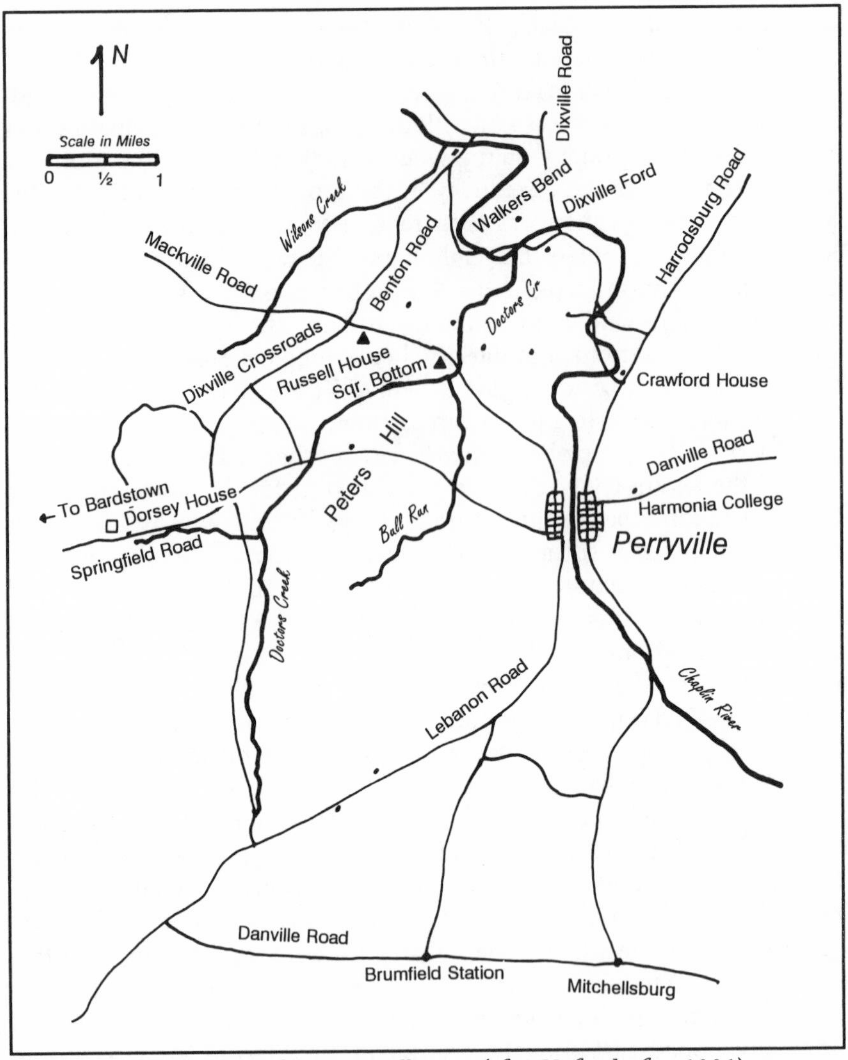

Overview map of the Perryville area (after Hofendorfer, 1991).

Union right flank, and Wheeler's artillery. Arrayed against the Confederate forces now moving into the area were the Union III Corps on the Springfield Road entering Perryville from the west, Crittenden's II Corps moving up the Lebanon Road to the south, and McCook's I Corps moving into Mackville to the northwest. Gilbert's III Corps was the most advanced Union corps that day, particularly Capt. Ebenezer Gay's cavalry which camped near Doctor's Creek where it crossed the Springfield Road. Confederate infantry (7th Arkansas) and Wheeler's artillery occupied Peters Hill just east of Gay's position, hoping eventually to deprive the Blue Coats of the water in Doctor's Creek. By sunset of the 7th, Buell, injured from a recent fall from his horse, was resting in his headquarters at Dorsey house on the Springfield Road, and Bragg was in Harrodsburg unaware that Buell's forces were merging on Polk and Hardee at Perryville. Finally made aware of the situation late on the morning of the 8th, he made his way to Perryville and set up headquarters in the Crawford House on the Harrodsburg Road.

At the risk of oversimplification, the main elements of the battle on the following day involved two major clashes. These were the fight for Peters Hill along the Springfield Road in the morning, and the attempted envelopment of the Union left flank by Cheatham (Polk's wing) and general assault on the Union left in the afternoon. The latter action involved Ormond Hupp's 5th Indiana Battery, thus the role of his unit in that conflict will be emphasized.

Peters Hill

Modern tourists entering the Perryville area from the west will most likely travel from Bardstown on U.S. Route 150, known in 1862 as the Springfield Road after the town located seventeen miles west of Perryville. Entering the area from the west, a sign marks the site of the Dorsey house (Buell's headquarters) on the left (north) About two miles east is a sign marking Peters Hill, named after the owner of the land, and situated between Doctor's Creek and its tributary, Bull Run, where these streams cross the road (the old road ran north of the current highway). Early in the battle, this hill was contested because of its strategic position between two water sources, particularly crucial during this time of extreme drought.

As noted above, the hill was occupied by the 7th Arkansas on the evening of the 7th. The first Union assault on this stronghold was made around midnight of the 7th by the 10th Indiana Infantry Regiment who had earlier replaced Gay's cavalry along Doctor's Creek. Sneaking through the brush on a reconnaissance mission in the darkness, they somehow managed to avoid the 7th Arkansas (of whose presence they were unaware). They eventually made contact with rebel pickets who chased the Hoosiers back to Union lines after a few shots were exchanged. This mini-skirmish, which occurred in the very earliest minutes of October 8th, is considered the first action of the Battle of Perryville.

At daylight the next morning, the battle for Peters Hill began in

Figure 4-6 – Union Brig. General Philip Sheridan, commander of the 11th Division (from A Photographic History of the Civil War in Ten Volumes, *vol. 3, p. 165).*

earnest with Union forces under Brig. General Speed Fry (a local boy, raised near Perryville) and Brig. General Daniel McCook (Alexander's brother; later killed at Kenesaw Mtn., Atlanta campaign) forcing the retreat of the 7th Arkansas to General Liddell's lines at Bottom Hill to the east. After turning back a fierce counter attack, mostly by the 7th and 5th Arkansas, at 7 A.M. the hill belonged to the Federals.

Later in the morning, Union troops under General Philip H. Sheridan (whose exploits at Perryville initiated his rise to prominence), using mostly battle-tested German-American troops from Missouri and Illinois (Laiboldt's Brigade), threw the Confederates off the east slope of Peters Hill. By late morning they had captured the Bottom Hill, as well.

It was at this juncture that the choice of Gilbert as Nelson's replacement as III Corps commander proved disastrous. Gilbert demanded that Sheridan remove his troops from Bottom Hill and retire to Peters Hill, and rebuked Sheridan for defying Buell's order not to advance until the main body of the army was concentrated in the area. The consequence of this was that, later in the day, Sheridan had to watch helplessly as Confederate reinforcements (Adams' brigade) passed under his nose on their way to pound the beleaguered Union left.

Polk and Hardee's Assault on the Union Left

Ormond Hupp had just settled into camp at Mackville and was relishing the luxury of a cup of coffee made from stagnant pond-scum water. But such revelry was not to last. His commanding general, Alexander McCook, received orders from Buell to move out toward Perryville at 2:30 in the morning of the 8th. By 5 P.M., McCook's column was winding its way toward Perryville. The men anticipated a fight later in the day, but many would probably have had second thoughts about the adventure had they known what lay ahead. McCook's Corps, particularly James Jackson's 10th Division, was to receive the lion's share of Confederate ire that day. More than a few of these marchers would earn their final rest at Perryville, or would soon be on wagon trains full of wounded headed for Louisville.

Rousseau's Division led the troops out of Mackville, with Col. Lytles

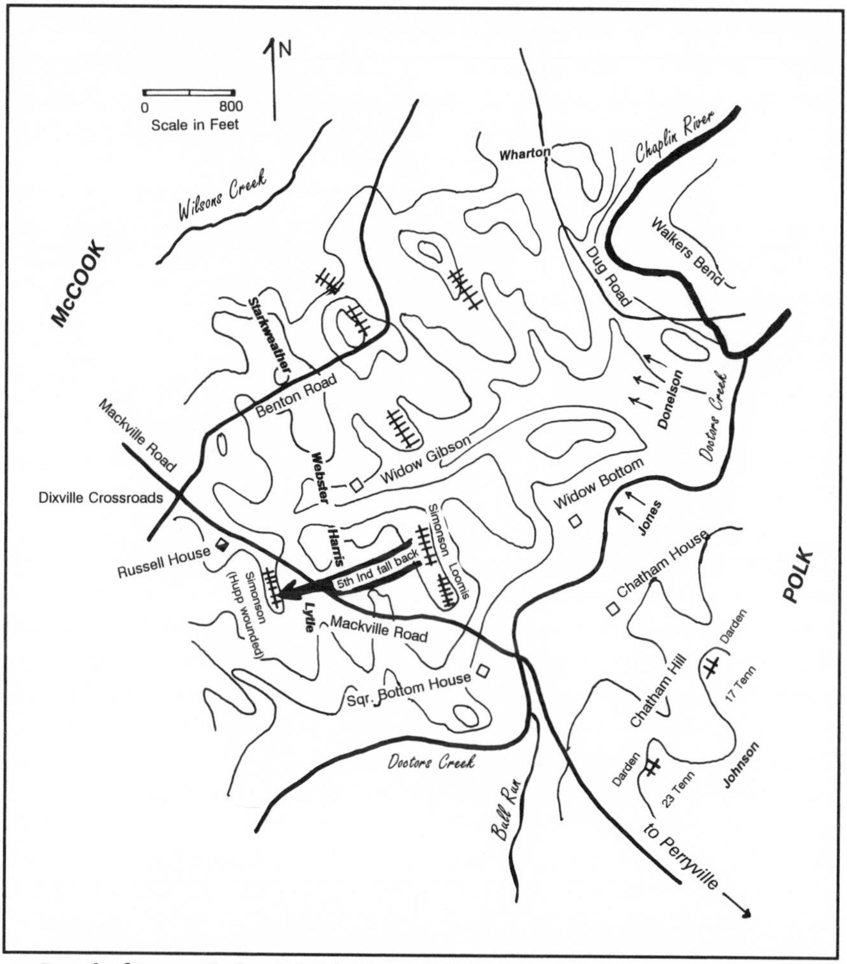

Detail of Perryville battlefield, Union left flank. First position and fall back position are shown for the 5th Indiana Battery (Simonson's). Other artillery battery positions occurred early in the battle (Union west of Doctors Crk.; Confederate – Darden – to east; after Hofendorfer, 1991).

17th Brigade first, followed by Harris' 9th which included the 5th Indiana Battery.

Brig. General Lovell Harrison Rousseau (1818-1869) was a native Kentuckian who had fought in an Indiana regiment in the Mexican War. He served with Buell at Shilo, and after Perryville led his division during the Murfreesboro and Tullahoma campaigns, but was absent for Chickamauga. He later commanded the garrison forces at Nashville as a Major General. After the war, he became a controversial political crony of President Andrew Johnson who rewarded him with a commission as brigadier general in the regular army in 1867. Later, he commanded the troops who took over Alaska from the Russians ("Seward's Folly"), and died while in charge of the occupation of Louisiana. He was considered to be a competent field commander and, as Hupp attested, was well regarded by his troops.

By around 9:00 A.M., McCook's corps arrived near the intersection of a narrow farm lane called the Benton Road (now called White's Road) and the Mackville Pike along which they were marching. This intersection, known locally as the Dixville Crossroads, was about three miles from Perryville. McCook was supposed to move far enough along so to extend the Union line on the left of III Corps (Gilbert) but at first saw no evidence for this line as he reconnoitered from his high vantage point overlooking most of the battlefield. He did hear the sounds of battle between Liddell and Sheridan at Peters Hill and soon spotted both the Confederate and Union lines.

After ordering cavalry and some infantry ahead to scout out the front, Rousseau spotted a two story house belonging to the Russell family on the right of the Mackville Pike just past the intersection. He and Alex McCook were later to make this house their headquarters; after the battle it was used as a field hospital, as were many of the local farm houses in the area. After surviving the ravages of war and time, the Russell House was burned to the ground in the late 1970's by arsonists; only the foundation and an historical marker sign mark the spot today.

Shortly after he crossed the Dixville crossroads, McCook got word from General Gay that he would appreciate artillery support for his line arrayed on the bluff west and east of Doctor's Creek where it crossed the Mackville Pike. McCook sent his chief of artillery, Captain Cyrus Loomis, down the road with two Parrot guns to reinforce the shorter range guns of Captain William Hotchkiss (2nd Minnesota). Loomis and Hotchkiss now poured their cannon fire into Liddell's retreating troops as they moved back toward Perryville. Eventually they ceased firing when it was obvious that the "Johnnies" were out of range.

At around 11:00 A.M., McCook, in his headquarters at Russell House, informed Rousseau that he should form his troops along a line extending north from the Russell House on the other side (east) of the Mackville Pike. He placed General James Jackson's (later killed) 10th Division in a similar north-south array but on the other side of the Benton Road. This troop positioning indicates that McCook was not exactly sure of the position of the enemy before him. As it turns out, he had placed them in a line nearly perpendicular to the Confederate line now being readied by General Braxton Bragg.

Buell, back at Dorsey House, realized that delays in assembling his entire army in the Perryville area (particularly with Crittenden's II Corps) would mean he would not have sufficient daylight to put his battle plan into full effect. Convinced that he faced the combined armies of both Bragg and Kirby Smith (Smith was still in the Lexington area), Buell decided to postpone his attack until he could amass his combined forces on the 9th.

Bragg, however, had not been informed of this vacillation, and sat in the Crawford House busily planning his own offensive – for that day, the 8th. He would place Buckner's division plus two of Anderson's brigades (both from Hardee's wing) with their left anchored at the bridge where the Mackville Road crossed Doctor's Creek (just below where Loomis and Hotchkiss had placed their artillery). To Buckner's right, he placed Cheatham's division of Polk's wing. Wharton's cavalry was to assist Cheatham on the extreme right of the confederate line. Bragg's idea was for the Confederate line to sweep around the Union left like a giant wagon spoke centered at the Mackville Road–Doctor's Creek bridge. Within sight of this bridge is a small white frame house belonging to Squire Henry P. Bottom, the man who would take it upon himself the next day to bury the Confederate dead.

Meanwhile, some time before noon, Sheridan had given an order withdrawing Gay's and Hotchkiss' men from the ridge overlooking Doctor's Creek (Hotchkiss' cannon were placed next to the Russell House). This greatly concerned General Rousseau until he and Loomis observed dust in the direction of the Harrodsburg Road. This was Cheatham's troops moving into position on the Confederate right, but the two Union officers interpreted the movement as a retreat. Feeling more secure now, Rousseau ignored McCook's order to stay near the Russell House and allowed some of his troops to go forward to Doctor's Creek in search of water. What these men found waiting for them just beyond Doctor's Creek must have been enough to make any soldier forget his thirst. Their advance skirmishers had run smack into Bragg's battle line and they were promptly chased, firing as they went, across Doctor's Creek. The time was 12:30 P.M. and the Battle of Perryville was about to explode in a furry on the unsuspecting Federals.

Bragg had chosen 12:30 as the time to commence the battle and, as ordered, the Confederate batteries of Carnes, Darden, Lumsden, and Semple opened up with their big guns almost precisely at that time. Their cannon, belching fire and smoke, lobbed shells from their positions on the east side of Doctor's Creek into the Union lines on the bluff to the west. The battle to crush the Union left had finally begun; this was no minor skirmish. Buell, it turns out, was not even aware that fighting was going on at his left flank until 4:00 that afternoon. Wind conditions and the acoustic shadowing effect of the local hills kept the sound of battle from him as he nursed his horse-fall wound at Dorsey House and conversed and dined with Gilbert. As a result of Buell's immobility and ignorance (remember that he had earlier decided not to fight until the next day), and Gilbert's instructions to Sheridan and other III Corps commanders not to advance, McCook's corps was left alone to do most of the fighting on the Union left.

After the Confederate bombardment commenced, Rousseau ordered Loomis to bring down the rest of his artillery and ordered Lytle to form his infantry in two lines of battle behind the artillery now returning fire for all they were worth on the creek bluff. It was now time to order Captain Simonson's 5th Indiana Light Artillery to the front.

After the artillery was in place, the rest of Harris' 9th brigade was also ordered forward from their resting place north of the road across from the Russell House. The position of the 5th Indiana Battery was probably near to where some modern farm buildings now stand overlooking Doctor's Creek. To their left was General James S. Jackson's 10th Division. Jackson was later killed in the battle, as were two of his brigade commanders, Brig. General William R. Terrill (33rd) and Col. George Webster (34th). The spot where Jackson fell near Parson's battery is marked by a commemorative sign in the present state battlefield park.

The cheering Hupp described above was in celebration of their battery's particular effectiveness at punishing the advancing Confederates. Their armament consisted of two 12 pounder howitzers, two 10 pounder Parrots (with identifying metal rings around their breeches), and two James Rifles. The latter two types of cannon were rifled, highly accurate long range guns and were capable of inflicting severe damage on troops and other artillery pieces.

As the artillery battle progressed, Simonson's battery eventually forced the partial withdrawal of Semple's battery and forced Brig. General

Sterling Wood's brigade to head for cover a short distance to the rear. The 5th Battery also damaged one or two of Capt. Carne's smooth bore cannons. A few shells from the 5th also landed amid Cheatham's troops waiting to come into line on the Confederate far right.

The cessation in shelling from the Confederates described by Hupp as eliciting the "shout" from the Union ranks, was not caused by the Union shells, but was part of Bragg's battle plan. At that point, General Polk was to order Cheatham's division forward across Doctor's Creek. His delay in issuing this order was prompted by his fear that Buell was about to heavily reinforce his extreme left flank, the one Cheatham was about to attempt to turn. Bragg then personally came to the field and, because Buell's left was already extended, issued the order to extend Cheatham's position farther to the right. These men would have to cross the Chaplin River at Walkers Bend in order to obtain the field.

Colonel John C. Starkweather, part of the contingent of reinforcing Union troops that had caused Polk to delay his attack, led his 28th brigade to the extreme left of the Union line. These men, along with Jackson's troops, would receive the major punishment from Cheatham's attack, which at 1:30 P.M. had still not materialized. However, sometime before 2:00 P.M., Cheathams forces attacked the Union left, preceded by a clearing action on the high hill above Walker's bend by Wharton's Cavalry.

Sometime after the full scale Confederate attack, Harris' 9th Brigade came under attack, which was described by Pvt. Hupp on page 32 of his diary.

Hupp could not have known that the troops advancing toward him with bayonets glistening were three brigades from Brig. General James P. Anderson's 2nd Division of Hardee's wing. The men who were trying to kill my great-grandfather and his mates were from the deep south, the 27th, 30th, and 34th Mississippi infantry regiments, along with Captain Charles Lumsden's Alabama Battery (he had been involved in the initial shelling of the Union left). This Brigade was commanded by a Virginian, Col. Thomas M. Jones.

Simonson's Battery on the west bluff of the creek was supported by the 10th Wisconsin Infantry. Loomis' guns had retired to the Russell house because his long range shells were exhausted. The battle between this part of Buell's line commenced at 2:30 P.M. as Jones' brigade moved forward down the hill toward Doctor's Creek and Lumsden unlimbered his field pieces.

Before Lumsden could ready his cannons, Simonson opened fire and killed one of Lumsden's horses. Shortly thereafter, Simonson fired canister (essentially oversized shotgun shells) at the oncoming Mississippians, felling a great many of these inexperienced troops. Nevertheless, they closed ranks and continued on. Meanwhile, to Simonson's left, the Union line was being battered by Cheatham's attack resulting in General Jackson's death from two balls to the chest.

This first assault finally slowed and stalled but was followed later by an attack by Brig. General Bushrod Johnson's 3rd Brigade of General Simon Buckner's 3rd Division. Composed mostly of Tennessee regiments, they were later repulsed by Col. William Lytle's forces above Doctor's Creek and replaced by Brig. General Patrick Cleburne's brigade and Daniel Adam's brigade of Louisiana volunteers who had crossed in front of Sheridan's forces to the Union right unmolested.

Remember that Gilbert had ordered Sheridan not to advance, and that Buell, who planned to meet the enemy the next day, had given no orders to attack. Bushrod Johnson's Tennesseans had been given no such order from Bragg, however, and took cover in Squire Bottom's front yard and attempted to turn McCook's right, then defended by the 3rd Ohio and later replaced by the 15th Kentucky (both from Lytle's brigade), on the bluff north of the Mackville Road. The Confederates were supported by Slocomb's battery which was dueling with Simonson farther to the Union left (later supported by the 38th Indiana).

It was now around 3:00 P.M. and Jones' Mississippians made a final attempt to charge the Leonard Harris line which included Simonson's battery. However, the 5th Indiana's withering canister fire and the 10th Wisconsin's musket fire caused the ground in their front to bleed with the bodies of numerous rebel soldiers. Bushrod Johnson's men were also badly mauled and eventually fell back beyond Doctor's Creek to be replaced by Patrick Cleburne's forces. Finally, however, ammunition began to run out for Simonson's guns and, fearing that the battery might be overrun, McCook's Chief of Artillery, Charles Cotter, ordered Simonson to move to the rear toward the Russell House. Hupp described the action, beginning with Tom Jones' first attack:

> Everything was put in readiness to receive them and at about this juncture their batteries opened a cross fire which seemed to make the earth quake, this fire from the enemy was doing much damage but we could only stand as best we could, our line reserving their fire until their infantry got within thirty rods, we then opened on them and finally after about fifteen minutes they fell back.
>
> They came up this way the third time and did their

utmost to take our batteries but met with the same results each time.

The third charge they made on our battery they came within twenty yards, but were forced to fall back with half their number.

Our battery was then ordered to fall back and we left with one man killed and four horses, also four men wounded." [actual casualties to this point, 14 killed, wounded, or missing, 16 horses killed]

The 5th Indiana fell back to the west-northwest, crossed the Mackville Road, and redeployed to the west of the road on a wide, north-south ridge to the front (southeast) of the Russell House. Loomis already occupied the south flank of the Russell House knoll, and Hotchkiss' two cannon were directly across the road to the north. Simonson sited his guns on the first defensible high point he came to as he moved toward Russell House, the aforementioned ridge now owned by the Townsend family (their family cemetery adorns the ridge just south of the Mackville Road).

By 4:00 P.M., the situation for McCook's Union forces on Buell's left had become critical. The far left of the Union line had sustained a fierce and determined turning maneuver by General George E. Maney's 3rd Brigade (under Cheatham). It had resulted in the routing of General Terrill's forces, as well as the general's mortal wounding. In one of the climactic actions of the Battle of Perryville, Starkweather's 28th Brigade and Webster's 34th brigade ultimately held the left flank but at the expense of a severe mauling to men and horses and the loss of some artillery.

The situation on McCook's right, however, was much worse. Lytle's line finally collapsed from the pressure of Cleburne's brigade, followed by a determined advance by Adams' brigade on Hardee's far left south of the Mackville Road. Leonard Harris' line also fell back as his troops ran out of ammunition. As these Confederate forces gradually pushed the Federals back toward Russell House, an artillery exchange broke out between Simonson's Battery and Calvert's Battery of Cleburne's Brigade. It was during this point in the conflict that Ormond Hupp was about to find himself headed for the rear – as one of the many casualties of battle. In Hupp's words, this is what transpired:

We had but just got in battery and ordered to lay on the ground, holding our fire for close action, as our ammunition was near gone, when I had to help take one of the lead horses out that had been shot with a minie ball.

The bullets and shells came thicker and faster here than I ever want to see them again.

We had just got this horse out when one of mine was shot with a minie ball which reached his heart, killing him instantly.

The battle was general and raging now all along the line, and it was plain to be seen that the enemy was too strong for us.

Reinforcements had been sent for which were within four miles, but were refused, as the General Commander [Buell] said it couldn't be possible that any musketry fighting was going on.

Gen. Rousseau sent another message for reinforcements and stated if they weren't sent his whole division would be killed, but the traitor in reply said he brought the fight on and might end it the best way he could, he would not send a man.

It would have been a very easy matter for Buell to have turned the left wing with the men he had lying idle and ruined their army what could not have been captured, but he was too much of a traitor for this and our men had to suffer the consequences.

When my horse got shot I was lying close by him on the same side.

I immediately called one of the boys to help take him out and run around to the near side in order to unbuckle the breast strap.

I had it but half unbuckled when a shell from the enemy struck me on the left arm and passing on, struck the ammunition chest, exploded and caused the cartridges in the chest to explode.

It was all done in an instant and resulted in the instant death of F. Eric [Frederick Ehrich] who was struck in the head with a piece of shell and the wounding of four others, C. Miller, burnt, A. Farg [Abraham Forry], arm broken and badly burnt on head and face; A. Pettit, lip cut and wounded slightly in the head and myself cut in the left arm, right arm, and face.

When the chest blew up it took me in the air about ten feet.

Figure 4-7 – "Townsend's Ridge," the first ridge east of Russell House, where the 5th Indiana Battery fell back and where Ormond Hupp was wounded by an exploding artillery shell.

> I had my thoughts during the operation and concluded I was torn to pieces, but after striking the ground and lying there about three minutes, I jumped up and saw that I was badly wounded, my clothes were all torn off, and the burn from the powder set me near crazy.

The comments concerning Buell's treachery in not sending reinforcements to Rousseau (actually it was McCook who needed them) call for some examination.

Hupp's suspicions of Buell represented a prevalent attitude among his men, as noted previously. But in this case, the accusations were unfair and inaccurate. Alexander McCook waited until after 3:00 P.M. to finally send a messenger to Buell requesting assistance. Buell did not receive the urgent request until about 4:00 P.M., and up to that time was not aware that his I Corps was engaged in mortal combat with Bragg's army. He did order that reinforcements be sent to McCook at once, but only sent two brigades, being unconvinced that the situation was as serious as the messenger described.

Why did McCook wait so long to inform Buell that he was about to be driven from the field? Kenneth Hoffendorfer, author of the definitive work on Perryville, *Perryville, Battle for Kentucky*, has advanced the premise that the answer lies in the "sickness" that pervaded the Army of the Ohio manifest as misgivings and mistrust among Buell's soldiers, from bottom to top. McCook, in his view, probably thought he could prevail against Bragg, but besides that, to have asked for reinforcements would have invited Buell's predictable orders to fall back until the whole army was assembled and victory was assured. The aggressive McCook and his fellow officers were sick of avoiding the enemy as they had done in Tennessee and at Munfordville; they wanted to fight and win. For his part, Buell (and Gilbert) could have done a better job of assessing McCook's predicament whereupon he would have sent many more than two brigades.

Back at Simonson's Battery, the now badly wounded Ormond Hupp found it imperative to move to the rear for help.

The first "hospital" he approached was a log house described as being a "quarter [mile?] of the left of our line of battle." If by this he meant the left flank of the whole Union army, he was probably heading northeast down the Benton Road which would have placed him close to Terrill's retreating troops.

The surgeon in this hospital offered to relieve Ormond of his wounded arm, but he decided to ask for a second opinion.

Hupp was eventually rescued by one of his battery mates, Jacob Kurtz, who took him by horse to another farm house hospital (he recounts being at three in all) where his wounds were cleaned and dressed and he was given a blanket to wrap around him. Kurtz then returned to the battery, but later returned to inform Hupp about the situation in the field:

> I was eager to hear how the battle had terminated so in the course of two or three hours he returned and stayed with me the rest of the night, telling me all he knew concerning the battle – that all my things [including his original diary] had fallen into the hands of the enemy and that the loss in the battery was two killed, sixteen wounded [actual count: 13 wounded; 6 captured/missing] and twenty horses killed and that the rebels held the field.

Jacob Kurtz, incidently, the good Samaritan who very likely saved Hupp's life through his efforts to see him to help and safety, died in battle on May 27, 1864, at Dallas, Georgia, during the Atlanta Campaign. He was still in Hupp's unit at the time, but Ormond made only scant note of the event in his diary.

In the early evening of the 8th, Kurtz returned from the battlefield and informed Hupp that "the rebels held the field." He was right, particularly if "field" is defined as the Union left flank (roughly, Mackville Road to Chaplin River) where most of the Battle of Perryville was fought. A late afternoon assault by the Confederate 3rd Brigade under Col. Samuel Powell on Peters Hill (Powell thought he was attacking a small force; not an entire army Corps) was turned back by Sheridan's forces. Powell's single brigade was eventually driven back through the streets of Perryville and across the Chaplin River after a courageous, but foolish, assault on the hill. Other actions had occurred southwest of town along the Lebanon Pike involving Wheeler's and Dan McCook's cavalry, but most of the heavy fighting and blood-letting was clearly to the north where McCook's boys had taken a terrible pounding by most of Bragg's combined Confederate wings.

By 6:30 in the evening (sunset had been shortly after 5:30 P.M.), most of the fighting had ceased on the Union left, with the early contestants on both sides exhausted and spent. A spirited and, at times, ferocious battle still raged between the two brigades sent by Buell to reinforce McCook (Col. Michael Gooding, supported by Brig. Gen James Steedman) and the Confederate brigades of Brig. Generals Sterling Wood and S. J. Liddell. The Confederates had moved west to the vicinity of the Russell House virtually unopposed. Nearly all of McCook's corps were now licking their wounds and out of action in the fields north of the Dixville crossroads. Gooding's line west of Russell House was all that stood between salvaging some semblance of stability from what otherwise would have been a total Confederate victory and Union rout. Russell House itself was now occupied by Wood's rebel forces.

The battle was to rage on by moonlight until 7:00 P.M. Simonson's battery, although situated in the northwest quadrant of the Dixville Crossroads at the extreme left of Gooding's line, did not participate further in the battle. After taking terrible losses from Wood and then Liddell's infantry, Gooding finally pulled back to the west (after breaking Wood's assault), and, though badly bloodied, was never fully overrun by the rebels. Gooding, himself, was captured during a period of intense hand-to-hand combat in the dark. General Polk finally told Liddell to call off the fighting because of darkness and the Battle of Perryville was over.

Gooding's staying action had cost him over 30 percent of his men; McCook had lost over 25 percent of his. In addition, McCook's officer corps was devastated by the loss of several officers, including Generals James Jackson (10th Div.), Terrill 33rd Brig, 10th Div.), and Webster (34th brigade, 10th Div.).

During the battle described above, McCook's battered soldiers retreated north toward Wilson's Creek. The rebels eventually controlled all of the Benton Road to just past the Dixville Crossroads, so it is likely that Ormond Hupp had been taken to a hospital north along the Mackville Pike where he would have eluded capture. This is indicated indirectly by this passage from his diary:

"Orders came that all those that could must get back about two miles toward Maxville [Mackville] to a large meeting house that had been converted into a hospital."

Bragg and his forces were on the retreat, in spite of their overwhelming victory the day before. Bragg now fully appreciated the fact that most of Buell's entire army lay before him, ready to pounce on him the next day to avenge the drubbing Bragg dealt McCook on the 8th. Bragg would be criticized for this retreat then and later, but it was probably a wise decision. Even if Buell had faltered on the 9th, reinforcements from Louisville, Cincinnati, and other points would have eventually made the Confederate position untenable. As it was, Bragg had always been badly outnumbered at Perryville; his advantage had been in pitting his whole army of mostly determined veterans against a single Union corps composed of many green troops.

To their credit, each side had fought bravely and each had sacrificed dearly over those contested hills north and west of Perryville. Most historians would later conclude that the battle was a tactical victory for Bragg, but a strategic victory for Buell in that Bragg's army shortly thereafter left Kentucky for good. With fewer leadership and intelligence errors on both sides, the results of the battle might have been different. For now, though, Kentucky was saved for the Union in a battle that today is largely unknown to the average American. In fact, it was one of the pivotal battles of the Civil War, easily the equal of Antietam or Gettysburg in strategic importance to the Union cause.

Buell's lack of enthusiasm for pursuing Bragg at this time, along with all that had gone before, finally cost him his job. On October 24th, he was replaced by General William S. Rosecrans, who chased Bragg across Tennessee the following year.

Hupp's story must be typical of many of the wounded of this, and other Civil War battles. He was one of the lucky ones, however. Not only did he survive an explosion that killed one man and wounded three others including himself, he suffered no broken bones and required no amputations. Hupp's long convalescence was now beginning.

On the 13th, Hupp was on a wagon train heading for Louisville. Squire Bottom and his friends had finished collecting and burying the fallen Confederates, and the Chaplin Hills and Perryville were left in peace.

Chapter 5
Life and Love in Wartime New Albany

I know not how, but martial men are given to love: I think it is but as they are given to wine, for perils commonly ask to be paid in pleasures.

Francis Bacon, Of Love

New Albany is the worst laid out town I ever saw and is noted for its many foundries and shops built for the construction of boats.

*Ormond Hupp (*Journal; *March, 1863)*

With festering wounds on both arms and burned over much of his body, Ormond Hupp began the ninety mile journey from Perryville to the Ohio River city of Louisville. It was a scene that had been well rehearsed from previous battles, and would be reenacted again in the aftermath of many more. The long train of wagons, some covered, others open farm wagons or buckboards, wound along the narrow twisting roads, first to Bardstown and then north toward Louisville. For many a badly wounded soldier, the constant bouncing was an unendurable torture, and many begged to be left in a ditch to die in peace. To have endured three days on hot, dusty, rutted roads in wagons that magnified every jolt was a major accomplishment. Many perished before the Ohio came into view.

Security and attention to long neglected wounds awaited in New Albany, Louisville's neighbor – and competitor – on the north shore. Why New Albany and not Louisville? Although Louisville also had hospitals, New Albany, with eleven military hospitals in all, was located in a strictly northern state with a wide river separating the town from potential Confederate raiders. Of course Hupp may have been assigned to New Albany for the mundane reason that the Louisville hospitals had

Figure 5-1 – Ambulance train like the one that transported Hupp from Perryville to New Albany (from A Photographic History of the Civil War in Ten Volumes, *vol. 7, p. 313).*

reached capacity. In any event, Ormond and his fellow wounded comrades crossed the river on pontoon bridges constructed in late September to facilitate the evacuation of civilians from Louisville in anticipation of Bragg's depredations. Their construction was necessary because the only other way to cross the river at that time was by ferry (the Kentucky-Indiana bridge was not opened until 1886).

Ormond and his buddy, Charlie Miller, arrived first at Hospital no. 4, the former Ashbury Female College (later, Depauw College for Young Women) at Main Street and upper 9th street (in New Albany the streets east of the city center are "upper", those to the west are "lower"). They soon were escorted by "Dr. Sloan" to their more permanent home, Hospital no. 1, one block away at upper 8th street. Dr. John Sloan, a prominent New Albany practitioner, was the head surgeon at Hospital no. 1 (his home, built in 1852, still stands at 600 E. Main). Before conversion to a military hospital, it had been the Upper City School, a public elementary school. More recently, until 1992, it had been the school administration building. Pvt. Hupp made himself as comfortable as possible in Ward 3 on the second floor. This would be home for the next year and a half of his life.

New Albany was, and remains, a geographically northern city, but with many southern customs and attitudes. Its location on the Ohio River across from a major city (Louisville) in a contested border state made things all the more interesting. On top of the serious social tensions caused by the war, New Albany more than once faced very real invasion threats by hostile forces, and it served as a major refuge for the wounded in the western theater. It also contributed several military regiments to the war effort, and some war materiel in the form of armored river boats (like the *Tuscumbia* in Hupp's journal).

The city that would serve as Ormond Hupp's temporary haven from the noise and smoke of battle, was founded at the time of an earlier American battle, the War of 1812. It was the brainchild of the Scribner brothers, Joel, Nathanial, and Abner, staunch Yankee Presbyterians from Connecticut.

The Scribners arrived in the area known as the "Falls of the Ohio" in 1813. It was a double bend with several islands, an unusual stretch of the river in that it was fraught with rapids or "falls." To pass this natural barrier, ships enroute to Pittsburgh were required to keep to a precise safe route. Louisville (pop. 1,000) had already been settled, as had nearby Jeffersonville and Clarksville, the latter founded by George Rogers Clark of "Lewis and Clark" fame. Recognizing the area for its potential as a center of commerce in the western frontier, the brothers Scribner purchased a quantity of land from Colonel John Paul which, upon survey, consisted of nearly 840 acres. They paid Paul $8,000.

In essence, the Scribners founded the town by building a homestead and advertising for others to come join them in the venture, for a price, of course. The first subdivided lot was sold in 1813 at auction to a William Summers for the price of $234. By 1820, the population numbered nearly 500 and was the seat of a new county, Floyd, named after a colorful local politician. The name "New Albany" was chosen to honor the state capital of New York.

By fits and starts, the new town eventually prospered, weathering the nation's first depression, disease epidemics, and some mismanagement and dead-end commercial and public works ventures.

By the 1830's, New Albany could boast Baptist, Methodist, and Presbyterian churches, a public school system, a library of sorts (in Pettet and Downey's drug store), a cotton mill, and boat builders, among other enterprises. Until just prior to the Civil War, New Albany was the most populous city in Indiana, finally surpassed by Indianapolis during the early war years.

It was in shipbuilding that New Albany eventually excelled like no other. The 1850's saw the heyday of the fabled paddle-wheeled steam river boats. In 1856, peak year of shipbuilding in the era, New Albany masters turned out 22 packet boats. Such famous floating luxury palaces as the *Leviathan*, the *Eclipse*, and the storied *Robert E. Lee* (built in 1866) were legendary craft even in their own times.

The *Robert E. Lee* is famous for beating the *Natchez* in the 1870 St. Louis to New Orleans race, but its manufacture in New Albany posed revealing political undercurrents. Built just after the Civil War and named for one of the South's greatest military leaders, the name had to be painted on in Louisville to avoid the possibility of public protest. Eventually the rise of the railroads dashed to ruin the once magnificent and profitable river boat trade. By 1867, New Albany's shipyards were virtually silent. Interestingly, Pvt. Hupp spent considerable time socializing with the daughters of a certain Dowerman family. Could this be Jacob Dowerman (or a relative) of "Dowerman and Humphreys" shipyards? If so, he was hobnobbing with some highly placed (and wealthy) citizens in New Albany society.

The New Albany that gave shelter and comfort to the wounded Ormond Hupp had already seen its glory days as a ship manufacturer, but the city was hardly moribund. In the early 1860's, the population numbered about 10,000 who attended a wide variety of churches, some of which were sampled by Ormond as he continued his recovery. By 1862, New Albany had Baptist, Presbyterian, Lutheran, Catholic, Christian, Episcopalians, and Methodists. A new branch of the latter group built the Centenary Church in 1839, a favorite of Hupp during the later stages of his stay. He is also on record of having attended the First Presbyterian, Third Presbyterian, Christian, Baptist, and German Catholic churches. His upbringing had been exclusively Baptist.

As Ormond notes in his journal, New Albany had a state-wide reputation as a center for education. The many schools included public schools through high school (including the first in Indiana), several parochial schools, and various colleges. Many schools were taken over during the war for hospitals, a blatant example of the rude insinuation of war on the civilian populace. Incidently, New Albany, which had acquired a very high population of blacks during and after the war (see below), responded to a state legislative decree in 1869 and built "colored schools" in the 1870's. Schools in New Albany were not integrated until 1950, 85 years after the end of the Civil War.

The military hospital system in New Albany grew from the use of private homes, churches, and hotels to care for the few wounded who trickled in from western skirmishes, to a major complex of eleven public buildings in 1862. A large government hospital, the Jefferson General Hospital, was later constructed in 1864 in nearby Port Fulton, Clark

County. However, previous to its construction, the wounded were mostly cared for in school buildings rented to the military as hospitals.

Figure 5-2 – Portrait of Hupp, at the age of 23, taken in November 1863 while he was serving as a nurse at Hospital no. 1, New Albany, Indiana.

Some hotels, a saloon, a river boat, and other businesses were also leased as hospitals. The first of these was the Upper City School building at Upper 8th Street, later known as Hospital no. 1. It was procured in February of 1862 by the Union Aid Society, a group of dedicated women, formed early in the war, to care for the wounded. They also provided the men with supplies, distributed mail, and saw that reasonable sanitary standards were maintained in hospitals.

In April of 1862, the U.S. Sanitary Commission took over the temporary hospital system as casualties from the Battle of Shilo in northern Mississippi began to fill available beds. Previous wounded had mostly come from Grant's successful campaign to take Fort Donnelson in western Kentucky. John Nunemacher's New Albany *Ledger* reported that most of the patients suffered from measles, pneumonia, fever, and colds in addition to their wounds. The early patients apparently survived as the *Ledger* reported that none had died as of February of the year. That was to change later on. Ormond Hupp, who recovered sufficiently to become a ward nurse, described helping with autopsies, and comforting the widows of departed soldiers.

The wounded were mostly shot in the shoulders, thighs, and lower legs, the *Ledger* reported. One "seccesh" soldier had the bone of his right arm, from the elbow nearly to the shoulder shot away, the arm hanging by a mere ligament of flesh and muscle. The arm was amputated soon after arrival. His brother, a civilian, gave himself up to capture to help care for his injured sibling.

The doctors who staffed the New Albany military hospitals were a mixture of local civilian doctors, like John Sloan at Hupp's Hospital no. 1, and military doctors attached to army units. The latter, like Dr. Frey

Figure 5-3 – Upper City School building which was converted into Hospital No. 1, one of the eleven hospitals in New Albany. (1992)

mentioned in Hupp's diary, served as high-level administrators. Dr. William Clapp, another prominent New Albany physician, served as an assistant surgeon at Hospital no. 5 and was also attached to the 38th Infantry for battlefield duty. New Albany provided one black doctor to field service, Dr. William A. Burney of the 28th Colored Regiment.

Much of the work of tending to the wounded, however, fell to the ladies auxiliary groups and female Sanitary Commission workers. Recovered soldiers also saw service as ward stewards and nurses, the position Hupp came to occupy. His account showed he was responsible for minor nursing, house cleaning, food and supply procurement, and bookkeeping.

His journal accounts indicate that he continued as a patient during some of that time, continually bothered by one common ailment or another. Some of his illness was related to his old Perryville wounds, but other ailments probably arose in consequence of living in close quarters with roomfuls of diseased men.

Given even the best of sanitary conditions for the times, the prevention of disease and its proliferation was not a perfected art during the Civil War (Louis Pasteur's "germ theory" was not developed until 1880). Malaria, typhoid, diphtheria, small pox, dysentery, cholera, yellow fever, and other tools of the grim reaper threatened many towns along the Ohio and elsewhere, with the constant threat of deadly epidemics.

It did not help Pvt. Hupp that the small coal burning stoves used to heat the wards were inadequate to maintain comfortable temperatures during cold winter evenings. This sometimes necessitated sleeping closely entwined with fellow ward mates to stave off the winter chill. Such close contact was a sure prescription for the spread of whatever contagions were presently infesting the hospital.

The war brought many changes to New Albany, but social activities were not entirely interrupted. In fact, the onslaught of wounded soldiers, those encamped at Camp Noble on the Floyd County fair grounds and those passing through on their way to the front were a source of new diversions and, for some, new friendships. However, many townsfolk were much relieved when a heavy contingent of troops would leave en masse for battle, as they did prior to Perryville and other hostile actions. As Hupp noted, the troops could be noisy and rowdy at times, and near riots broke out from disagreements between whiskey-fortified soldiers and local citizens.

For 23 year old Pvt. Hupp, safe again in his own home state, New Albany presented temptations that would try the soul of any Baptist in Heaven. By March 1863, he had recuperated sufficiently to venture beyond the hospital grounds to sample the local hospitality. His journal entries permit no doubt that he found it in abundance. In addition to the many friends he made in the hospital (Keggie, Turner, Wilson, and the rest), he seemed to have an almost uncanny knack for charming the locals into invitations to home and hearth. The locals in question were nearly exclusively female. A more or less complete list of Ormond Hupp's New Albany lady friends is displayed below (bold indicates multiple references):

Fanny Bird
Hattie Brannon
Mary Ellen Dottson
Alice Dowerman
Miss S. E.
Nan Miller
Miss Qualey
Emma Sebastion
Miss Shaw
Miss West(s)
Miss Fowler
El Neate
Annie Stokes

Hupp also mentions many married women, in some cases mothers of his young women friends; in others the relationships are less clear. Who, for example, were Mrs. Warren, Mrs. Warner, Mrs. Rogers, and Mrs. Monroe? One can only imagine that these were caring townspeople who genuinely enjoyed Ormond's company (as many did before and after), and wished to show their appreciation for a wounded defender of the

Union. He probably made many an acquaintance in the several churches he attended; Mrs. Sebastion and her daughters, for example, attended the Centenary Methodist church, one of his favorite spiritual and social haunts.

The many references to pleasant days and evenings spent with Mary Ellen Dottson suggest that she was his favorite woman companion, although the relationship was not so serious as to hold his exclusive allegiance. He divided his time among the Wests, Dowermans, and many others. However serious the relationship was, or might have become, Mary Ellen's particular memory never emerges again in his journal after leaving for the front in the spring of 1864. He lamented having to leave all his female friends behind, not just her. In camp at Cleveland, Tennessee, he wrote, "felt very lonely at night as is natural in consequence of being taken from such an interesting society of the opposite sex."

Proper activities for "dates" in those days included evenings at the young lady's home eating "jelly cake and sipping blackberry cordials", or consuming delicious oyster suppers. Oysters must have been quite the delicacy in those days, and whole establishments (like Harris' Oyster Saloon) sprang up just to accomodate the demand. The oysters were served stewed or fried, and came in cans from the east coast via riverboat or by rail.

Other favorite parlor activities included playing cards, checkers, or listening to a piano recital by the hostess. Playing "philopena" games was also popular. This game, imported from England, consisted of two people sharing the two kernels of a nut. If one of them failed to satisfy a specified condition , that person had to pay the other with a "philopena gift." Presumably they lost the nut kernel, too.

Daytime adventures might include a walk in the Fairview Cemetery, attending a circus or menagerie show (travelling zoo), or, in these days before movies, one could attend a panorama show. These consisted of pictures, generally photographs, that were rolled scroll-like on either side in a box with a rectangular front opening for viewing the pictures. Advancing the pictures by winding the scrolls caused a series of pictures to appear, which, in sequence, told a story or illustrated a lesson. Many panorama shows in those days depicted recent actions in the war, and thus represented forerunners of movie newsreels.

Of course, there were also opportunities for rides in the country to go "nutting", to pick berries, or just to enjoy the scenery. The New Albany area had plenty to enjoy with the nearby Ohio river and its tributary, Silver Creek, the hilly "Knobs" wooded area to the north, and "Boiling Spring." The latter feature emerged from the ground, turbulent and roiling, and emitting gas bubbles that were flammable (probably methane from buried coal deposits).

As Ormond Hupp and his lady friends ate their oysters and exchanged philopena gifts, a war still raged to the south of the great river that served to insulate New Albany from the worst of the turmoil. On the other hand, the reality of war pervaded the city and touched all inhabitants.

During Ormond's stay there (fall 1862 to spring 1864), newspapers began publishing detailed accounts of battles from reporters in the field. Lists of the dead and wounded began to appear in early '63 and they generally included members from more than one New Albany household.

On the fairgrounds at newly built Camp Noble, men were mustered in for service in Kentucky, Tennessee, and, later, Georgia. These were Colonel William Sanderson's 23rd, Benjamin "Frank" Scribner's (Grandson of Joel) 38th, Walther Gesham's 53rd, DeWitt Anthony's 66th, and Colonel William Caldwell's 81st. They all saw heavy action and suffered severe losses. Many survivors eventually joined Sherman's "March to the Sea."

New Albany was directly threatened by war at two different times, the first by Bragg's forces in October 1862. Had Bragg not been halted at Perryville by Buell's forces marching down from Louisville, he and Kirby Smith may very well have made their threatened entry onto northern soil via New Albany. Of course, it was just this battle that landed Ormond Hupp in his "interesting society of the opposite sex."

The second threat came even closer to making life interesting for the ladies and gents of New Albany. John Hunt Morgan and his band of Confederate cavalry raiders, ignoring orders from General Bragg not to cross the Ohio, did just that on July 2, 1863. His troops were transported across the river at Brandenburg (25 miles downriver from New Albany) on two captured steamboats. They overwhelmed the home guard at Corydon (15 miles away) and were expected to march on New Albany but, to everyone's relief, swung north instead. Later, however, Floyd County farmers filed damage claims amounting to $11,000 arising from lost horses and other livestock and equipment confiscated guerrilla-style by Morgan's raiders. Morgan was eventually captured on July 26th at New Lisbon, Ohio, trying desperately to escape into Pennsylvania. New Albany was never again directly affected by the war (except to accept its refuse).

Like other northern cities, political issues surrounding the war were hotly debated in New Albany, often causing long lasting rifts in the social fabric. The burning questions that had served to divide the country and thrust it into war in the first place, were still being debated as the war raged around them. Most people in the north were united in their opinion that the Union must be preserved, but at what cost and under what conditions? Certainly slavery was a central issue. Should the north insist on the total abolition of slavery advocated by "Radical Republicans"; should slavery be accepted as the price for peace and unity as advocated by the "copperheads"; or should the Union be saved with or without slavery, the position of Lincoln?

Hupp notes in his entry of February 24, 1864, that the Dottsons were unhappy about the Emancipation Proclamation issued by Lincoln in the fall of 1862. This sentiment probably reflected the views of many Floyd County residents of the time as the political bent in the area was decidedly Democrat. New Albany area residents voted for Douglas over Lincoln in the election of 1860, and McClellan over Lincoln in '64. Most of the rest of Indiana was in Republican hands, but the state was fairly racist on the whole.

Ormond Hupp, a Hoosier to the core, was given to some severely racist observations in his journal, particularly in describing the "disgusting" sight of negro "contrabands" trailing the troop trains leaving Fort Stevenson in Alabama.

Southern Indiana, in particular, also had its share of outright Confederate sympathizers and turncoats. In fact, the property used to build Jefferson General Hospital in Clark County (mentioned above) was built on land confiscated from a Confederate supporter, Indiana Senator Jesse D. Bright. Bright fled to join the confederacy shortly after secession.

Given the political sensitivities of the area, it is interesting to note that New Albany was "plagued" by a sudden and seemingly unrelenting influx of freed negro slaves. At one point, New Albany had the highest concentration of black citizens in the state, 8 percent of the population. They were mostly crowded together in an area known as "Contraband Quarters" where as many as 23 people might be crammed into two-room shacks.

July 22, 1862, (about two months before Hupp's arrival) saw one of the bloodiest race riots in Indiana history. It lasted 30 hours and was precipitated after two white men were shot by blacks after a fierce argument. Eventually the riot was put down by troops, but hostilities toward blacks persisted. Those blacks caught on the streets without passes were confined to military barracks before being mustered into service. This helped to alleviate the population problem, but post-war years saw a new rise in black immigrants. A major complaint of the white population was the competition posed by blacks for limited jobs, an issue not yet fully resolved as the 20th century draws to an end.

Ormond Hupp eventually tired of his situation in New Albany and decided to return to his regiment. It was not the company he was keeping that drove him away, but good old fashion army bureaucracy. As the need for military hospitals waned in mid-1864, many of the temporary hospitals like no. 1 were closed and returned to their former function as schools, saloons, or whatever. In the process, live-in staff were shuffled from one hospital to another, an obvious inconvenience.

Hupp soon lost patience with the situation and realized that to stay in New Albany meant constant hassles. His service obligation was due to expire in November, and he probably could have petitioned for an early discharge. However, if this option occurred to him, his journal fails to record it. Nonetheless, the March 10 journal entry reveals his decision to return to the front with the 5th Battery. On April 7, he left New Albany and Mary Ellen Dottson, who at that moment lost forever the opportunity of becoming my – and many others' – great-grandmother.

Hupp embarked by train from Louisville on the 8th and arrived in Nashville on the 9th. Taking a route that led through Stevenson, Alabama, to Chattanooga, Tennessee, (which his battery had helped to "liberate" in November of the previous year), he reached his unit encamped at Cleveland, Tennessee, on the 12th. There he was reunited with his battery mates, particularly his friend, Charley Miller and, as he described it, he "took a long walk and had a talk over things which had origin since last we met."

Pvt. Ormond Hupp had arrived just in time to participate in one of the most famous, climactic actions of the Civil War – Sherman's Atlanta Campaign.

Chapter 6
Meanwhile, Back with the Boys . . .

It is well that war is so terrible – we would grow too fond of it.

Robert E. Lee to James Longstreet
Fredricksburg, Dec. 13, 1862

There is many a boy here today who looks on war as all glory, but, boys, it is all hell.

William T. Sherman
G.A.R. convention, Columbus, Ohio, Aug. 11, 1880

Newspapers and magazines (Ormond Hupp read *Harper's* and others), whose reporters followed the troop trains from camp to camp, filtered back news from the front to the towns and villages that had provided so many of their young men for the conflict. One of these towns was New Albany, Indiana, where Ormond Hupp found refuge from the noise, depravation, and terror of the battlefield, and a reasonably comfortable place to stay until his burned and torn flesh healed.

The news from the front was not particularly disturbing but, just the same, it did not inspire great confidence in the Union war effort in Kentucky and Tennessee. Of particular concern to Pvt. Hupp, however, was the fate of the "boys" of the 5th Battery and the rest of the Army of the Ohio as he lay in pain from his wounds at Perryville. His diary entries for the period show that he did receive correspondence from battery mates, who kept him somewhat up-to-date on their activities.

This chapter follows the exploits of the 5th Battery (sans Pvt. Hupp) all the way from Perryville to Chattanooga, and finally to winter quarters in Blue Springs, Tennessee, in early 1864. Hupp rejoined the battery shortly thereafter. Battles in which Simonson's battery was actively involved are described here in some detail, with emphasis placed on aspects of a given battle where this unit played an active role.

The recent battle in Kentucky had been something of a draw, although unquestionably the Federals took the greatest punishment and lost the most ground. In retrospect, Buell had probably been right to want to concentrate all his forces for a battle with Bragg on the 9th, an option denied him by Alexander McCook's rash forward deployment of his corps. In the final analysis, though, Bragg failed to deliver a knockout punch, and Buell was credited by many for "saving" Kentucky. Many Northerners, however, saw the battle as an inglorious defeat. This impression was reinforced by the subsequent escape of Bragg's forces from the Union grasp.

Buell had made powerful enemies among his troops (note Hupp's diary entries to this effect), his officer corps, and among some of the most powerful politicians of the day. These included the impetuous governor of Indiana, Oliver P. Morton, and no less a figure than the future president of the United States – now military governor of occupied Tennessee – Andrew Johnson. Morton and Johnson were mortified by Buell's singular lack of interest in pursuing Bragg, and Johnson, for one, resented Buell's orders barring the sacking of southern residences and other property. Johnson advocated that all Southerners, civilian and military, should be made to pay dearly for the sins of secession.

Buell, for his part, only added volume to the rising chorus demanding his ouster by only half-heartedly pestering Bragg after Perryville. Bragg's forces finally eluded the pursuing bluecoats and made their getaway through the Cumberlands. Buell, content to have chased the two invading Confederate armies from Kentucky without destroying them (Kirby Smith and Bragg retired their armies to Knoxville), was enroute to Nashville to gather strength and make preparations for driving Bragg and Smith from Tennessee as well.

But such was not to be, for Abraham Lincoln had finally reached the limit of his patience. He sacked Buell, encamped at Bowling Green, on October 24 and handed his command to Major General William Starke Rosecrans (1819-1898), an eccentric genius, and favorite of General George B. McClellan (sacked, himself, on Nov. 9). The Army of the Ohio was reorganized at Nashville and renamed Fourteenth (XIV) Corps of the Department of the Cumberland. This soon to be refurbished unit (boasting over 81,000 effectives) was divided into three wings, the Left under Thomas L. Crittenden, the Center under George Thomas, and the Right under Alexander McCook, Hupp's former corps commander at Perryville. The 5th Indiana Battery remained under McCook during this transition period, attached to the 3rd Brigade of the 2nd Division. After the Battle of Stones River in January, XIV Corps was renamed the Army of the Cumberland, with the wings reverting to corps. McCook's Right Wing became the Twentieth Corps at that time.

Figure 6-1 – Major General William Starke Rosecrans, commander of the Army and Department of the Cumberland. (from A Photographic History of the Civil War in Ten Volumes, *vol. 10, p. 173).*

Braxton Bragg, Buell's Confederate opponent, fared a bit better but also had his ardent critics. Among them were his own wing commanders, Polk and Hardee, who lay much of the blame for the failure of the Kentucky campaign on Bragg's indecisiveness, and inability or unwillingness to follow up on his successes (witness Perryville). They urged Jefferson Davis to replace Bragg with Joseph E. Johnston, now recovered from wounds suffered at Seven Pines (Fair Oaks) during McClellan's "Peninsula Campaign" aimed at the Confederate capital. Davis, however, was not a great admirer of Johnston and decided to stay with Bragg for the time being. Thus, as Rosecrans reorganized and resupplied his army at Nashville, Bragg moved his to Murfreesboro some 30 miles down the pike to the southeast. His new army was now called the Army of Tennessee.

The soldiers of the Fifth Indiana Battery who had escaped the casualty list at Perryville marched to Harrodsburg a few days after the battle, and from there to Crab Orchard, where Buell decided to call off the chase of Bragg. They turned west and arrived in Bowling Green in late October. (From here, Hupp noted that Capt. Simonson visited his wounded in New Albany, bringing them gifts of food, and news from the company.) Now under their new commanding general, Rosecrans, they moved into Nashville on November 9. It was on December 24, 1862, that they were transferred to the 2nd Division under Brig. General Richard W Johnson. Johnson (the "W" stood for nothing; he had no middle name) had been captured by John Hunt Morgan, the elusive Confederate cavalry raider, while pursuing Morgan. He was exchanged on December 20 in time to take over the 2nd Division of McCook's wing for the advance on Murfreesboro, which culminated in a battle now generally called "Stones River" ("Murfreesboro", in the South).

Before venturing further, we should examine the grand scheme behind the troop movements in middle Tennessee that were about to begin in late December of 1862. As before with Buell, Rosecrans' charge from Washington was to push southeast from Nashville with all due haste, the ultimate goal being the capture of Chattanooga, major rail crossroads and gateway to the deep south. In the process, all or most Confederate forces would be cleared from Tennessee which meant that Knoxville would also have to be taken. General Ambrose Burnside, operating in the east, was given that task. Chattanooga, however, was the first priority, with Atlanta soon to follow.

Bragg, of course, was given the daunting task of stopping the Federal advance and saving as much of middle and eastern Tennessee for the South as possible. True to past performance, however, Bragg continued to fight and then fall back, eventually yielding Chattanooga to Union forces who had retreated there after the climatic – and disastrous – Battle of Chickamauga in September of 1863. More on that later.

On the eve of Stones River, as Ormond Hupp still lay in his hospital bed too weak yet to resume his journal entries, the overall tenor of the war for the Union was taking a dismal turn. In the east, Ambrose Burnside, recently tapped to replace McClellan as commander of the Army of the Potomac, had failed his first leadership challenge by being repulsed by Lee at the bloody Battle of Fredricksburg (Dec. 13). He was attempting to cross the Rappahannock in northeastern Virginia in another attempt to assault Richmond.

In the west, Grant and Sherman launched the Vicksburg Campaign in late December with the Battle of Chickasaw Bayou (or "Bluffs"; also, Walnut Hills) in which Grant attacked Vicksburg by land from the east, and Sherman moved down the Mississippi River to attack simultaneously from the north (Yazoo River). Confederate forces were successful in repulsing the attack and Grant temporarily withdrew, whereupon the city eventually came under siege. Lincoln and Halleck were thus under considerable pressure to produce a Union victory. Prevailing wisdom dictated that even the appearance of Confederate success on the battlefield would be enough to impel the British, and possibly the French and Russians, to intervene in favor of the South. With his army now rested, reorganized (including a more effective cavalry with new repeating rifles), and amply resupplied, Rosecrans was urged to quit Nashville and engage the enemy with all due speed. On the 26th of December he finally complied.

Stones River

The Federal advance from Nashville toward Murfreesboro was preceded by three major Confederate cavalry raids aimed at cutting Rosecrans' supply lines and communications to the north. John Hunt Morgan was particularly successful at this task; in early December he had captured the two-thousand-man garrison at Hartsville. He followed up this triumph with another at least as impressive. On the 27th of December (as Rosecrans was on his way to Murfreesboro) he captured the Union garrison at Elizabethtown, Kentucky, then moved to Muldraugh's Hill where he captured that garrison and burned the huge wooden trestle bridge on which the Louisville and Nashville Railroad crossed the Rolling Fork River. However, neither Morgan nor Nathan Bedford Forrest were present for the upcoming battle at Murfreesboro.

Bragg, confident that Rosecrans would stay the winter behind the entrenchments of Nashville, deployed Forrest westward to harass Grant (along with a detachment of infantry), and sent Morgan to Kentucky. Both were absent for the battle, a critical mistake. Bragg retained only Wheeler's cavalry (with Wharton) who had performed some daring stunts of his own prior to the battle. On a two-day foray behind Union lines beginning December 29, he succeeded in destroying four supply trains (Crittenden's and McCook's) and in returning to the Army of Tennessee with badly needed rifles, horses, and other supplies.

As at Perryville, the advance on Murfreesboro was to be accomplished by sending the separate corps (in this case, "wings") along divergent routes to combine later at their objective. The objective this time was the northwestern outskirts of Murfreesboro, west of the nearby Stones River, a tributary of the Cumberland. It was here that Bragg had concentrated most of his forces (he brought more up as Rosecrans approached), divided into two corps headed by Generals Polk and Hardee.

The Union troops moved along three major routes, McCook's divisions taking the middle approach (Nolensville Pike), George H. Thomas' wing taking Wilson and Franklin Pikes on McCook's right, and Crittenden's wing marching along on the most eastern and direct route, the Murfreesboro Pike.

Simonson's battery was encamped the night of December 25-26 at Mill Creek Camp, five miles south of Nashville. Their commanding general, as at Perryville, was Alexander McCook who received orders from Rosecrans to move out at 4:30 A.M. The first day of marching was

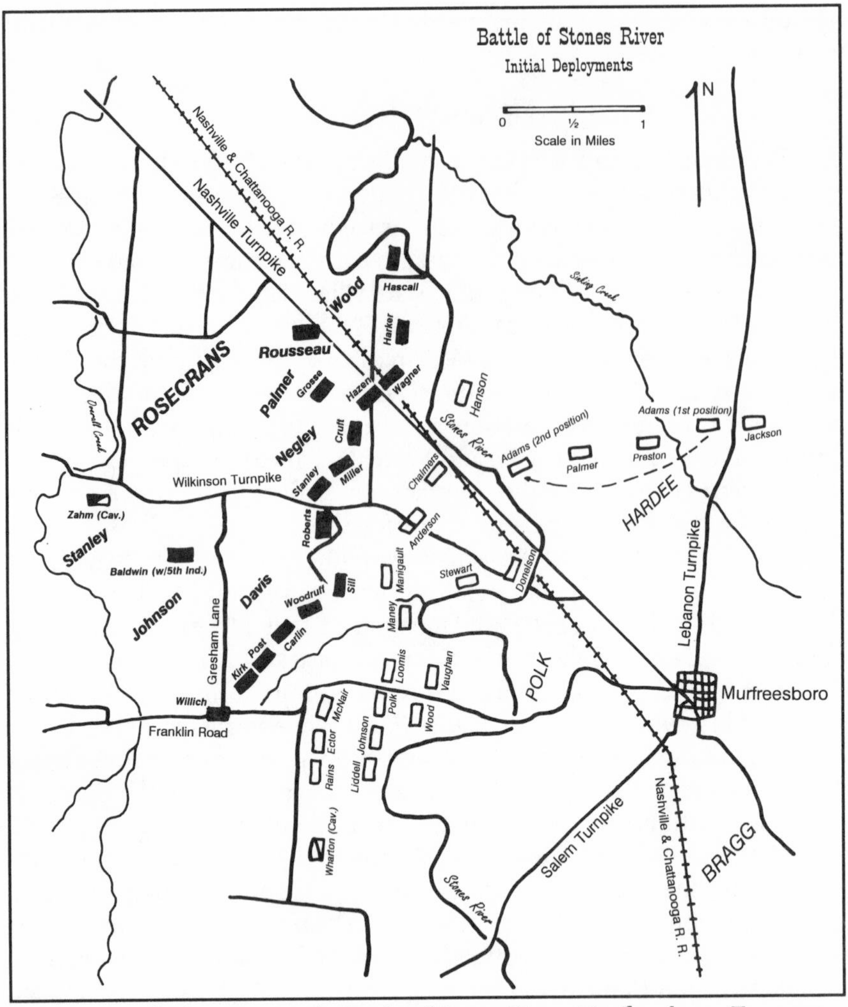

Initial troop deployments at the Battle of Stones River, Murfreesboro, Tennessee, 1862-1863 (Union = filled symbols; Confederate = open symbols; after Cozzens, 1991).

extremely arduous as a steady rain turned the dirt roads to the consistency of paste, miring wagon and artillery wheels, and the muddy boots of the Union volunteers, slowing their progress to a crawl. Late in the day, Jefferson C. Davis' (General Bull Nelson's murderer) division made contact with Wharton's cavalry and drove him back toward Triune, but otherwise the day for McCook's wing was uneventful.

Sheridan's and Johnson's divisions reached the outskirts of Nolensville at 4:00 after encountering only sporadic fire from Confederate cavalry. They bedded down for the night there in the rain, after consuming a supper of salt pork and hardtack washed down with coffee. Not much nourishment, but under the circumstances it was a meal to be relished.

The next day (Dec. 27), dawned chilly, misty, and wet. The night before, Rosecrans had ordered McCook to Triune due south of Nolansville, where some of Hardee's units were waiting. After an afternoon skirmish with Wharton's cavalry and Wood's brigade of Mississippians, the Confederates decided to yield Triune and fell back toward Murfreesboro, due east on the Franklin Road. Official records relate that Simonson's battery was heavily involved in fending off these cavalry attacks. They were involved in skirmishing with Confederate cavalry, for that matter, through to the 30th. Chief of Cavalry, General Stanley, and Johnson's division (including the 5th Indiana Battery) were ordered to bivouac one mile south of Triune, while Sheridan occupied the town and slept there as temperatures now dropped below freezing.

The 28th was a Sunday so Rosecrans, a zealous Catholic convert, ordered a badly needed spiritual and physical respite for his exhausted troops. Bragg took advantage of the lull in the Union advance to dig fortifications and maneuver troops so as to take the best advantage of the terrain. The topography around Murfreesboro and west of Stones River where most of the battle would be fought, was hardly conducive to providing defensive cover, being mostly open and relatively flat. Thick cedar and oak woods with numerous limestone outcrops made up some of the area. Bragg would be criticized then and later for his choice of Murfreesboro to make a stand when more suitable terrain (i.e., hilly) existed to the southeast.

By afternoon of the next day, most of Rosecrans' troops were to have been in position to form a continuous line of battle with McCook on the right, almost due east of Murfreesboro (opposed by some reserve units from Hardee's corps), Thomas in the center (opposed by Polk), and Crittenden on the Union left, northwest of town near the west bank of Stones River (opposed by Hardee). On the left, Union forces under Col. Charles Harker had made an abortive, but almost successful, assault on a strategic high point across the river called Wayne's Hill. On the right, McCook was late in moving his troops into position to the right of Negly's division (Thomas' wing) and had not communicated with headquarters for some time. After repeated orders from Rosecrans to close the gap between his troops and Negly's, McCook, who had a difficult time finding Negley's right in the darkness, finally gave up trying and went to bed. Richard Johnson's division arrived on the field at 8:00 and was placed at the far right of the Union lines. It was here that Capt. Simonson's battery spent the evening of the 29th.

After further chastisement from Rosecrans, McCook finally moved forward at 9:30 the next morning. After fighting a rather heated battle with elements of General McCown's forces in the afternoon, McCook was finally in position by evening. He had left most of Johnson's division in reserve, placing Baldwin's brigade far to the west of the line in a wooded area just west of Gresham Lane. Simonson's battery bivouacked there on the eve of the battle. During the night, Rosecrans ordered camp fires set extending out from the Union right to give Bragg the impression that a large concentration of troops was posted there.

As it turns out, Bragg was, in fact, planning to attack the Union right first, then to employ a turning maneuver to jack-knife this wing back toward the rest of the Union line positioned along Stones River. Rosecrans' battle plan called for a similar tactic against the Confederate right. Had both movements proved successful, the two armies would have rotated clockwise like a giant wheel, but it was Bragg who did most of the rotating the next day. Alexander McCook was about to experience Perryville all over again, but this time the rout would prove even more extreme and costly. And once again, the 5th Indiana Battery would be caught up in the maelstrom.

Despite persistent reports of troop and artillery movements opposite their lines in the dark, McCook dismissed the anxieties of his officers that the Confederates were moving to reinforce their left flank heavily. He assured his worried colleagues that Crittenden's attack on the Confederate right would take care of any threat of reinforcements. His job was to hold his position, or advance if he could, as Crittenden turned the Rebel right.

This "Fighting McCook" was ready for whatever the Confederates could throw at him, which in his estimation was not much. However, McCook's complacency was misplaced. Arrayed against him and ready to charge at first light of the new year were Hardee's divisions of McCown and Cleburne, the latter having helped maul McCook at Perryville. As most of McCook's troops greeted the last day of 1862 by casually munching breakfast and conversing around their campfires, the Confederate lines silently inched their way forward to within striking distance. At 6:22 A.M., Union pickets saw the butternut-clad "Johnnies" materialize from the foggy mist in full battle formation. Mars was about to paint the valley of the Stones River in his favorite color – blood red.

As McCown's veterans were poised to pounce, McCook's forces were arrayed with Johnson on the far right (Willich, Kirk, and Post's brigades; Baldwin in reserve), Jeff Davis to his left, followed by Phil Sheridan.

Negly's division held the center (Thomas' wing) of the Union line, and Crittenden's divisions of Palmer and Wood held the left flank to the river.

The opening Confederate charge soon forced the surprised Union pickets back to their lines, alerting the soldiers of Willich and Kirk's brigades (Johnson's division), many of whom were in the midst of breakfast, to the impending onslaught. They were attacked at the double quick by McCown's brigades of Rains, Ector, and McNair. As the Union right collapsed under the weight of the Confederate charge, Cleburne moved his troops up on McCown's right and joined in the melee. Before long, both Willich and Kirk's forces were in retreat, and the Union right was rapidly collapsing. Toward the middle, however, Davis and Sheridan held off attacks from Hardee's three divisions, and McCown and Cleburne's attack became disorganized and stalled. This gave time for Post, who was being pressed by Bushrod Johnson, to organize his defenses in coordination with Baldwin in echelon at his right rear. It was at this point in the battle, not yet 7:30 in the morning, that the guns of the 5th Indiana Light Artillery came into action.

Baldwin's brigade had been held in reserve, but it was obvious now that his forces should be deployed at once to help save what was left of the Union right. For his part, Peter Simonson split his battery with his 12-pounder Napoleons in advance of the 6th Indiana infantry and his four Parrot rifles in a cornfield behind the 1st Ohio. Baldwin's forces were threatened by Liddel's brigade of Arkansas infantrymen, with McNair pulling up to his left and rear. Some of the retreating blue infantrymen from Kirk's and Willich's brigades collapsed other brigades which had stopped to extend Baldwin's line to the right. They didn't have long to wait for the next Confederate attack.

As Liddell led his men forward, Simonson opened up with his guns as the 1st Ohio fired a vicious volley that staggered Liddell's left. Liddell's artillery reply had tragic consequences for the Arkansas regiments as some of the shells fell among the Rebels, killing and maiming large numbers. Finally reinforced by McNair, Liddell's minions, primed by the whiskey they had been served for breakfast, dislodged the dispirited Union soldiers who scrambled to join the growing multitudes at the rear.

As the battle raged around them, Simonson's battery alone stood their ground at a cost to the Arkansas regiments of 24 killed and two guns destroyed. Eventually, however, they too retired from the field to save their remaining guns from capture. In all, the 5th battery lost two guns and 32 horses, but more importantly, three men were killed (D. Rickard, J. Waters, and P. Gaddis) and 16 wounded, one mortally. In his New Albany hospital ward, Hupp noted in his March 1863 journal entries that

"There is at the present time a jolly lot of boys in this ward, who were wounded at Murfreesborough [sic] on the 1st of Jan. 1863 [actually, Dec. 31, 1862]" He further noted that these wounded men were ". . . getting along fine and needed little attention".

Before the battle was fully an hour old, five Union brigades were in full retreat.

Informed of the situation on his right flank, Rosecrans called off Crittenden's attack on the Confederate right, and ordered him to reinforce the beleaguered Union right being turned in his direction.

By noon, the Federals had retreated northeastward in the face of repeated assaults to their final defensive position in a four-acre oak forest called Round Forest, but dubbed Hell's Half Acre" by the soldiers who fought there. Here, astride the L&N rail line, the blue-clad soldiers put up an organized defense to repeated attacks during the afternoon and evening, mostly by elements of Breckinridge's division, Chalmer's brigade (Whither's division), and Donnelson's brigade of Cheatham's division. Although several Federal units held the Round Forest during the course of the 31st, most of the work fell to Palmer's 2nd Division and his gallant brigade commanders, Charles Cruft, William Hazen, and William Grose. Regiments in these brigades were mustered from Ohio, Indiana, Kentucky, and Illinois.

As the day wore on, Bragg sent brigade after brigade at the seemingly impregnable forest fortress, only to be torn to pieces and repulsed in blood in the open fields where the Federals had trained their cannon and rifle fire. Later in the evening, the 15th and 57th Indiana regiments (Wagner's brigade under Wood, Crittenden's wing) staged a briefly successful counter attack along the west bank of Stones River in which they drove back the Rebels in their front. They had to retreat eventually in the face of enemy artillery.

Bragg had succeeded in closing the Union "jack-knife", but he could not dislodge the stubborn Rosecrans from "Hell's Half Acre." Sundown came at about 4:30, followed later by a rising moon that shone over the now quite fields and thickets. Losses on both sides had been heavy. Bragg's casualties amounted to over 9,000; Rosecrans lost over 12,000 with literally thousands captured (paroled the next day). No one could argue that Bragg had badly stung his Union guests, and his fervent hope now was that they would take the hint and repair back to Nashville.

The next day, the first one of 1863, the Union commander did consider leaving the field but decided to hold his position to await Bragg's next move. To straighten his lines, Rosecrans had ordered a pull-back from the Round Forest during the night. Polk promptly occupied that ground without opposition in the morning.

Bragg took advantage of the new year's day calm to send Wheeler's cavalry out to harass Rosecrans' supply trains, capturing and destroying a 30 wagon supply train and variously disrupting Rosecrans' communication to Nashville. Otherwise, the guns were silent that New Year's day, but the morrow would be different.

Polk, in trying to emerge from the Round Forest toward Union lines, found that Rosecrans had sent Van Cleve's division (commanded by Col. S. Beatty; Van Cleve was wounded) across the river to take a hill overlooking the ford. Bragg found this situation intolerable and decided that the Federals must be removed from the hill before Polk could advance.

On the 2nd, Bragg ordered John C. Breckinridge, former vice-president under Buchanan, to assault the Union-occupied hill with his five brigades of Kentucky volunteers. Breckinridge, no favorite of Bragg's (Bragg unjustly accused him of willfully delaying joining him for the Kentucky campaign), protested what he considered a suicide mission, since his troops would have to traverse the open river valley to reach the hill. Bragg insisted that the mission move forward, leaving Breckinridge no choice but to order his troops to charge the hill, which they did at 4:00 in the afternoon.

Met with the predicted canon and rifle fire from Beatty's legions, the Kentuckians took heavy losses but continued to surge up the hill yelling and screaming. The startled Federals broke under the determined assault and Breckinridge's troops chased them down the other side of the hill whooping and hollering in their triumphant exuberance. However, the Federals had planned for just such an event and opened up on the charging Rebels with 58 guns positioned on the west bank ridge of the river manned by Chief of Artillery, John Mendenhall. As Breckinridge had predicted, the Kentucky boys never had a chance and were decimated by the enfilading Union fire. Losses amounted to 1,700 out of 4,200 who had started the assault. The survivors finally dragged themselves back to their starting point, having failed to dislodge the determined Federals whose defensive position – and fighting spirit – were now stronger than ever. The tragic charge by Breckinridge's "poor orphans", as he called them, lamenting their slaughter, was to be the last engagement at Stones River.

In all, the South lost 1,294 killed, 7,945 wounded, and 2,500 captured or missing (11,739 total casualties). Rosecrans lost 1,730 killed, 7,802 wounded, and 3,717 captured or missing (13,249 total). In total casualties on both sides (24,988) the battle was bloodier than either Shilo or Antietam. At Perryville, by comparison, total casualties were "only" 7,600.

On the 3rd, realizing that Rosecrans was being reinforced and resupplied from Nashville and could oppose him with over 70,000 effectives, Bragg reluctantly made preparations to withdraw. Once again, he had won the field, but, unable to capitalize on his victory, was forced to retreat. That night his army silently slipped away: Hardee to Wartrace, Polk to Shelbyville, and Bragg to Winchester and then to Tullahoma and the Duck River valley where he established his new headquarters. Rosecrans, true to form, made no attempt to follow, but established his new headquarters in occupied Murfreesboro. The troops spent the next five months in Murfreesboro drilling and preparing for their next movement on the road to Chattanooga, now known as the Tullahoma Campaign.

Figure 6-2 – General George Henry Thomas, commander of XIV Corps, Army of the Cumberland. He later took over the Army and Department of the Cumberland from Rosecrans (from A Photographic History of the Civil War in Ten Volumes, *vol. 10, p. 171).*

Tullahoma

Soon after settling into their winter quarters at Murfreesboro, Rosecrans' army was renamed The Army of the Cumberland and the "wings" given corps status. Thus, McCook's Right Wing became the Twentieth (XX) Corps with division and brigade numbers left in tact. Thomas's wing became the XIV Corps and Crittenden's wing became the XXI Corps. The cavalry was greatly enhanced by the arrival of John Wilding (of Munfordville fame) whose horse soldiers were equipped with seven-shot Spencer repeating rifles purchased by Wilding himself (the men repaid Wilding).

During most of the nearly six months that Rosecrans' army drilled at Murfreesboro, Bragg's cavalry did its best to make them feel less than welcome. With the arrival of Major General Earl "Buck" Van Dorn's horsemen from Mississippi (over the objections of General Pemberton, in charge of saving Vicksburg from Grant), the art of rear guard sabotage and mayhem took on new and exciting dimensions. Together with Bedford Forrest, they succeeded in making life extremely dicey for Rosecrans and company.

In early March, Van Dorn and Forrest succeeded in capturing most of Col. John Coburn's infantry column which had been dispatched south to attack Columbia on the Duck River. Phil Sheridan, who had marched down on another road, barely escaped a similar fate but was warned to retreat by the sound of gunfire in Coburn's direction. Forrest later succeeded in riding into the southern suburbs of Nashville within sight of the capitol tower, causing panic and confusion within the Union garrison there. Later (May), he led his cavalry on a wild chase across northern Alabama in pursuit of Col. Abel D. Streight who was leading a "commando" expedition against southern railroads and the cannon foundries at Rome, Georgia. His capture of Streight and his men before they reached their prime objective was the cause of great rejoicing in Bragg's camp, and resulted in sealing the legendary reputation of "The Wizard of the Saddle." It also garnered him a promotion to Major General, and appointment to replace Van Dorn who had been assassinated by a local citizen in Columbia on May 7.

Wheeler also joined in the fun, shooting up troop and supply trains on the L&N Railroad, tearing up tracks, and otherwise harassing and cutting Rosecrans' vital rail connections to the north. In January, he had used cannon fired from the bank to sink some supply packets and a gunboat on the Cumberland River, now a major supply route for the Federals. Cavalry raids made up most of the action in Tennessee until June, when Rosecrans finally decided to move against the Confederate pests arrayed along the Duck.

After repeated "encouragements," some in the form of less-than-veiled threats, from Halleck to move against the enemy, Rosecrans sent this message to Washington on June 24: "The army begins to move at 3 o'clock this morning. W. S. Rosecrans, Major General." Needless to say, it was well received. If for no other reason, an attack against Bragg at this time (earlier would have been better) would preclude any notion of his helping to reinforce Pemberton at Vicksburg, where Grant was moving in for the kill.

Rosecrans' battle plan involved moving his troops south along three routes (sound familiar?). The main column led by Thomas and followed by McCook would travel southeast through a mountain pass called Hoover's Gap, then toward Manchester. From there they could move on

Tullahoma (Bragg's headquarters and supply base), or move farther to the southeast if required. He sent one division of General Gordon Granger's Reserve Corps (the rest were garrisoned at Nashville) accompanied by Stanley's cavalry southwest through Guys Gap as a feint which would be seen as a threat to Polk at Shelbyville. Crittenden's corps was sent east through Bradyville toward McMinnville. The latter movement, also a feint, was designed to fool Bragg who was sure to recognize it as a feint, and to infer that the real thrust was coming from the opposite direction, i.e. Granger.

As the troops moved out, it was raining: a hard drenching shower that continued for most of the next fifteen days. This situation considerably slowed the pace of the moving columns of blue soldiers, nevertheless, all drenched to the skin, they moved down the mud rivers that had been roads.

McCook's XX Corps, with Simonson's battery, moved out a few miles along the Murfreesboro-Shelbyville Pike to deceive Bragg, then moved toward Hardee's position around Wartrace. On the first day of their march, they passed through Liberty Gap located west of Hoover's Gap where Thomas had taken his column. Thomas was able to pass because of an earlier bold clearing action by Wilder's Spencer-toting "Lightening Brigade." Wilder's cavalry pushed back the Confederate pickets and stormed the breastworks at the south end of the pass enabling Thomas to move into Hardee's rear.

Meanwhile at Liberty pass, XX Corps had contacted Confederate cavalry and infantry guarding the pass and defeated them with a persistent attack accompanied by artillery, including the guns of the 5th Indiana. The next day (25th), Bragg, now realizing that Crittenden and Granger were feints, ordered Hardee to attack McCook in force. Again the 5th battery was involved in the heat of the battle that ended in stalemate; Hardee failed to drive XX Corps from the pass, but neither could McCook move forward.

Realizing an opportunity when he saw one, Bragg ordered Polk to march through Guy's Gap the next day to attempt to gain McCook's rear. Polk, as was his way, protested the order, and Bragg later relented and had it rescinded. The reason he relented stemmed not from Polk's obstinacy, but the realization that Thomas, with Wilder blazing the way ahead, was headed for Manchester from where he could easily move southwest to threaten Bragg's base at Tullahoma. Crittenden had abandoned his feint and was moving down to support Thomas. Rosecrans' plan, or a variant of it, was working beautifully. Bragg had no choice but to move to protect his base at Tullahoma and abandon his fight with McCook.

On the 27th, with the rain still driving down on the retreating southerners, both Hardee and Polk moved their wings to Tullahoma. Bragg was now in a position to do battle with the Union hordes behind fortifications prepared for that event. But Rosecrans disappointed him by moving his troops to his flanks instead of confronting him head on. Granger and McCook occupied Shelbyville and Wartrace, Wilder was striking the railroad at Decherd in Bragg's rear, and other troops moved southeast toward Hillsboro and Pellam, a move that further threatened Bragg's rail supply line. Rosecrans now had Bragg precisely where he wanted him: outflanked and nearly surrounded. It was time to retreat – again.

Crossing the Elk River on July 2, Bragg reached Bridgeport on the Tennessee River the next day – the town where Hupp and the boys of Simonson's battery had kept watch over the Rebels the year before. He entered Chattanooga on the 4th, the rest of his army arriving on July 6. The Army of Tennessee arrived back at Chattanooga nearly one year after starting on their Kentucky Campaign as the Army of Mississippi.

It was one of Rosecrans' greatest triumphs of the war, one for which he was much praised in some (but not all) official circles, among his staff and men, and among the northern populace in general. The cost to the Union forces was 570 casualties, less than 100 dead. In his diary, Ormond Hupp, writing from New Albany, mentions no additional wounded from his unit at this time; there were none. Events occurring around this time that Hupp does include were the climactic clash between Meade and Lee at Gettysburg (July 2-3). The July 6 entry notes:

> The news from the Army of the Potomac is glorious if it can be relied upon; we have it that Gen. Meade has captured 20,000 of Lee's army, most of his artillery and is pursuing his flying columns with Cav. capturing great numbers.

Grant finally succeeded in taking Vicksburg on July 4. Hupp's July 8 entry states:

> Yesterday at 2 p. m. a dispatch arrived telling of the fall of Vicksburg on the 4th, with 24,000 prisoners: and a grand jubilee was held in the evening: speeches were made by the Adjutant, Dr. Fry, and several others whose names I am not acquainted with, the Choral Association sang several patriotic songs and during the time the air was filled almost continually with fire works.

Figure 6-3 – General Alexander McDowell McCook (second from left) with staff at Chickamauga, commander of Right Wing, XIV Corps, and later XX Corps, Army of the Cumberland. This is the same McCook who led the 1st Corps at Perryville (from A Photographic History of the Civil War in Ten Volumes, *vol. 2, p. 279).*

The Confederacy was now clearly at a depressing nadir, made worse perhaps for Braxton Bragg when he heard the news that his flamboyant cavalry raider, John Hunt Morgan, had been captured in Ohio on July 26 after disregarding orders not to cross the Ohio. Hupp wrote on July 28:

> News of Morgan's capture reached us yesterday morning: with all his force he was overtaken by Col. Shackelford when a short fight ensued which resulted in the capture of Morgan and his force.

The next passage may refer to Col. Abel D. Streight's abortive raid into northern Alabama and Georgia (mentioned above) finally stopped by Forrest on May 3:

> The prisoners [Morgan & Co.] are to be held as hostages in retaliation for those held by the enemy in Georgia under ___________.

"Old Rosy", the fond nickname given Rosecrans by his grateful troops, now centered his new base around Tullahoma, recently abandoned by Bragg. The wet and exhausted Union volunteers finally had a chance to rest after nine days of jousting with the Rebels. In August, rested and reinforced, they would be ready to march with Old Rosy to Chattanooga.

Chickamauga and Chattanooga

One might conjecture that Rosecrans' victory at Tullahoma would have been greeted at the White House with grand accolades for the General Commanding who had pulled off the feat. After all, the victory was won with so few casualties as to go virtually unnoticed compared to the frightful numbers produced in most other battles between major armies. In addition, the winning side had employed stealth, cunning, and initiative of a magnitude virtually unprecedented compared to previous Union battle campaigns.

However, perhaps because the Tullahoma occupation had been won with a minimum of fireworks and human sacrifice, the powers pulling the strings in Washington put little value on the effort, and gave only sparse credit to its architect, Rosecrans.

Secretary of War Stanton saw the easy victory as evidence that it all could have been accomplished much sooner, and Halleck saw Tullahoma as a mere first step towards denying Chattanooga to the Rebels. On July 24 he wired Rosecrans, "You must not wait for [Joseph E.] Johnston to join Bragg but must move forward immediately . . ."

The Army of the Cumberland's commander responded, true to character, that he needed more time to plan strategy, repair rail lines and bridges, and attend to other necessary matters. He was also concerned that General Burnside had not yet moved on Knoxville, deeming his army's presence there as necessary to protecting his left flank. Burnside, however, had his hands full trying to deal with Morgan's mischief makers on their hell-raising raid across the Ohio.

After many more messages from Halleck inviting him to again take the offensive, Rosecrans issued orders on August 15 to his four army corps (IV, XX, XXI, and Granger's Reserve Corps) to begin their perilous advance toward the Tennessee River over some of the most forbidding terrain tread by any army in the war. To reach Chattanooga from any direction, they would have to traverse the rugged Cumberland plateau which consisted of a monotonous series of north-south trending hills and valleys north of the city that could easily sap the energy and enthusiasm of the most determined army. But on the 16th, the blue soldiers once again marched out in pursuit of Bragg, in divergent routes that Rosecrans had meticulously planned.

Figure 6-4 – Brig. General Jefferson C. Davis, served as a division up through corps commander from Stones River through Atlanta and the Carolinas campaigns. Before Perryville, he murdered Gen. William "Bull" Nelson in Louisville (from A Photographic History of the Civil War in Ten Volumes, *vol. 10, p. 189).*

It might be useful here to outline briefly the events from mid-August to late November 1863. Rosecrans' objective in this particular campaign was the capture and occupation of Chattanooga, and he eventually accomplished that when Bragg, as at Tullahoma, decided to evacuate the town without offering resistance. Without stopping to regroup, he then overshot Chattanooga (leaving a force of occupation) and pursued the Army of Tennessee to the banks of Chickamauga Creek in northwest Georgia. Taken as a whole, the movement from the Tullahoma area to Chickamauga, including the climactic battle there, was called the "Chickamauga Campaign," even though the initial objective was Chattanooga.

As a result of actions on the final day of fighting at Chickamauga (Sept. 20), the Union army was forced to retreat back to Chattanooga where Bragg held it under siege for nearly two months. The battles involving the efforts of Grant, Hooker, and Sherman to rescue the Army of the Cumberland are collectively known as the "Chattanooga Campaign." Ormond Hupp's unit, the 5th Indiana Light Artillery, was actively involved in the

Figure 6-5 – Brigadier General Richard W Johnson, commander of 2nd Division, Right Wing, XIV Corps, and XX Corps, Army of the Cumberland. 5th Indiana Battery was under his command from Stones River to Chickamauga (from A Photographic History of the Civil War in Ten Volumes, *vol. 10, p. 85).*

Chickamauga Campaign, essentially the last major action they would see before Hupp rejoined them in spring of 1864.

For this campaign, the plan that Rosecrans set into motion assigned different tasks to each corps, most of them deceptive in nature. That especially described Crittenden's XXI Corps' directive, which was to move into the Sequatchie Valley north of Chattanooga and demonstrate with sufficient noise and other activity to simulate the presence of a much larger army. Meanwhile, Minty's cavalry would ride north along the Tennessee on a reconnaissance mission that was to convince Bragg that the Federals planned a crossing north of town. Wilder's Lightening Brigade was given the most challenging task of demonstrating against Harrison's Landing opposite Chattanooga, and against the city itself, with orders to fire artillery shells into its center.

George Thomas' XIV Corps was to move as discretely as possible from their base at Decherd and Cowan to the banks of the Tennessee where they were to prepare boats for a secret crossing. Alex McCook's XX Corps held the right flank of the Union Army. He was to advance Johnson's Division to Bellefonte, Alabama, for a crossing of the Tennessee, while Sheridan and Jefferson C. Davis would cross at nearby Stevenson. In other words, Crittenden acted as a feint, threatening to cross the river north of Chattanooga, whereas the real crossing was to be effected southwest of the city, in Alabama.

Attached as before to McCook's Corps (Johnson's 2nd Division; Baldwin's 3rd Brigade), Simonson's 5th Indiana Battery moved by train from Winchester to Salem, Tennessee, and then was transported by boat along the Paint Rock River in Alabama, eventually entering the Hurricane fork of that river. They then had to march overland through the Cumberland mountains until they reached Bellefonte.

The 5th Battery eventually moved to Stevenson (where they had started on their pursuit of Bragg one year previously) and, on August 31, crossed the Tennessee River at Caperton's Ferry. Like most Union contingents, they encountered only sporadic resistance from Rebel pickets from the 3rd Confederate Cavalry, who were quickly brushed aside (most simply ran away) by the well armed landing parties. From their landing point, Johnson and Davis were ordered east on September 3 across Sand Mountain where they would join with Thomas' corp in taking Winston's Gap on famous Lookout Mountain.

Figure 6-6 – C.S.A. General James Longstreet. Known as Lee's "Old War Horse", he was detached from the Army of Northern Virginia to help Bragg in Georgia. Troops under his command achieved the climactic breakthrough at Chickamauga that led to the Union Rout (from A Photographic History of the Civil War in Ten Volumes, *vol. 10, p. 2450).*

By September 4, Rosecrans succeeded in transporting his entire army across the Tennessee River barrier, one day after Burnside entered and occupied Knoxville. Bragg, whose information regarding the disposition of his enemy was woefully inadequate, was completely fooled by Rosecrans' ruse. After he had shifted most of his troops to the northeast to counter the perceived threat there, Thomas and McCook had an easy time crossing at the virtually undefended southwestern embarkation points.

On August 21, Bragg ordered all non-combatants to evacuate the town. Outnumbered by Rosecrans' forces which he estimated at 70,000 (actually about 60,500 Union troops with another 20,500 in reserve), Bragg appealed for more troops to augment the 37,000 available to him. John C. Breckinridge and W. H. T. Walker's 9,000 strong combined divisions were called up from Joe Johnston's army in Mississippi, but Bragg appealed for more, hoping he could peal a few divisions away from Lee's Army of Northern Virginia. Help from this quarter would come eventually, but not in time to launch an offensive that would save Chattanooga.

In the meantime, unbeknownst to Bragg, McCook and Thomas were slowly and painfully making their ways across the mountains west of Lookout Mountain: McCook across Sand Mountain and Thomas across Raccoon Mountain to the north. The dusty roads up Sand Mountain, in particular, were a nightmare to traverse in the blazing heat of late summer. Most had to be widened and repaired to allow the transport of wagons and artillery, which had to be pulled by extra teams of mules and horse. Many of these animals were killed by runaway wagons careening down the steep slopes after slipping on the narrow trails.

A few days after McCook's forces broke out of the eastern side of Sand Mountain to gaze upon the beautiful sight of their next objective, Lookout Mountain, Bragg finally had access to Rosecrans' plans courtesy of an article in the Chicago *Tribune* written by a reporter in the Union general's camp. The article noted the movements of Crittenden directly opposite the city, and the rapidly closing forces of McCook and Thomas from the west. Were Crittenden to be successful in driving Bragg from Chattanooga, McCook and Thomas were to move on Rome, Georgia, in preparation for an ultimate assault on Atlanta.

Bragg finally decided that he was in no position to wait while the combined Union corps closed in on him. On September 7, the first soldiers evacuated Chattanooga and by the next day most of the others would join them. Rosecrans' army, led by Col. Smith D. Adkins' 92nd Illinois Infantry, triumphantly entered the city on the 9th, the same day that Confederate troops under Longstreet began moving out by rail from Virginia enroute to northwest Georgia. Lee and Davis had finally agreed to substantially reinforce Bragg with veteran soldiers from the Army of Northern Virginia, even as Bragg slipped away yet again, this time to the banks of a river called Chickamauga.

Naturally the fall of Chattanooga was greeted in all quarters of the North with great jubilation. It had been accomplished, as at Tullahoma, by a combination of a brilliant plan hatched and executed to perfection by Rosecrans, and unexplainable gullibility and lack of foresight and careful planning by Bragg.

Of course, the individual skill and perseverance of the Union officers and individual soldiers in the field had added considerably to the project, although notable weak links were apparent. This was particularly true in the weak or non-existent performance of Stanley's Cavalry (Wilder's brigade had performed brilliantly as usual), and Thomas Wood (under Crittenden) who had refused an order to demonstrate against Chattanooga

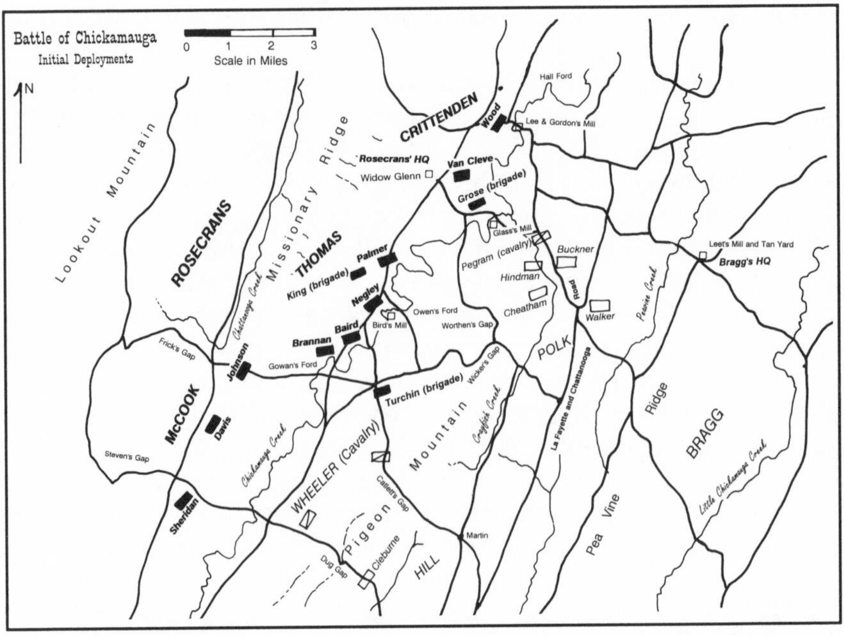

Initial troop deployments at the Battle of Chickamauga Creek, 1863 (Union = filled symbols; Confederate = open symbols; after Cozzens, 1992).

to test Bragg's commitment to the city. Most other army units had performed up to or beyond expectations.

Flushed with a victory that he certainly saw as a vindication of his previous methodical actions, Rosecrans immediately sought to pursue Bragg, whom he mistakenly presumed was in retreat. Bragg, however, was not retreating, only repositioning with the intent of choosing the time and place to spoil his adversary's victory celebration. With that in mind, Rosecrans' uncharacteristically rash enthusiasm for the chase (without even stopping to regroup) may have resulted from having Stanton's and Halleck's previous rebukes playing upon his sensibilities. Here was a chance to show Washington that he could act quickly and decisively.

Bragg's plan called for nothing less than trapping and annihilating his Federal foe in a place where this could be done without the complicating factors of mountains and mountain passes. Thus, he pulled back to the vicinity of La Fayette, Georgia, nearly due south and 20 miles distant from Chattanooga, and, more importantly, just beyond where the Cumberland mountain passes spilled out into the plains. Here he planned to pounce on the unsuspecting Federals as they emerged from the mountains – as three, separate troop columns.

Adding to Rosecrans' exuberance over his recent coup were reports coming in from Confederate "deserters" that Bragg's army was demoralized and fleeing for their lives. These men, it turned out, were specially selected scouts that Bragg had enlisted to give the false impression that his army was whipped and would not put up a fight. Spurred on by these reports, Rosecrans did not hesitate to put his three regular corps in motion with the objective of neutralizing Bragg's army and scattering it to the four winds. He sent Crittenden (minus a small occupying force at Chattanooga) through the Rossville Gap cutting Missionary Ridge just south of the city, his force thus constituting the Union left flank. Thomas formed the Union center and was directed through Steven's Gap across Lookout Mountain enroute to a restricted valley salient known as McLemore's Cove.

McCook, on the right, took his troops south then east through Winston Gap at the far southwestern terminus of Lookout Mountain and thence to Alpine, Georgia, near the Alabama line. He reached Alpine on the 10th and stayed in camp there for two days hoping to open communications with Thomas to the north. McCook discovered, through the spying of a Union-loyal mountaineer, that Bragg was lying in wait at La Fayette, not retreating toward Resaca as had been anticipated previously. He prudently decided to backtrack across Lookout Mountain to Winston Springs. On the 13th, he finally received orders to unite with Thomas in McLemore's Cove in the Chickamauga Valley to the north. Confused by an unintended error in his orders and unaware that a more direct route existed that could have united his troops with Thomas' corps in about one day, McCook took a more circuitous route through Lookout Valley to Steven's Gap. For the soldiers, this was an arduous march over hot dusty mountain trails that took fully three precious days. Only the torpor of the Confederate commander, who had lapsed into a bit of a funk after losing an opportunity to crush Thomas in the "Dug Gap" affair (see below), saved McCook from being attacked on the flank and mauled before he could join up with Thomas.

After evacuating Chattanooga, Bragg had reorganized his army into four corps under Polk (right flank) stationed at Lee and Gordon's Mill on Chickamauga Creek, Buckner behind Pigeon Mountain to the southwest, D. H. Hill positioned near Dug Gap in Pigeon Mountain, and Walker stationed near La Fayette on the left flank. Wheeler and Forrest remained in charge of the two cavalry units – Wheeler on the left flank of Walker, and Forrest to the right (north) of Polk. The Confederate units were disposed in positions designed to prey upon any army entering the confined cul-de-sac of McLemore's Cove, now the objective of Thomas' onrushing corps. Forrest and Wheeler were assigned the job of keeping

McCook and Crittenden occupied and delayed while the centrally concentrated Rebel army set upon and devoured Thomas. After that, the plan called for the Confederate forces to combine and whip whichever Union flank happened to be most convenient. Rosecrans, believing that he was chasing a demoralized and vanquished foe, had seriously divided his army in this mountainous terrain where the prospects for rapid mutual aid in the event one column was attacked were practically nil.

On September 11th, the trap was set with Cleburne's division (Hill's corps) ready to attack through, and plug Dug Gap in Pigeon Mountain, and Hindman's division (Polk's corps) ready to move up (to the southwest) the Chickamauga Valley from Lee and Gordon's Mill, effectively sealing off McLemore's Cove from escape. However, because of delays in troop movements and confusion concerning their orders from Bragg, the Rebel advances were delayed. Thomas eventually saw through Bragg's plan for his demise, and retreated through Steven's Gap to the north side of Missionary Ridge. Bragg was furious that his subordinates had allowed such an extraordinary opportunity to slip from their grasp, and of course they blamed him for the debacle. The "Dug Gap" incident would not be the last the Confederates would miss a golden opportunity to ensnare one of Rosecrans' corps.

Bragg, still stewing over the escape of Thomas, directed Polk on the 13th to attack two isolated divisions of Crittenden that had ventured far beyond Missionary Ridge and were attempting to capture Ringgold on the Confederates' rail supply line. Polk protested that Crittenden had, in fact, withdrawn these divisions (after Thomas' scare at Dug Gap) and they were now reunited with three others just beyond Chickamauga Creek. Although Polk's information was accurate, Bragg nevertheless insisted on an attack to be concentrated in the area of Lee and Gordon's Mill. Polk, however, delayed the advance and assumed the defensive, allowing Crittenden's forces to escape beyond Missionary Ridge.

Old Rosy, now cognizant of Bragg's designs, hurried to reunite his scattered forces (leading to McCook's orders to reunite with Thomas described above) which were eventually deployed along the Chickamauga Valley. In addition, rumor had it that Bragg would soon be reinforced by battle-hardened troops from the eastern theater under no less a general than James Longstreet, Lee's "Old War Horse" of Gettysburg fame. It was under Longstreet's command that Picket made his famous charge up Cemetery Ridge (also known as "Longstreet's Assault").

On the 18th of September, the rumors proved true as three of Longstreet's brigades under General John Bell Hood arrived to reinforce Bragg. Longstreet arrived with two more brigades by rail the next night. Rosecrans now had reason to fear that he had overextended his army beyond Chattanooga and Lookout Mountain. What is more, Burnside was unavailable to reinforce him, leaving him alone to face the Rebels massed in his front. He was soon to reap the consequences of his bold advance. The coming battle would be the greatest battle in the western theater in terms of troops deployed, casualties, and general destruction. For the troops engaged, it was also the bloodiest contest of the entire Civil War.

By the night of September 17, the two armies lay facing one another in a northeast-southwest alignment roughly paralleling Chickamauga Creek (an Indian word meaning "stagnant water"). The now fully reunited Union forces occupied positions west of the creek, with the Confederates to the east. McCook's Divisions, constituting the right flank, were camped at Baily's Crossroads just east of Steven's Gap (Sheridan) on the southern tip of Missionary Ridge (Davis), and Johnson's division (including Hupp's friends in Simonson's battery) was a mile-and-one-half north of Davis on Missionary Ridge. Thomas was encamped in the vicinity of Pond Spring further downstream (north), and Crittenden was even farther north positioned between Glass Mill and Lee and Gordon's Mill.

Arrayed against them on the other side of the creek were Polk's corp to the north (Confederate right) and D. H. Hill's corps to the south (left flank) as far as Dug Gap, now occupied by Cleburne's division.

Although there would be plenty of shifting around over the next few days, this general alignment along the creek valley and surrounding heavily wooded hills and bluffs would hold for most of the upcoming conflict. The principal overall changes in alignment over time would be steady movement of troop concentrations toward the north, and a general crossing of Chickamauga Creek by the Rebels, eventually placing most of them on the west side of the creek.

Bragg took the initiative on the 18th with a plan that would concentrate the initial attack on Crittenden at the Union left. Polk would demonstrate on Crittenden's right, while Buckner and Walker (and Hood, if he arrived in time from the east) would cross the creek to the north and sweep south hitting the Union left flank and driving them toward Polk who would then help drive the blue soldiers into McLemore's Cove where they could be entrapped and slaughtered at will.

This plan was similar in some respects to the one that was designed a week earlier to insure Thomas' demise. However, the plan went a wry for a number of reasons. One was that Rosecrans, having heard reports of large enemy troop movements across the creek, moved to protect his left flank and supply line to Chattanooga by extending his line northward.

Accordingly, he moved Crittenden north of Lee and Gordon's Mill which meant that, from Bragg's perspective, the Union "left," as he had envisioned it in making his battle plan, was now closer to the Union center. Thomas was also moved north to Crawfish Springs, and McCook moved into Thomas' old position at Pond Spring.

Bragg's plan was also thwarted by the usual slow execution of his subordinates, and by superior work by Federal cavalry, particularly Wilder's Lightening Brigade and their rapid-fire Spencers. On the other hand, by late afternoon and evening, Bragg had most of his infantry across the creek, and on the morning of the 19th was ready to try his plan again – now fully reinforced by Longstreet and Hood.

Meanwhile, however, still concerned about his left flank, Rosecrans continued to extend his line to the north during the night of the 18th. Thomas was ordered to abandon Crawfish Springs and to march around Crittenden's rear to a new position that extended the Union line two miles to the north. McCook then moved into Thomas' old camp as before. Thus, on the morning of the 19th, the Union forces actually outflanked the Rebels on their right, a point unknown at the time to both commanding generals. The battle began in earnest on the morning of the 19th, with a second and climactic phase on the 20th.

The 19th began with Thomas sending Brannan's division out to attack what he thought was an isolated Confederate brigade at Reed's Bridge. Brannan ran into Forrest instead who skirmished with the Federals to buy time while calling up an infantry brigade for support. The battle raged back and forth prompting Thomas to call for reinforcements. Rosecrans, ever concerned for his left, sent Palmer from Crittenden's corps and Johnson from McCook's. It would soon be time for the boys of the 5th Indiana Battery to see some action.

It should be noted here that the battle of Chickamauga was not known for its artillery duels. The thick forests limited visibility and impeded the flight of most shells over any distance. Nevertheless, artillery was used as infantry support by both sides – at times with deadly effectiveness (particularly by the Rebels during the last hours of fighting on the 20th).

Col. Philemon Baldwin directed his brigade off the La Fayette road and into double line of battle on the left flank of the division. To his right, was Willich's brigade, with Hazen on his right. Simonson's battery was ordered to stay well to the rear of the infantry to avoid capture during a frontal assault. In their front was General John K. Jackson's brigade of Cheatham's division, Polk's Corps.

By noon, Willich had marched his brigade forward and had engaged Jackson's troops, training the guns of Goodspeed's 1st Ohio, Battery A, on

Scogin's Georgia battery, who had sighted in on Willich's infantry. By 1:00 P.M., both sides were exchanging a steady fire but maintaining their positions. Baldwin's brigade hung back at first but was soon also engaged in the action. Although no specific references exist noting the role of Simonson's battery, they no doubt acted in support of their infantry. By early the afternoon, in fact, Baldwin had moved forward and was succeeding in turning Jackson's right. Jackson was finally forced to retire whereupon Cheatham ordered Maney up to the front from his reserve position in the rear. At 2:30 P.M. Baldwin nearly gained Maney's rear but was impeded by the heavy forestation.

Later in the afternoon, around 3:30, the Union lines had moved forward so that Baldwin's brigade was positioned to the west of an open field belonging to the Winfrey family. On the eastern side was Walthall's brigade of Mississippians and Govan's Arkansas brigade. At one point in the action, Baldwin grabbed the flag to rally his troops. "Rally round the flag, boys!" he shouted while ordering the 93rd Ohio forward on the double quick. The charge was enough to panic Govan's Arkansans, who by now were also being shelled by Simonson's battery. Walthall's brigade joined in the rout and fled before the charging Ohio and Indiana infantrymen. Although Willich was all for pursuing the Rebels for a knockout blow, most of the weary Union men and their officers did not have the endurance or bodily strength to continue the fight. Most were sure that they had seen the last of the Rebels for this day, but as the sun set they found they were in error.

Bishop Polk, himself, issued the order at 4:00 P.M. for a renewed attack at Winfrey's field to be led by Pat Cleburne who had to move north from Thedford's ford. The wet, tired Rebels now had to leave their fires for another assault when, as it turns out, Thomas had already decided to withdraw Johnson and Baird's divisions from their forward positions. Before the attack, Baldwin was joined on his left by Scribner and Starkweather.

Johnson was distributing Thomas' order to withdraw when his attention was drawn to gunfire near the open field. It was about 6:00 P.M. and the Cleburne's brigades of S. A. M. Wood and Lucius Polk (Leonidas Polk's nephew) were attacking Baldwin and Willich across the same field where they had driven back the Arkansans and Mississippians a few hours before. Darkness was falling and the forms of the soldiers were difficult to distinguish in the gathering gloom. Eventually the firing across the field in both directions reached a torrid crescendo which lit up the surrounding darkened woods. In the dark, Rebel units fired into the backs of their fellow soldiers unable to distinguish them from the enemy. Simonson's battery then opened up and scattered the rebel lines attempting to cross the field. Particularly battered by their exploding shells was the 45th Alabama, also one of the units who later lost men to "friendly" fire.

Noting that the infantry was faltering, Henry Semple moved up the Alabama battery and began firing well-aimed shells into the Federal works. The Confederates then rallied as Jackson's brigade joined the fray. In order to steady his faltering lines, Col. Baldwin grabbed the regimental colors of the 6th Indiana, faced the enemy on his horse and yelled, "Follow me!", whereupon after a brief pause he tumbled from his horse dead. Shortly afterward, the 6th was rushed by Col. Adam's Alabamians who fought the Indianians in hand-to-hand combat until many of them were able to sneak off further back into the darkened forest.

Command of Baldwin's brigade now fell to Col. William Berry of the 5th Kentucky, who was for some time unaware of Baldwin's death. He was informed of his new responsibilities as he fell back with his men deeper into the woods. Following the retreating Ohio, Indiana, and Union-loyal Kentucky regiments was Simonson's battery who lost a gun as its limber crashed into a tree in the dense woods. These infantry, with Simonson's guns in the rear, made a stand and even rallied, hoping to maintain their position until help arrived.

Richard Johnson, seeing that Baldwin's (now Berry's) brigade was in deep trouble, ordered Baird to advance Starkweather to Baldwin's left. Scribner's brigade was also sent forward, but due to confusion on the darkened battlefield, both brigades performed half-wheel maneuvers that suddenly brought them face to face. They promptly fired into each others ranks in the murk, followed up by Lucius Polk's Rebels striking both brigades at once. The latter charge drove both Scribner's and Starkweather's confused and panicked troops from the field. Actually his nephew's success that evening was one of the few gained by the Confederates during Bishop Polk's evening attack. Finally, with their brigades intermingled in the darkness to the point where the troops were more likely to shoot at one another rather than the enemy, the Rebels quit the field. They had ultimately succeeded in moving the Federals back to where Thomas had ordered them in the late afternoon, at a cost of heavy casualties on both sides. This included poor Philemon Baldwin, who died with those very orders in hand.

Later that night, after searching in the dark for his lost brigade, a confused and forlorn Benjamin Scribner recorded this passage, interesting for what it revealed about his state of mind, and for the specific unit involved in giving him aid and comfort:

> My condition was indeed forlorn and miserable. A cup of coffee that morning was my only nourishment since the evening before Steven's Gap; my inflamed eyes itched and burned, asthmatic coughing and breathing and all the discomforts of hay fever added to my sorry plight. At length pity for my poor horse, who had fared no better, diverted my mind from my own privations to his. A rail fence was found to which he was hitched, but in removing the saddle, my pistols fell from the holsters, and with all my groping around I was unable to find them. Observing a light in the woods at some distance off, I called out and found that it was the bivouac of Simonson's battery. They knew me at Perryville and a party of them hastened to my assistance. They found my pistols, made my fire and spread my blanket before it, and would have shared their supper with me, had I permitted them to rob themselves.
>
> (Scribner, *How Soldiers Were Made* [Civil War Memoirs])

Scribner was a descendent of one of the brothers who founded the town of New Albany, Indiana (see Chapt. 5), where Ormond Hupp was now nearly fully recovered from his Perryville wounds. Hupp's best friend, Charley Miller, had already returned to his company in time to take part in the great clash of armies in the Chickamauga Valley. Hupp wrote, "Got a letter from C. W. Miller which was very interesting: gave me full details of the great fight . . ."

The savage fighting on the 19th saw every Union corps engaged; only Breckinridge and Hindman on the Confederate left did not participate. As profound darkness fell, no side had gained a critical advantage and the fighting finally subsided across the whole six mile front. For their participation in service of Richard Johnson's division, Simonson's battery lost one gun (to a tree during their "tactical withdrawal" from Pope) and several horses; remarkably they recorded no human casualties on the 19th. The Union left under Thomas, even after Pope's protracted evening attack, now bulged in a convex arc aimed toward the Confederate lines. This disposition attested to the efforts of individual brigades in staving off the Rebel thrusts, and the failure of Polk's nighttime rampage to collapse it significantly. As they shivered in the night chill, the Confederate soldiers could hear the sounds of felled trees being emplaced in breastworks along this new Federal line. These noises mixed with the cries and moans of the hosts of wounded, and reminded them of what obstacles they would have to overcome the morning.

As Sunday morning dawned, Bragg had a new plan and Rosecrans had new breastworks. Bragg decided to attack the breastworks in series, beginning at the far right (Thomas' left) and proceeding in successive waves southward (toward the Union right flank). Longstreet had arrived during the night and was placed in command of the Confederate left wing, while Polk retained command of the right. Breckinridge would attack first, followed by Cleburne and on down the line.

At 9:45 A.M. on September 20th, the battle got under way as Breckinridge did indeed assault the left side of Thomas' fortifications – more than four hours past the time Bragg had specified for the attack to start. Fifteen minutes later, Cleburne attacked on Breckinridge's left. Although the attacks achieved some local success (especially in areas where breastworks had not been constructed), as the morning wore on it was becoming apparent that Polk's assault was not forcing Thomas to budge. Thomas, nevertheless, felt sufficiently threatened to ask Rosecrans to move Negly's division, which was supposedly in reserve, north to reinforce him. In one of the most bizarre and tragic foul-ups in the history of the war, this request was to prove the untimely unraveling of the Army of the Cumberland, and would send its tarnished commander hurtling back to the sheltered confines of Chattanooga, and professional oblivion.

By 10:00 A.M., Rosecrans had already ordered McCook to send two of Sheridan's brigades north to aid Thomas, with some of Van Cleve's brigades already on their way. Again, Rosecrans was showing great concern for his left and was quite ready to concede the right to protect his escape and supply routes. The trouble for Rosecrans and the Army of the Cumberland began with a series of erroneous reports from Thomas' couriers that Brannan's troops were "out of line" to Reynolds right (Reynold's division occupied the southern curve of Thomas' bulging defense works). In fact, Brannan's division was very much in place but hidden from view in the woods. Rosecrans gave credence to this intelligence, however, because he had it from two sources that it was true. To close this grievous (albeit, bogus) gap in the Union Center, Rosecrans ordered Wood to "close up on Reynolds as fast as possible, and support him."

Wood occupied the very center of the Union line and had shortly before replaced Negly who had marched off to help Thomas. Negly had not been in reserve, but occupied the line that morning; Wood was in reserve and it was his division that should have been requested in the first place. Now with an urgent order to vacate his position, he did so promptly, spurred on by a stinging rebuke he had received from Rosecrans earlier in the morning for not responding with sufficient alacrity to a previous order.

With an assurance from McCook that he would send Sheridan and Davis in to replace him, Wood now marched his troops straight back, directed them to the rear of Brannan (who was very much in place in the line) for a hookup on Reynold's right. Before he encountered Reynold's position, Wood met Thomas, who told him that Baird, located farther north, was in much greater need of him than Reynolds. Assured that Thomas would take full responsibility for the changed orders, Wood marched off to the far left of the line. It was at this time, however, that Longstreet decided to deliver a blow to the Union center.

At about 11:30 A.M., before Davis had time to move into the gaping hole left by the departed Wood, Longstreet, with 16,000 men at his disposal, launched his assault on the Federal entrenchments. By pure chance, the Rebel spearhead happened to land precisely where the Union troops had evacuated their works. Whooping and hollering, they jumped the fallen tree breastworks and poured into the Union center unmolested.

Thus began one of the most thorough and, from the Union perspective, most ignoble routs of the entire war. Longstreet with fifty percent more troops – and these in better fighting condition – than he had during his abortive charge at Gettysburg, quickly brushed aside Davis and Sheridan who were rushing north to fill the gap left by Wood. They were obviously too late, and their demoralized troops were soon tripping over themselves to escape to the rear. The panic also infected the top brass; Rosecrans, Crittenden, and McCook fled toward Chattanooga, unable to rally their frightened men. General William Lytle, commanding Sheridan's 3rd Brigade, was cut down as he attempted a counter attack near Rosecrans' headquarter's at the Widow Glen's house. It was not long before the rout in the Union center was general and Longstreet's troops were succeeding in turning what was left of the Federal right flank in on Thomas at the Union left.

Thomas responded by positioning Brannan and Wood toward the south, and in spite of repeated attacks maintained his position through the afternoon as the rest of the army fled through toward McFarland's and Rossville gap and safety. By mid afternoon, Thomas had arrayed his forces over two defensive sites: a series of heavily wooded hills and bluffs called Horseshoe Ridge (Van Derver, Stoughton, Harker, and Hazen's brigades) as his right flank, and an open field flanked by woods called Kelly field just east of the La Fayette road as his left flank. Kelly field was occupied by Reynolds, Baird, Johnson, and Palmer's divisions. Berry's (formerly

Baldwin's) brigade was smack in the middle of these defenses. Opposing them were Wood's Confederates, with Lucius Polk and Jackson to their left and some of Cleburne's brigades to their right. The fighting was intense all afternoon at both Horseshoe Ridge and Kelly field. Fighting at times was hand-to-hand, and the terrific toll of captured, wounded, and dead mounted by the hour.

Thomas was eventually reinforced by Granger who had taken the initiative to disobey Rosecrans' orders to stay put at McAffee's Church. The addition of Granger's reserves helped to stave off a total rout of the Union army that would have included Thomas' defiant stalwart cadre. For his stubborn resistance against the encroaching Confederate legions, George Thomas was known thereafter as "The Rock of Chickamauga." Subsequently, he became one of the very few Union officers to gain fame and professional advancement after the affair.

Simonson's battery was heavily engaged in this part of the battle in support of Berry's infantry. Arrayed against them were no fewer than twenty guns in their front, in addition to artillery of Semple, Douglas, Calvert, and Scogin firing from the east (to their left). At 2:00 in the afternoon, Simonson was ordered to fall back, whereupon he lost another gun. General Johnson was handed orders at 5:00 P.M. to withdraw. Dodge and Berry's infantry was beginning to give way in any event by that time under heavy bombardment from Confederate artillery. One by one, Johnson's brigades headed for the rear and, by nightfall, harassed mercilessly by the cheering advancing Rebels were on their way toward Rossville.

In the confusion wrought by darkness, many Union regiments were captured, with some men able to escape amidst the chaos, some to be recaptured after wandering into Confederate lines. All in all, it was a pathetic scene, except that those who had delayed the Confederate advance with Thomas could be proud they had prevented an even greater disaster.

Meanwhile, angry that it was not his cherished plan that had turned the Federals out, but rather Longstreet's lucky late morning assault, Bragg went into another funk, leaving the direction of the battle to Longstreet and Polk. Thus, both commanding generals were sulking by day's end and were essentially divorced from the ever unfolding events. Bragg's profound melancholy prevented him from enjoying his victory, or from even admitting that he had won one. As he had not allowed for a reserve corps – and believing that he did not have sufficient supplies for a continued offensive – Bragg had no fresh troops to follow the retreating Federals for a *coup de grace*. His refusal to follow up on his victory angered many of his officers and men, especially Forrest who, at one point, stomped off muttering, "Why does he fight battles for?"

Casualties in Simonson's battery on that fateful Sunday amounted to one gun lost (for a total of two), one mortally wounded (Pvt. Michael McCarty, died Nov. 30 in Chattanooga), nine wounded, and two taken prisoner. A total of 26 horses died in the last two days of the heaviest action. Compared to many other Federal units, the 5th battery suffered few casualties. However, a letter from the company to Pvt. Hupp suggested a much greater loss of armaments than actually occurred: "Got a letter from the Co. the first since the battle of Chickamauga: sorry to hear they lost their guns." By Tuesday the 22nd, the battery was safe in Chattanooga after having stopped off at Ringgold. They were in the company of most of the rest of Rosecrans' worn out and dispirited Army of the Cumberland.

The Union army had lost 1,656 killed, 9,749 wounded, and 4,774 missing for a total of 16,179 out of 57,840 soldiers that had entered the contest. Northern casualties made up 28 percent of the whole. Estimates of Confederate casualties run from about 18,500 to 21,000 or about 30 percent of the 68,000 effectives Bragg committed to combat.

In the end, all Bragg had to show for the sacrifice was a Union army under siege in Chattanooga – but he did not have Chattanooga. In fact, from that point on, the strategic city on the Tennessee River was lost forever from the Confederacy. The way would soon be open to Atlanta.

By Wednesday, September 23 (the autumnal equinox), Bragg had occupied the heights of Lookout Mountain and Missionary Ridge overlooking the besieged city. Rosecrans quickly dispatched troops to enlarge and strengthen the earthworks surrounding the southern perimeter. Bragg's artillery soon brought these works under long-range bombardment, and by also stationing troops and cannon on Raccoon Mountain, he was able to interdict any supplies coming into Chattanooga from most points north and east of the river.

Wheeler's cavalry was also sent out to sever supply lines and destroy supply trains, a task that he performed well but at the expense of many casualties. Bragg finally deemed the cost of active raids too high, and decided to simply wait out the starving Federals. They were receiving only a trickle of supplies and rations over a necessarily long and circuitous route originating at Stevenson. Late September rains further slowed the trains until, by early October, the situation among the ill-fed Union troops was becoming critical.

It soon became apparent to Stanton and Halleck that to save the Army of the Cumberland from starvation, Rosecrans would have to be reinforced, and soon. By October 2nd, a 20,000 man detachment from Meade led by "Fighting Joe" Hooker had arrived by rail from the east (stationed at Bridgeport). Sherman came later from Vicksburg with another five divisions. On October 16th, Lincoln issued an order directing that U. S. Grant be made military commander of the "Division of the Mississippi" which combined the departments of the Ohio, Cumberland, and Tennessee. At the same time, with official confidence in him at a nadir, Rosecrans was relieved of his command of the Army of the Cumberland and replaced by George Thomas. Sherman now commanded the Army of the Tennessee and Burnside still commanded the Army of the Ohio. Alex McCook and Crittenden were out, and the four previous corps were recombined into two. Granger was given command of XIV Corps which included the divisions of Johnson, Baird, and Davis. Palmer now commanded IV Corps with the divisions of Cruft (Palmer's replacement), Wood, and Sheridan.

On October 23, Grant finally arrived in Chattanooga to see for himself the effects of deprivation on Thomas' men who had been on quarter rations for over a month. It was a pathetic and desperate situation and Grant would soon sit down with his associates to plan a breakout. But first they needed a more efficient supply route.

The task was given to Thomas' chief engineer, "Baldy" Smith, who devised an ingenious plan for shortening the route the supply trains would have to take from Stevenson. It involved securing two crossing points on the Tennessee and Cummings Gap through Raccoon Mountain east of town, all of which were under Confederate control. The Confederates were eventually cleared from the route and the supply line, dubbed by the grateful troops, "The Cracker Line," was open for business on October 28.

The next month was spent in planning and then executing the battles to break Bragg's hold on the city. Bragg had sent Longstreet with Wheeler's cavalry north to try to wrest Knoxville and the rest of eastern Tennessee from Burnside's control, taking the divisions of McLaws and Hood with him. Earlier, Bragg had canned Leonidas Polk, D. H. Hill, and Thomas Hindman, and had reorganized his ridge-top forces into two wings under Hardee and Breckinridge.

Soon it was apparent that the Federals were not only positioning themselves to break the siege, but also were threatening Bragg's supply line on his right. The detachment of Longstreet to Knoxville was beginning to appear a bit ill-conceived, although Longstreet was successful in putting Knoxville under siege on November 17th. In fact, for most of October, with all the reinforcements brought to Thomas' aid, the Union forces in Chattanooga actually came to outnumber the besieging Confederates.

Three major battles were fought in late November which ultimately resulted in Bragg's withdrawal, thus breaking the siege. These were the battles of Orchard Knob-Indian Hill (Nov. 23), Lookout Mountain ("The Battle above the Clouds"; Nov. 24), and Missionary Ridge (Nov. 25). Richard Johnson's division (now under Granger's XIV Corps) played a prominent role in the latter battle in which the Rebels were ultimately driven from Missionary Ridge, prompting Bragg to order a general withdrawal to Dalton, Georgia. No mention is made in the company records of any participation in this, or any other battle around Chattanooga by Simonson's battery – and for good reason. The 5th Indiana stayed in the city performing garrison duty for most of October, watching sadly as many of their artillery horses and mules died or sickened from starvation.

After the Cracker Line opened in early October the health of both men and surviving animals slowly improved and, sometime in November, Capt. Simonson and the boys were ordered to Shell Mound, Tennessee, to guard the river and road from Bridgeport to Chattanooga. Thus they were unavailable for duty with Johnson's division during the final assaults against the Rebels.

Shell Mound was located on the southern bank of the Tennessee opposite the northwestern flank of Raccoon Mountain west of Chattanooga. It was a station on the Memphis and Charleston Railroad and was strategically located on the water portion of the precious Cracker Line. No doubt the battery was assigned this position to protect this supply route from Confederate cavalry. To reach that point, the battery had to cross the steep bluffs of Waldron's Ridge (a northern spur of Raccoon Mountain projecting into a loop in the river) which bordered the Tennessee River on the south side. Artillery had to be laboriously pulled up the mountain (a three mile trek) with ropes attached to 100 soldiers for each artillery piece. This route was necessitated by the fact that Bragg still had artillery posted on Raccoon Mountain so that passage farther south through Whiteside Pass was deemed too perilous.

After Bragg was repulsed and Chattanooga was freed of the Confederate stranglehold, the battery went into winter quarters at Shell Mound until February 1864, when they were ordered to Blue Springs, Tennessee. After being attached to the 1st division (Stanley) of Palmer's IV Corps, they were actively engaged with Confederate troops during a reconnaissance mission to Buzzard Roost. They suffered no casualties in this encounter, but returned to Blue Springs to wait out the rest of the winter.

In the spring, Ormond Hupp rejoined the battery, as General William

T. Sherman was laying the grounds for his devastating thrust toward the Crown Jewel of the Confederacy, Atlanta. Simonson's battery had one more job to do, and this time Hupp would be there to record his impressions of the affair.

Chapter 7
Atlanta: The Final Campaign

To make war we must and will harden our hearts.
General William Tecumseh Sherman

In late 1863 and early 1864, the divided nation had endured nearly two and one half years of the most horrendous warfare ever seen on this continent or any other. Recent Northern successes, however, prompted many newspaper and magazine editors – and some government officials, including Lincoln – to declare that victory over the Confederacy was imminent. Union victories had created, in addition to hopeful optimism, a mind-numbing carnage of dead and wounded that served to try the patience and sensibilities of those who longed for the safe return of loved ones at the front.

Of about 2,000,000 men mustered into the northern armies, nearly 250,000 would never return, and many of the young wounded casualties lay horribly mangled, all too many with missing or paralyzed limbs. War weariness infected many northern communities, with political implications for Lincoln's ruling Republicans. Voters seemed poised to turn out the "War Party" and elect the generally more moderate and compromising Democrats in the fall congressional elections, if by year's end the war did not seem to be heading toward a victorious conclusion. Lincoln was painfully aware of this growing popular dissatisfaction with the progress of the war, and fully realized that his armies and navy must break the Confederacy soon, or he and his party faced sure political oblivion.

Symptomatic of the state of unrest in the North was the upturn in desertion rates among Union volunteers, many of whom refused to report back from leave, or who dallied in the relative luxury of military hospitals long after their wounds had healed. Most of the worst offenders were those men who volunteered or were drafted in 1863, some being induced to join more by generous government bounties than a fervent sense of patriotic duty.

On the other hand, earlier three-year enlistees, like Ormond Hupp, were mostly solidly committed to the Northern cause, and a few even reenlisted when their terms expired. Hupp was not quite that noble, but neither was he a coward or a skulker. He could have easily and justifiably served out his enlistment as a nurse in New Albany, but freely chose to rejoin his comrades, many of whom fully expected him to stay put. Like many other recovered wounded "boys of '61", Ormond bade caution farewell and once again placed his life in the line of fire.

Hupp probably knew little or nothing about the military campaign in which he was about to play a part. His friend, Charley Miller, no doubt informed him of the exploits of the 5th Indiana Battery at Stones River, Tullahoma, Chickamauga, and Chattanooga – battles fought toward the end of driving the Confederates out of Tennessee. The storming of Missionary Ridge outside Chattanooga in late November had resulted in the collapse of the Rebel armies and their retreat to Dalton, Georgia. By the end of the pivotal year of 1863, the siege of Knoxville ended in the Confederates being chased completely out of the state after the Battle of Fort Sandars (Dec. 29). But the job was not over in the west, any more than in the east where Lee continued to thwart the Army of the Potomac's inept attempts to take the Confederate capitol. Jefferson Davis' western forces, now licking their wounds in northwest Georgia, were stunned, but hardly finished off.

In Washington, Lincoln realized that the success of the war effort – and his political fortunes – depended upon the swift destruction of the Confederate Army of Tennessee. He and his advisers were also aware that any slacking of pressure on the western Rebel armies might allow them to send reinforcements to Lee in the east. Now, in early 1864, Lincoln finally had a military team in place with the ability and, more importantly, the willingness to do the job.

The team Lincoln assembled had been grooming in the wings for some time, but the necessity for demonstrable success against the enemy finally ushered them to the forefront in 1864. On march 9, General Ulysses S. Grant was formally promoted to the re-instituted rank of lieutenant general (formerly only held by Washington), and on the 12th he was given full control of all Federal Armies. He later took field command of the Army of the Potomac, and chose his friend, colleague, and fellow Ohioan, Major General William Tecumseh Sherman to lead the "Military Division of the Mississippi" which included, among others, General George H. Thomas' Army of the Cumberland at Chattanooga.

Figure 7-1 – General William Tecumseh Sherman wearing the uniform of a major general, the rank he held during the latter stages of the Atlanta campaign (from A Photographic History of the Civil War in Ten Volumes, *vol. 10, p. 75).*

Sherman, who had previously fought with various degrees of distinction at Shilo and Vicksburg (Chickasaw Bluffs, a disaster; Arkansas Post, a victory), was also put in command of all Federal armies in the west, which made him second only to Grant in the current military hierarchy. Sherman's strength was not necessarily in his abilities as a great tactician, but in his willingness to fight the enemy wherever he found him, a quality dearly lacking in many Union commanders. But Sherman went even further. He believed that the war would be won only by inflicting its horrors on the South's people, as well as its military. He was, in modern parlance, an advocate of "total war."

Sherman would first test his merciless theory of war during the "Meridian Campaign" in Mississippi. Grant knew that, were he to move most of the troops occupying Federal enclaves into the southern interior like Vicksburg, Memphis, and Natchez, he would have to destroy the ability of Confederate armies to harass northern shipping on the Mississippi, or to launch raids from there into the Tennessee interior. An attack on the vital supply center of Nashville would have been disastrous to his plans for northern Alabama and Georgia. Consequently, Grant sent Sherman on a raid into the interior of Mississippi which commenced from Vicksburg on February 3.

On their way to the major rail center of Meridian, the Union troops tore up miles of railroad tracks, looted farms and villages, and generally rampaged across central Mississippi, creating a fifty mile swath of destruction and an incalculable measure of resentment and outrage. Bishop Polk, who was serving his exile from Bragg and Tennessee as commander of the Army of Mississippi, did what he could to confront Sherman, which amounted to virtually nothing since his command included a mere 10,000 infantry soldiers (and another 10,000 cavalry scattered about the state) against Sherman's 26,000. Polk's cries to Davis for more troops were ignored. Meridian, like many other population centers in the west, was systematically destroyed over a 5-day period resulting in over fifty million 1864-dollars in damage.

Numerous diversions and feints were planned as part of the Meridian campaign, including naval demonstrations in Mississippi (Mobile Bay) and Louisiana, and an abortive attempt by Union cavalry under Brig. General Sooy Smith to destroy Bedford Forrest's command at Meridian (the wily Forrest defeated him on Feb. 22). Other feints were successful in keeping the Rebels off balance while Sherman did his dirty work. This included the late February demonstration by 25,000 of Thomas' troops (led by Gen. John Palmer) at Buzzard's Roost gap against Joe Johnston's Confederates holed up in Dalton, Georgia.

Joseph E. Johnston, one of the South's more capable generals, had replaced Bragg as commander of the Army of Tennessee in December (Bragg became Jefferson Davis' personal military adviser). Thomas' demonstration (officially a "reconnaissance in force") before Dalton included artillery barrages by Simonson's Battery, mentioned in Chapter 6. Its purpose was to test Johnston's strength and will to fight, and to prevent him from sending reinforcements to Polk in Mississippi. Inadvertently, this sortie also provided valuable intelligence about Buzzard's Roost that would prove useful during the upcoming spring campaign in northwestern Georgia, known to history as the Atlanta Campaign.

Prior to the launching of this campaign, the Union armies encamped in southeastern Tennessee were reorganized and the Army of the Cumberland, which had suffered through the defeat at Chickamauga and bitter suffering during the siege of Chattanooga, was joined by a supporting cast of previously far-flung armies. As noted previously, Sherman was now commander of the Military Division of the Mississippi, and thus became overall commander of the newly combined forces about to begin their push into Georgia. George Thomas, the "Rock of Chickamauga," remained in command of the Army of the Cumberland and was also second in command to the combined forces, serving as Sherman's chief adviser. The Army of the Cumberland was reconstituted into three corps: IV under Oliver O. Howard under which Simonson's 5th Indiana Battery served (attached to the 1st Division under David S. Stanley, former cavalry chief), XIV Corps under John M. Palmer, and XX Corps under "Fighting Joe" Hooker, late of the Army of the Potomac. He had come west to rescue some of his tarnished image as a less-than-successful commander of that army.

The man who commanded Hupp's army corps, General Oliver Otis

Howard, rates further comment. Howard had lost his right arm in the Battle of Seven Pines during the Seven Days battles of the Peninsula Campaign (an early attempt by Gen. McClellan to capture Richmond). He also fought at 1st Bull Run, Fredricksburg, Antietam, and Gettysburg at which place he temporarily took over command of the three-corps army commanded by General John F. Reynolds after the latter was killed on the first day of battle. At the time, he commanded the largely German XI Corps, which was later sent to Tennessee to help rescue the Army of the Cumberland trapped in Chattanooga. When this corps was later consolidated with XII Corps, Howard was transferred to command of IV Corps shortly before the first shots were fired in the Atlanta Campaign. Howard, noted since West Point days as an abolitionist, later founded Howard University in Washington and was its president from 1869 to 1874. In 1865 he became the first commissioner of the Freedman's Bureau, and championed the rights of freed blacks until he died in 1909.

To complete the forces concentrating for the attack on Georgia was another Ohioan, Major General James Birdseye McPherson, brilliant graduate of West Point (where he tutored fellow classmate Confederate Gen. John Bell Hood in math), and now placed in command of the Army of the Tennessee. This was Grant's and then Sherman's old command. A contingent of the Army of the Ohio (XXIII Corps) recently detached from Knoxville filled out the rest of the grand assault force. It was lead by John M. Schofield, a classmate of McPherson and Bell's at West Point, who became Commander in Chief of the Army after the war (1888-1895). Schofield, at the time, was the overall Commander of the Army of the Ohio (formerly led by Burnside); most of his troops remained in eastern Tennessee to guard Knoxville.

Facing the Union forces on the Confederate side was the Virginian, General Joseph Eggleston Johnston, who, as noted above, had replaced Bragg as field commander of the Army of Tennessee. Before that he was overall commander of the Confederate Department of the West which included Bragg's Army of Tennessee and John Pemberton's Department of Mississippi and East Louisiana (Pemberton commanded the forces which surrendered to Grant at Vicksburg). Johnston was indisputably one of the South's most capable leaders, possibly exceeding Lee as a military genius. His constant feuding with Jefferson Davis, however, reduced his effectiveness at critical times. During the upcoming Atlanta Campaign, he played a daring game of cat and mouse with Sherman, forestalling the latter's advance on Atlanta, but ultimately was unable to avert her capture. His constant withdrawals in the face of Sherman's stubborn attacks – coupled with his lack of favor with Davis – caused him to lose his command

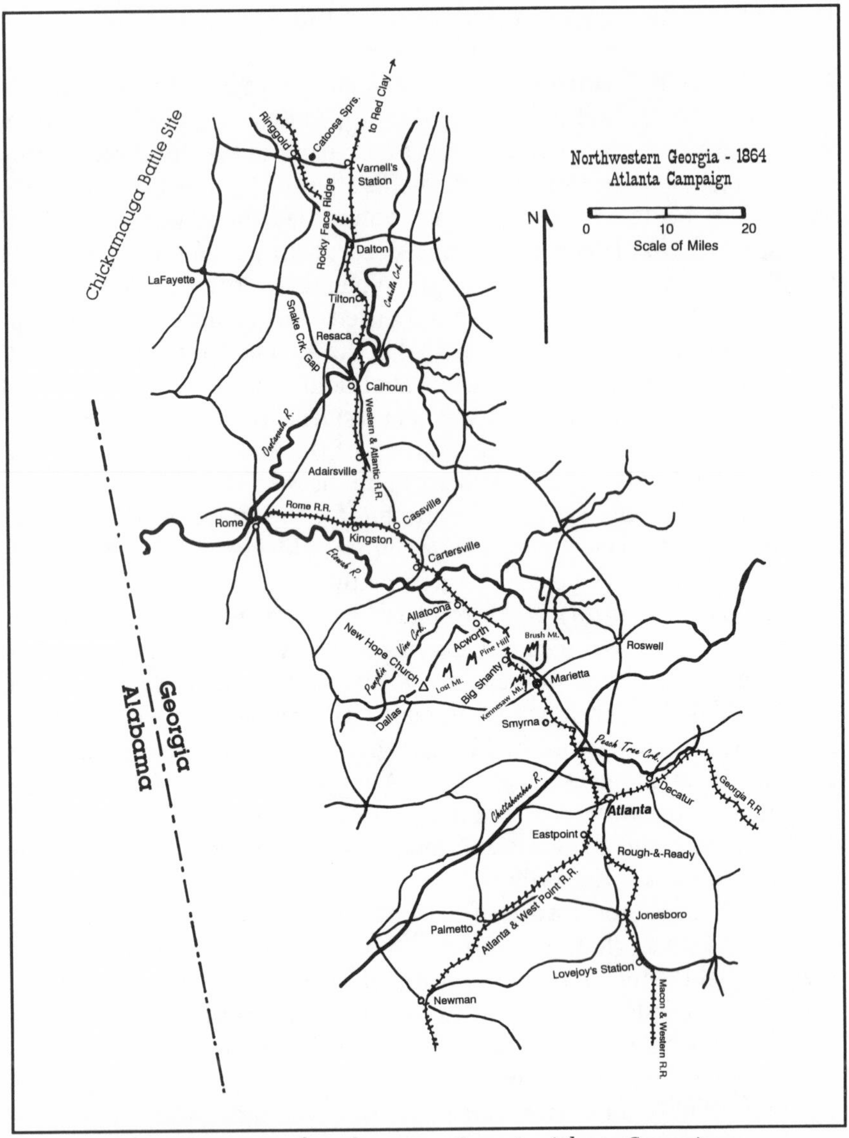

Overview map of northwestern Georgia, Atlanta Campaign.

outside the gates of Atlanta to another colorful southern leader, Lieutenant General John Bell Hood.

It was Hood's corps which, under Longstreet's wing command, broke through the Union lines on the last day of the Battle of Chickamauga to carry the day for the South. Before that he was involved in action during the "Seven Days," Second Bull Run, and Antietam, and also fought at Fredricksburg and Gettysburg where he suffered a severe wound to his left arm causing it thereafter to hang helplessly at his side. He was wounded again at Chickamauga, this time in the right leg resulting in its nearly complete amputation in the field.

Hood arrived at Dalton still recovering from this latest life-threatening trauma. He was noted as a daring, gallant, and perhaps reckless leader whose great victories had been won with a fair dash of luck, and with ample bloodletting. Even by Civil War standards, his men fell victim to enemy fire at an alarming rate. They loved him anyway for Hood was no coward, and willfully placed himself in danger in the thick of battle alongside his soldiers. His men saw his shattered body as a clear testament of his devotion to them, and they returned it in kind.

Also serving with Johnston were many of the leaders who bore witness to earlier campaigns against the Union invaders in Kentucky, Tennessee, and northern Alabama. Major General Benjamin Cheatham had fought from Perryville to Chickamauga and commanded a division under Johnston. Lieutenant General William J. Hardee, who had also served at Perryville through to Tullahoma, commanded Polk's old corps under Hood at Dalton. The Bishop himself, Leonidas Polk, came out of his exile in Mississippi (where of late he had been pushed aside by Sherman's Meridian pillagers) to lead a corps-sized "army." His troops had fought directly against Ormond Hupp's position with the 5th Indiana Battery at Perryville, and this battery was to play a significant role in his life, as will be explained later.

Rounding out the cast of notable Confederate leaders assembled under Joseph E. Johnston's command was another Perryville veteran, the very capable Brigadier General Patrick R. Cleburne, a native of Ireland. Cleburne, along with another division commander (under Hardee), Brigadier General William H. T. Walker, formerly proposed to the Southern leadership a plan to arm and free the slaves for the defense of the South. The plan was suppressed initially but eventually adopted by a desperate Confederate Congress shortly before the war's end. By that time, both Cleburne and Walker were dead, and the Confederacy was breathing her last.

Rocky Face Ridge

Ormond Hupp's diary presents a fairly detailed account of his battery's movements prior to the opening of hostilities on the road to Atlanta. On April 12, he rejoined a contingent of his unit encamped 1 mile from Cleveland, Tennessee, which was located where the East Tennessee and

Georgia Railroad, snaking southeast from Knoxville, splits in two: one spur going west to Chattanooga and the other (Western & Atlantic R. R.) heading south to Red Clay and then Dalton, Georgia.

On the 17th, Hupp reported "moving to the Battery at Blue Springs," the winter quarters of the 5th Indiana. Blue Springs was located just south of Cleveland, Georgia although it no longer appears on modern maps, nor is it plotted on period maps. He was posted in Brigadier General Walter Chiles Whitaker's 2nd Brigade of Stanley's 1st Division, IV Corps. (Refer to pages 94 -95 of Hupp's diary for a detailed account of some of the activities of the common soldier.)

On Tuesday the 3rd of May, things began to heat up as Hupp reported that the supply train had been ordered to Cleveland to obtain supplies, and then to commence to Red Clay. He washed and packed his clothes and cooked 5 days rations, an unusually high quantity compared to the more common 1 to 3 days carried on typical battle marches. They reached Red Clay at 7:00 that evening, but were on the march by 5:00 A.M. the next day, reaching a point on the Ringgold-Dalton Road by 2:00 P.M. that, by Hupp's account, was twelve miles from Dalton. At this time the main mass of the Army of the Cumberland was moving down from Chattanooga toward Dalton via Ringgold. It is likely that Simonson's Battery (and the rest of the 2nd Division) joined with Thomas' legions at Ringgold after cutting west at Varnell's Station. Schofield's Army of the Ohio was assigned the task of continuing straight south toward Dalton.

Hupp described conditions in this camp near Dalton as offering certain creature comforts even with the enemy within artillery range down the road. His impression of the local hill folk on the eve of battle reveals some firmly held prejudices and an ignorance of the "Dark Continent" probably shared by many contemporaries (see Wed. 4, page 90).

On May 5, Hupp reported heavy firing by pickets in the morning and noted that his brigade advanced about one-half mile, while the line was extended to the west. That night they slept near Catoosa Springs, a resort spa and playground for wealthy southern gentry who flocked there by rail to escape the heat and malarial swamps of the coastlands. It was located at the northern foot of Rocky Face Ridge, about 6 miles east of Ringgold. One soldier in Hupp's Brigade called it the "Saratoga of the South." Before Union occupation the hotel buildings there (a grand hotel with smaller duplex units) had been used as a 500-bed Confederate hospital. This area of Georgia was a collection point for wounded Confederate soldiers who had followed Braxton Bragg and Kirby Smith into Kentucky.

In present times the grand ornate three story brick hotel has vanished (burned in the late 19th century) and many of the springs Hupp enthusiastically described in his journal have dried up. Each of the several springs on the grounds was supposed to have a distinct composition (false) and medicinal value (false, again), but perhaps the simple pleasure of bathing in, and ingesting their mineralized waters held some curative value. The nearby town of Ringgold, incidentally, was founded in 1847 and named for Sam Ringgold, the first regular U.S. officer to fall in the Mexican War. Ringgold and a young colonel named Braxton Bragg were responsible for developing the fine art of light artillery combat tactics during the Mexican War, techniques now used by both sides in the Civil War.

The next day (May 6), like tourists on a grand excursion, Charley and Ormond inspected the abandoned but still magnificent grounds of Catoosa Springs. After describing the resort in uncharacteristic detail, Hupp's gay tone suddenly gave way to urgency:

> No time to take notes this evening: prepared to advance in the morning: received orders at 6 p. m. that no man should fall out of the ranks to assist the wounded from the field until after the battle is decided. Charley and I lay down at 9 but it was high 11 before my eyes closed in sleep.

The next morning was May 7, and because this day marked the beginning of the Battle of Rocky Face Ridge, the first battle of the Atlanta Campaign, I will allow a soldier in the ranks, Ormond Hupp, to describe his observations of the day in their entirety.

> **Sat. 7.** Reveille at 2½ a. m., all in readiness: our brigade (the 2d commanded by Whittaker) moves off in advance in the Tunnel Hill Road:
>
> 6 a. m. have halted a mile from camp: can distinctly hear skirmishing on the left: halt 15 min.: line of battle formed, move forward, advance ½ m.: meet with many obstructions which hinder us but little: advance to the top of Buzzard Roost Ridge.
>
> Halt 15 min., fire five rounds at about 3000 Cavalry, when they skedaddled and at once our line marched on Tunnel Hill without opposition, where I now write.
>
> The enemy are falling back on Dalton, such is the supposition at least.
>
> 1 p. m. have advanced this part of the line 1/2 m. took a position, fired 5 rounds which caused the enemy to fall back.
>
> The ground which we now occupy was covered with rebels troops to the no. of 10,000 so stated by citizens.

> The land is very rolling and before its occupation by the C. S. was heavily timbered, but is covered with rifle pits and log houses.
>
> 3 p. m. have not yet moved: pickets are being thrown out which indicates our staying over night, doubtless for the purpose of giving the flanks time to advance.
>
> 6 [p.m.] fire rounds at a squad of Cavalry.

The May 7th attack on Rocky Face Ridge by the Army of the Cumberland was part of a larger action initiated by Sherman in response to Grant's orders of April 4 "to move against Johnson's army, to break it up, and to get into the interior of the enemy's country as far as you can, inflicting all the damage you can against their war resources." Sherman's later actions and words, however, show that he was less interested in breaking Johnston's army (his prime directive) than he was in maneuvering around Johnston to take Atlanta. If the defending Confederate army could be neutralized in the process, so much the better, but Atlanta was the prize plum on Sherman's itinerary.

Sherman's combined army consisted of about 99,000 "effectives" (troops ready to fight). It was one of the largest single Union armies to be assembled during the Civil War, and was supported by about 25,000 non-combatants (teamsters, medical personnel, railroad workers, etc.) and could bring 254 cannons to bear against the Rebel army. The Army of the Cumberland was by far the largest of the three armies available to Sherman with about 62,000 men, most of them, like Ormond Hupp, from the Midwest. Hupp's IV Corps had about 20,000 men, similar numbers filling the ranks of XIV and XX Corps. The artillery batteries were served by 6,292 soldiers in 50 4-gun and 6-gun batteries (Simonson's battery had six). The Army of the Cumberland was well endowed with artillery batteries; the 5th Indiana was one of 24 artillery companies, nearly half the total Union batteries in the field.

Intelligence gathered during the February demonstration against Buzzard's Roost Gap (local name; its formal name is Mill Creek Gap) by elements of Thomas' command, including Simonson's Battery, revealed that Johnston had failed to adequately guard Snake Creek Gap west of Resaca (12 miles south of Dalton). Thomas proposed to Sherman that, while McPherson and Schofield occupied Johnston with a demonstration along the north and middle extent of Rocky Face Ridge, the Army of the Cumberland would march through Snake Creek Gap to the south to gain the Confederate rear. Sherman had earlier proposed sending McPherson even farther south to Rome but decided that his Army was too weak to take on Johnston if he happened to retreat to Rome. He eventually accepted Thomas' plan (after first rejecting it) but sent McPherson's Army of the Tennessee to Snake Creek Gap where they were to destroy the railroad north of Resaca, then retreat back to the gap. This would effectively cut Johnston's communications with Atlanta just as Thomas (at Buzzard's Roost) and Schofield, marching south through Crow Valley east of Rocky Face Ridge, were attacking the Rebel army frontally near Dalton. The plan, if carried out to perfection, could have destroyed Johnston's army in a matter of days.

On the 8th, Thomas advanced on the 700 foot quartzite escarpment of Rocky Face Ridge as McPherson's army made its way toward Snake Creek Gap. Thomas' army faced troops under John Bell Hood (Stewart's Division) and William J. Hardee's Corps (Bate's Division) who put up an extremely stiff resistance. After easily taking Tunnel Hill, they made little progress against the determined Confederates until C. G. Harker's brigade of the IV Corps scaled the northern face of the ridge and attempted to move south. They met with stiff resistance, however, and made little headway. Ormond Hupp described his brigade's activities as the action heated up on that very warm Sunday in May:

> 8 a. m. The signal Eng. fired for the line to advance: at once the Army threw out the skirmish line and started down the valley which lay in our front: the ground which has been gained up to 4 p. m. has been hotly contested for: skirmishing commenced within 40 rods from where they started: up till 4 p. m. our 2 pieces which have been in front from the start, held their position taken yesterday, occasionally firing a shot at Buzzard's Roost: 5 p. m., move out to the skirmish line where firing and musketry is going on quite brisk, both to the right and left: I know not the object in taking this position, but suppose it is for the purpose of opening an old Rebel Fort about a mile in front.

He went on to describe more skirmishing and the sound of heavy fighting to the right (south). These sounds probably did not come from McPherson's army because his column, although just entering Snake Creek Gap, had encountered virtually no enemy resistance. Hupp probably heard Geary's Division of Hooker's XX Corps assailing Rebel positions in Dug Gap about 4 miles south of Buzzard's Roost Gap.

Casualties were high for the Federals trying to assault the rocky heights of Rocky Face Ridge. From their defensive positions among the rocks, the Rebels were able to fell many a blue clad soldier with withering musket fire, but many others were crushed beneath falling boulders dislodged from above. The Confederates suffered comparatively few casualties during the first days of the fighting.

On the next day, the 9th, Harker's troops brought up two cannons to the ridge in an attempt to move farther south, but his position on the narrow rocky precipice proved untenable and he made little progress. In the meantime, farther south, McPherson advanced from the eastern mouth of Snake Creek Gap toward Resaca just as Schofield to the north was repulsed by Stevenson's and Hindman's Divisions (Hood's Corps) as he attacked from Crow Valley.

As McPherson moved ever closer to Resaca, he was informed by locals and captured Confederates that the town was held in great force by the rebel armies. Alarmed at the potential danger he faced deep in the enemy's rear, he panicked and turned tail back to Snake Creek Gap. Better intelligence would have informed him that the town was only lightly defended; he had missed the chance of a life time. Taking Resaca would have trapped Johnston's army between McPherson to the south and Thomas and Schofield to the north, with no means of escape toward, or resupply from, Atlanta.

On May 10, when he learned of McPherson's blunder, Sherman decided to send most of the rest of his army to Snake Creek Gap to threaten Johnston's rear in force, knowing that this would force the Confederate army to retreat to Resaca. Johnston did not accommodate Sherman immediately. He sent Hood south to counter McPherson but, upon learning of the Union general's retreat, he ordered Hood north again, fearing that Sherman would attack him from the north from Crow Valley.

Eventually, when it was obvious that most of the Union forces had pulled out for Snake Creek Gap, Johnston ordered a full withdrawal to Resaca where he was joined on the 12th by elements of General Polk's army. The Bishop and much of the rest of his Army of Mississippi would soon arrive to join in the fray.

The next battle, for Resaca, would involve a flanking movement similar to what Sherman had performed at Rocky Face Ridge. He was bitterly disappointed that he had missed an opportunity to greatly shorten the campaign, but he now had a proven strategy for driving Joe Johnston to the gates of Atlanta.

Resaca

With Resaca now fully reinforced, Johnston prepared to do battle again by deploying his forces to the west and north of the village. His new

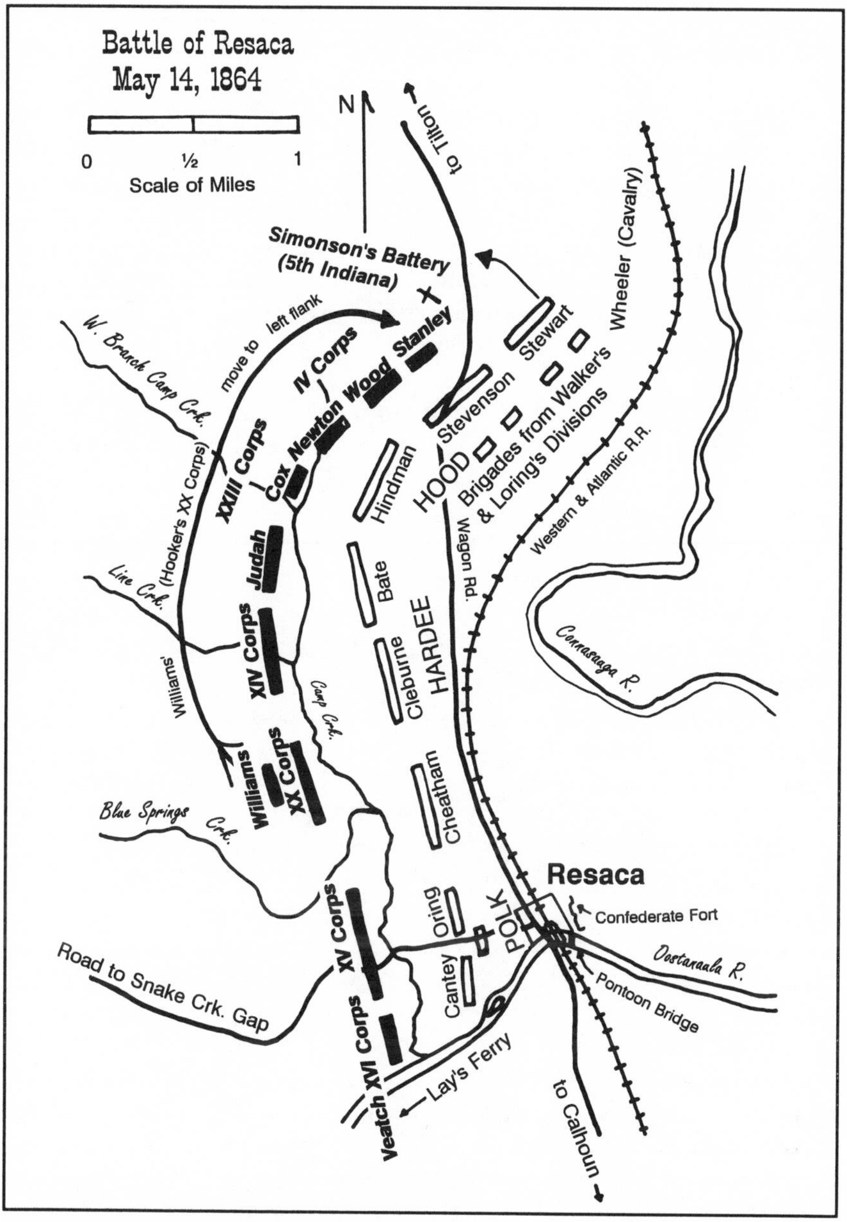

Troop deployments during the Battle of Resaca, May 1864, Atlanta Campaign. Arrow in rear of Union left flank (northwest) shows movement of Alpheus Williams' division of Hooker's XX Corps coming to the aid of Stanley's beleaguered division (Union = filled symbols; Confederate = open symbols; after Castel, 1992).

line was far less defensible than the craggy cliffs of Rocky Face, but in the chess game being played out with Sherman, retreat to Resaca was his only move.

Johnston placed Hood on the right with his lines extending east to the Connasauga River. Hardee was in the center, and Polk occupied some hills on the right near Camp Creek, a tributary of the Ostanaula River which flowed west of town. This river was a key topographic feature in the battle; Johnston's forces were hemmed in by the river to their rear which added an element of suspense should they to be forced to retreat. Also, a crossing in force to the eastern side of the Ostanaula by the Union army would give Sherman Johnston's rear, assuming the river could be easily forded.

On the 13th of May, Sherman began moving out of Snake Creek Gap to pounce upon the Confederate defenders at Resaca. McPherson led the way, pushing back Rebel pickets until he stalled near the butternut lines. Thomas then moved his troops to the left of McPherson and Schofield moved north to Thomas' left. Howard's division of Hooker's XX Corps, left back at Dalton as a rear guard during the advance toward Resaca, moved onto the Army of the Ohio's left. In the evening, the Union and Confederate lines roughly paralleled one another. The stage was set for Sherman to attack in earnest the next day.

Just after noon on the 14th, the Union attack began, concentrated mostly on the Confederate right. The advance toward the Rebel lines was led by Schofield's army and Palmer's XIV Corps of the Army of the Cumberland which had a difficult time trying to march over the rough terrain. Although some early gains were made, the attack faltered and died in confusion as different units became entangled and mixed together, nearly eliminating the possibility of coordinated attacks.

The Federals suffered severe casualties, many attributable to bungled leadership, particularly by Brigadier Henry Judah. One particularly uncoordinated and confused attack resulted in Judah marching his division (part of XXIII Corps, Army of the Ohio) through and past troops of other Union units, thus attacking alone without support. He was repulsed by a barrage of bullets and bursting shells, his men taking refuge along the muddy banks of Camp Creek.

Another of Schofield's division commanders, Jacob Cox, was a bit more successful and finally succeeded at occupying some of the Rebel works along Camp Creek. By 3:00 P.M., however, the Union assault on the Confederate right stalled for good. Artillery was then brought up to shell the Confederate positions along the creek, a tactic that would have been better employed earlier, before the futile infantry assaults. The experienced Union artillerists soon found their range and throttled t in the Confederate works. The startled and frightened Confe lerymen returned only a feeble counterfire.

Later in the afternoon, as Brigadier General Thomas Sweeny (Army of the Tennessee), along with director of pontoon trains for the Army of the Cumberland, General George P. Buell (no relation to Don Carlos), were effecting a crossing of the Ostanaula to gain Johnston's rear, the Confederates noted a vulnerable position of the Union left. This was where Stanley's IV Corps stood face to face with Hood's forces stretched to the east nearly to the Conasauga River. At 4:00 P.M., aware that Stanley was hanging exposed on the far left, Johnston ordered a flank attack to crush the Union left, and possibly cut Sherman off from his rearward communications with Snake Creek Gap. If Hood were successful, Sherman would surely be destroyed or forced to surrender.

Scouts soon reported to Stanley that the Confederates were massing for an attack in force. Hood had placed A. P. Stewart's Division and C. L. Stevenson's Division in double line of battle, with brigades from Walker's command in reserve. Stanley calmly ordered Captain Peter Simonson, who now served as his chief of artillery, to move the six cannons of the 5th Indiana to the rear of Cruft's brigade on the extreme left. This was a logical move designed to give his extreme flank maximum protection. It was 5:00 before Hood's troops began their advance.

In spite of Stanley's attempts to extend his line as much as possible, the Rebel right extended farther to the east than the Union left which was soon engulfed and routed. After chasing Cruft's panicked troops from their entrenchments, the rebels paused for a brief rest and then flooded down the side of a wooded hill and into an open field beyond. But the rebel yell of the gray attackers was cut short by the sudden explosion of shells being blasted forth from the six guns of the 5th Indiana posted on a hill one half mile distant. As at Perryville, Stones River, and Chickamauga, their time to stand and deliver a blow – while all around them the infantry was fleeing the field in terror – was again at hand. The soldiers they were now blowing to bits in the open field belonged to Stevenson's Division whose survivors, stunned by the barrage, regrouped and continued the attack, now intent on taking the murderous Yankee battery on the hill.

At 400 yards range, Simonson switched to the bane of the charging infantryman, canister. The effect of loading canister was to turn his Rodmans and Napoleons into giant shotguns hurling one-and-one-half-inch iron spheres at the bodies of the onrushing Rebels. The survivors this time took refuge in a forest to the north of the battery and Simonson ordered the cannons turned in that direction to repulse their expected attack. When it came a short time later, the 5th was ready with double canister charges. The slaughter made a horrifying spectacle as the limbs, heads, and torsos of Stevenson's troops littered the battlefield. Those who were spared being ripped apart retreated. Any who doubt the effectiveness of artillery during the Civil War should note that Simonson's six guns had held off an army of over 5,000; no mean feat.

In the meantime, Cruft and Whitaker managed to form a ragged line of infantry on either side of the battery to fend off a renewed attack, expected at any time. In the distance, however, help was on the way as Alpheus Williams' division of the Army of the Potomac veterans came into view with General Hooker at its head. As expected, the battery was again assaulted and just as it was about to be overrun on the flank, Williams' eastern veterans arrived on the scene to save the day in true Hollywood style! Arranged in several ranks, the first line would fire a volley, then drop down while the next line fired theirs, repeating over and over until the torn and bleeding rebels finally turned tail and retreated back toward their original lines.

The other Confederate unit involved in Hooker's offensive, Stewart's Division, had swung far to the right and had become separated from Stevenson's bloodied division. It moved so far right, in fact, that it had nobody to fight, and also retreated.

As the dazed Confederates were still retreating across the fields and woods toward Resaca, General Hooker told Simonson's embattled soldiers, "Every one of you are heroes" – and so they were.

Even as he wrote about the battle nearly a week later on the 20th (stationed near Kingston), Hupp expected orders to move out at any time. These must have been rather frantic times for the men of both armies. On the road to Atlanta, rest was a rare luxury.

On the 15th, Sherman ordered Hooker to attack Hood on the Confederate right. Ironically, Johnston had been contemplating having Hood do the same to Hooker, but vacillated as he concerned himself with Sweeny's attempts to cross the river into his rear. Hooker's assault was eventually repulsed, but a future president, Benjamin Harrison, leading the 70th Indiana, captured a small fort on the Rebel lines and attempted to take back the guns of a captured Georgia battery. Because of determined Confederate fire, they were unable to hold the fort, however, and had to retreat. Not to be outdone, that night they stole back into the darkened fort and made off with the guns through a hole in the wall. This valiant exploit was used in later years for political gain.

Of greater importance was the progress made by Sweeny and crew in crossing the Oostanaula on Buell's pontoon bridge on the afternoon of the

15th. When Johnston realized he was about to be flanked again, he gave up any ideas of cutting off Sherman from Snake Creek Gap and began to contemplate yet another tactical retreat. Besides, Sherman – specifically General John Logan's XV Corps of McPherson's army – had succeeded in placing cannon on a high hill west of Resaca and was pounding the railroad and its bridges across the Oostanaula river. Attacks on the Confederate right and center by Thomas' IV Corps (under Howard; including Simonson's cannoneers) and Hooker's XX Corps met with little success other than to spill more blood on both sides of the lines. Many of the dead from these futile charges were in Benjamin Harrison's heroic 70th Indiana regiment, the cannon thieves from the previous night. Despite the setbacks and bloody failures to the north and west of town, Sweeny's crossing marked the end of any hope the Confederates had of holding on. At midnight that night, the Rebels began the evacuation of Resaca, crossing the Oostanaula south toward their next appointment with their Union pursuers.

The next morning, Sherman entered Resaca, quickly repaired a bridge over the river, and sent a force out to follow Johnston's retreating troops. Rome, Georgia, was also abandoned at that time, and a force under General Jefferson C. Davis was sent there to take the town from remaining pickets and stragglers.

The next confrontations for the two main armies lay south at Cassville and Kingston. Ormond Hupp noted in his journal that he and the 5th were very much involved in chasing Johnston in that direction.

Cassville and Kingston

The IV Corps was given the honor of being placed in the vanguard of the forces pursuing Johnston's troops south from Resaca. By 1:00 P.M., they were crossing two newly repaired bridges over the Oostenaula, damaged or destroyed by the fleeing Confederates. By late in the afternoon, as they advanced south, they skirmished for some distance with Wheeler's cavalry. After dark they reached Calhoun where they camped for the night.

Hupp commented in his diary that the rebels were "retreating toward Atlanta." How far toward Atlanta was a matter of conjecture. To the south of Resaca lay the Etowah River and beyond that, to the southeast, is a pass through the mountains called Allatoona. Sherman, in moving south of Resaca, was very much in danger of overextending his supply line to Chattanooga and wanted badly to force Johnston into a major engagement in the fairly open country between Resaca and the Etowah. He guessed that Johnston would try to cross the Etowah and make a stand in the more rugged and defensible hills near Allatoona farther to the southeast. He therefore issued orders to his corps commanders to spare no time in their pursuit of Johnston, which accounted for a lack of rest for Hupp and the boys after Resaca.

For his part, Johnston initially headed for Adairsville, a little town about half way between Resaca and the Etowah where the Rebel commander had his sights on a defensible ridge and narrow valley nearby. On the morning of the 17th, Howard's IV Corps, with Simonson's Battery in tow, passed through the mostly abandoned Calhoun on their way to Adairsville. Their progress, however, was greatly impeded by Wheeler's cavalry which was serving the important function of covering the main Confederate army's retreat. Having served with many a retreating army, Wheeler was well practiced in this role, and his tactics were driving Howard to distraction, slowing the pace of the IV Corps to a crawl. Every half mile of so, Wheeler would throw up a log barricade on the road and fight it out with the advancing Union columns, then retreat to repeat the process.

Because the IV Corps was trailing a long line of supply wagons to the rear, their slow progress also impeded the progress of the other corps in their rear. Within sight of Adairsville they finally encountered a larger contingent of rebel forces apparently spoiling for a larger fight. Evening arrived, however, before any serious sparring could begin.

During the evening, Sherman brought up most of his other corps, directing Schofield and McPherson to approach Adairsville from the east and west on Johnston's flanks. He also sent General Stoneman's cavalry south to cut the rail line in Johnston's rear between Cassville and Cartersville (near the Etowah). Thomas hurried Hooker's XX Corps forward as well as Baird and Richard Johnston's divisions who had lingered for a while back at Resaca. The stage was now set to attack Johnston's forces from three sides and to cut his rear communications to Atlanta. If all his far flung army could be brought together, Sherman was in position to deliver a knock-out punch to Johnston, greatly shortening the present campaign and delivering a morale- boosting victory to the North. This accomplishment would contrast mightily with the trouble Grant was having with Lee in the Virginia "wilderness."

Johnston declined to participate in Sherman's grand designs for his premature demise. On the morning of May 18, Hupp and his blue-clad comrades awoke to find the rebel fox once again in retreat from the Union hounds. There would be no battle that day, but Johnston had a plan of his own, one that he and his associates were certain could turn the tables on Sherman. Johnston planned nothing less than to trap Sherman's army near the town of Cassville, relying on Sherman to divide his army between the roads to Cassville and Kingston (Hupp's unit moved toward the latter). His mood was also bolstered by the news that Forrest was on the way to harass Sherman's supply lines in middle Tennessee. A bloody repulse at Cassville coupled with Forrest's threat in his rear could surely nail Sherman's campaign shut.

Johnston's battle plan called for concentrating all his forces near Cassville where their combined strength would assure victory over whatever Union forces Sherman would send in that direction. After destroying Sherman's left flank at Cassville, the plan called for the Confederates to march on Kingston, where the rest of the Union army would be crushed.

On the morning of the 18th, finding the Rebels gone from Adairsville, Ormond Hupp and IV Corps marched through Adairsville toward Kingston, again forming the advance of the Union column. Sherman believed that Johnston had fled with his entire force toward Kingston, so he directed his forces there and instructed them to prepare for battle the next day if Johnston turned to challenge them. Only the IV Corps marched as far as the outskirts of Kingston by evening, although "Fighting Joe" Hooker's XX Corps managed to come within sight of Cassville where they encountered some determined Confederate skirmishers. Hooker's intelligence suggested that he was facing a substantial Rebel force near Cassville, but Sherman persisted in believing that Johnston had concentrated his forces near Kingston to the west. In view of that presumption – erroneous, as it turns out – Sherman ordered Hooker, Schofield, and McPherson to hurry over to Kingston to join with Howard's corps.

As the 19th dawned, Sherman found Kingston abandoned and finally realized that Johnston's forces were massed closer to the Etowah to the east at Cassville. He ordered the IV Corps to move from Kingston in that direction, followed by XIV Corps. Hooker was at this time pressing down the road from Adairsville from the northwest and the XIII Corps was advancing southwest toward Cassville on the Marseller's Road.

Johnston had arrayed his armies with Hardee on the left, Polk in the center, and Hood on the right. By mid morning, Hood was about to initiate the first blow against the divided Union forces when a line of Union cavalry was spotted off to his right flank. These highly unexpected intruders were Edward McCook's and George Stoneman's troopers galloping toward their objective of cutting the railroad between Cassville and the Etowah, and wholly unaware that the entire 74,000-man western Confederate army lay in their path. Their serendipitous but timely arrival, however, was enough to wholly unnerve Hood and Johnston who ordered an immediate retreat to just south of Cassville instead of an attack.

Thus, Sherman's army was spared a disaster that may well have put an end to, or significantly delayed, the Atlanta Campaign.

At around the same time, Stanley's division of the IV Corps led the Union advance on Cassville from the west. They soon spied a heavy contingent of Rebel troops massed near Two Run Creek who charged forward as if to initiate a major attack. Then, inexplicably, the butternut troops suddenly ceased their surge, reversed direction, and fell back toward Cassville. This demonstration was put on by Hardee's Corps, and was designed to buy time for a planned retreat to new lines south of Cassville precipitated by the surprise arrival of the Union cavalry. Later, Stanley's division continued to push the rebels back beyond Cassvile. That afternoon, most of the Union corps formed a battle line extending north-east and paralleling the re-formed Confederate lines to the southeast.

Late in the afternoon, Sherman ordered Captain Simonson (Stanley's chief of artillery) to commence a 40-gun artillery barrage on the rebel lines. The Confederate batteries soon fell silent under the bombardment and the Confederate situation soon turned critical as horses, men, and equipment all fell prey to the terrifying explosions that burst in the air and on the ground. After considerable argument and debate with his senior commanders, Johnston was finally convinced of the futility of maintaining his position. Before midnight he ordered a withdrawal toward the Etowah. Simonson's battery, combined with several others, had succeeded in driving Johnston closer to Atlanta. Private Hupp described the action at Cassville thus:

> Our lines were formed at once and at 1 p. m. we advanced driving them 1½ miles with considerable opposition: but no general engagement: darkness closed the scene and gave way to the ambulances which scattered themselves over the field picking up the wounded and dead.
>
> It is hard to name any accurate no. we have lost so far: probably 400 would be too low an estimate.
>
> It is generally believed the great battle will come off a few miles in advance of this place, as their men are getting tired of running.

Sherman, by contrast, had been convinced for some time that Johnston would not give him a fight any time soon; that he would retire beyond the Etowah, maybe in the high country between there and the Chattahooche. Were it not for his cavalry blundering smack into the Confederate right flank he would most certainly have found out differently on May 19. As things stood now, however, it was time for another chase. As Johnston's forces crossed the Etowah south of Cartersville, Sherman's forces now stood only fifty miles from Atlanta.

Dallas

On the 23rd, Sherman's legions marched again after a brief respite to carry the wounded and other ineffectives to the rear, receive new recruits (many from Hupp's home state of Indiana), and to resupply an army that would soon be leaving its rail lifeline back north. The latter situation would inevitably result in foraging by the men, both officially sanctioned and otherwise. Sherman and Thomas' edicts barring unauthorized scavenging of food and souvenirs, and inordinate vandalism went unheeded by many of the troops who knew that they would probably escape punishment by junior officers in any case. The temptation to carry off a chicken or pig, or even to butcher a cow to supplement the camp bill of fare was simply too great to worry about edicts, particularly when the alternative was hardtack and water, or worse.

IV Corps and Thomas crossed the river at Gillem's bridge near Kingston and headed toward the next objective, the town of Dallas. From there they intended to proceed to Allatoona, a railroad station village near a strategic pass of the same name through the high ridge to the south. Sherman's other corps crossed the Etowah in their own time, a process that did not go unnoticed in the Confederate camp at Allatoona. Certain that, based on past behavior, Sherman would march on Dallas, Johnston ordered Hardee and Polk in that direction to cut him off. Sherman, as usual, was confident that Johnston would make a stand farther south, perhaps at Marietta. On the 24th, Hooker's corps reached Burnt Hickory, a small village only 7 miles north of Dallas, with other elements of the Army of the Cumberland pulling up the rear. Sherman's army camped in this area for the night and, in spite of intelligence from a captured rebel courier indicating that most of Johnston's army was moving toward Dallas, Sherman ordered a march past that town in the morning.

By the evening of the 24th, it was obvious to Johnston that Sherman was planning to flank him again by moving his troops around to the west. Realizing that Sherman's goal was probably Marietta to the east, Johnston now also ordered Hood to Dallas where the Confederate line was formed the next morning across the Marietta road just east of town. The rebel line extended from Hood's position near a log Methodist church called New Hope Church northeast of Dallas, with Polk in the center and Hardee holding the left flank. Here they intended to make a determined stand although many of the rebel soldiers were feeling cynical and demoralized after their recent retreat at Cassville. They needn't have worried, however, for they were about to do battle for real this time. The battle that was to come is now variously known as the Battle of New Hope Church, Pumpkin Vine Creek, Burnt Hickory, or Dallas. By whatever name, it spelled trouble and frustration for Sherman whose flanking movement was soon halted in short order.

The shooting started on the morning of the 25th. Hooker, in advance of the rest of the Army of the Cumberland, led his troops across a bridge over Pumpkin Vine Creek and marched toward Dallas. Earlier, Hooker had helped save this bridge from being burned by Confederates, an act attributed – erroneously – to McPherson by Pvt. Hupp. After crossing this bridge, Hooker and General Geary (2nd division) came to a fork in the road and decided to split their forces along the two roads, assuming they both led to Dallas. Only one of these roads did, in fact, lead to Dallas. And the Union troops marching along this road, Geary and Dan Butterfield's (3rd) divisions, soon met with heavy resistance from Rebel skirmishers. They had blundered into range of Hood's troops (A. P. Stewart's Division) dug in around New Hope Church and, to add to their woes, they found that they were isolated from the rest of the Army of the Cumberland who was marching east along a road that carried them ever farther from their imperiled comrades.

By 2:00 P.M., Hooker and Thomas were painfully aware of the predicament of Geary's troops (Geary himself was not with them; he had gone with Hooker on the "spurious" road). Word was soon sent back to Howard and IV corps to move up in support. By that time Geary's division was under full attack by Hood, although by late afternoon they were finally reinforced by Butterfield and Alpheus Williams' (1st) divisions. Hupp described the situation from his vantage point (recorded on May 29):

> The enemy has made a stand: the 20th corps (Hooker's) engaged the enemy on the 25: had a brisk fight and lost heavy as the enemy had great advantages.
>
> Our corps was got in position at 11 p. m., next morning [26th] the battery was taken along the lines to the left 1½ mi. where we went in position which we held 2 hrs., at which time were relieved by Bridges' Batt. Our Howitzers were then sent to reserve: our section then moved ½ mi. farther to the left in Gross's brigade where a cross fire was opened on us, compelling us to keep silent, the sharp shooters kept a continual pecking at us until darkness closed the scene of action.

> We were then marched back to the Batt.: on the following day [27th], the Co. was ordered to a close support at 8 a. m., but owing to the sharpshooters' fire were soon taken back out of their range as we were not wanted on the line: in the afternoon of the same day Cap. took the cannoniers [sic] to a point on the line but a short distance from the enemy's works for the purpose of fortifying for the guns: before 2 hrs. had passed had 1, Jake Kertz [Kurtz] shot dead and 1 wounded both with the same ball.

This passage illustrates the danger that artillerists faced from sharpshooters – specially trained marksmen (snipers) usually armed with deadly accurate rifles sporting precision sights and, rarely, primitive telescopic sights. Their mission was to pick off officers or other officials, or generally to harass and terrorize whatever troops happened to lie before them. Artillerymen, most of whom were virtually unarmed as they worked around their guns, were favorite targets of sharpshooters. Jacob Kurtz, mentioned above as one of their victims, was one of the soldiers who gave critical aid and comfort to Ormond Hupp after his wounding at Perryville (see Chapt. 4).

All through the afternoon near New Hope Church, Hooker's men (particularly Williams' division) took a vicious pounding. Stewart's forces had the advantage of cover (trees and tombstones near the church, and entrenchments) and could open up on Williams' soldiers with sixteen cannons placed on the forward lines. The Confederates also had the foresight to cut the brush away from their front, providing a clear view of fire for both marksmen and artillerymen.

The massed Union forces repeatedly assaulted the front of the Rebel line which greeted them with bursting shells, canister, and withering musket fire. By nightfall, amidst a drenching thunderstorm, the frustrated Union troops began to fall back and the Confederates to advance. As the fighting finally ended with the coming darkness, Hood's forces were the obvious victors; Hooker's troops, in spite of holding a numerical advantage over the rebels, had been convincingly repulsed at a cost of over 1,800 casualties. An angry Sherman blamed the results on Hooker, whom he despised, and at least in part on George Thomas, for delaying their attack while waiting for reinforcements. But at least part of the blame lay on the commanding general's shoulders, he who could not shake the conviction that Johnston would surely not fight at Dallas. Now, with no room to doubt the determination and ability of the Confederates to hold him at bay at this spot north of the Chattahoochee, Sherman ordered up the rest of his forces for a major battle the next day.

Most of the 26th, however, was spent by both sides digging entrenchments and building earthworks in the sweltering heat, humidity, and all-pervasive mud. The soldiers dubbed the place "Hell-Hole", a name befitting of such a dank and miserable swamp. The Civil War brought many refinements to warfare, one of which was the idea of the fortified trench. Although such works had been in use before in both theaters, the Atlanta campaign saw their use expand to routine practice. Although the time-honored practice of forming lines of marching men was not wholly abandoned during the campaign, the construction of "works" became an integral part of battlefield tactics. This means of troop deployment presaged the "trench warfare" of World War I.

On the 27th, the combined batteries of Hooker, Howard, and Schofield were brought up for a major bombardment of the Rebel lines. Of course, the 5th Indiana was a part of this call up, and they took their place at the front lines with Stanley's division in the afternoon, replacing Thomas Wood's division which was ordered to lead a planned attack on the Confederate right. Hupp noted that his battery had previously been deployed in a forward position early in the morning, but had then been called back in reserve. During both periods at the front, the battery was engaged in "softening up" the Confederate lines with concentrated artillery fire, but the rebel batteries' return fire was at least as effective as the Union gunners'. As Hupp observed, rebel sharpshooters also made things "hot" for anyone lingering at the front, as attested by J. Kertz' demise in the afternoon. The Union bombardment of Rebel entrenchments was meant as a prelude to a flank attack Sherman planned for the Confederate right. He hoped that by crushing the east side of the rebel line he could cut Johnston off from his rail supply line.

The attack on the Confederate right flank, now manned by Pat Cleburne's Division (2 miles northeast of New Hope Church at Pickett's Mill), got underway at about 4:30 that afternoon. It was led by Wood's Division (IV Corps; Cumberland) with Hazen's brigade in the advance. Sherman hoped that by breaking the Confederate right he could eventually move on their rail supply line to Atlanta, but the attack was doomed to failure from the beginning. Because of confusion in the dense forests and underbrush and delays in deploying supporting brigades, Hazen was repulsed with numerous casualties by Cleburne's well-entrenched infantry supported by Hotchkiss' battery. After Hazen fell back, he was replaced by Gibson's brigade which, by 6:00 P.M., had met the same fate. A third brigade was eventually sent in (Knefler) to hold the Rebels in check while the many wounded and dead could be removed where they were pinned down and otherwise massed before the Confederate line. The affair at Pickett's Mill added another 1,600 casualties to Sherman's mounting list. By this time, Sherman had had all he could stomach at Hell-Hole and made the decision to vacate Dallas.

But the fighting did not cease during this withdrawal – far from it. On the morning of the 28th, Johnston decided to attack the Union lines near the right flank but then withdrew after realizing he was attacking a numerically superior Union force. From the 28th to the 31st, the two sides exchanged deadly fire by sharpshooters and cannon, with much time spent reinforcing and otherwise embellishing their works and rifle pits. The effect was like mutual siege warfare, with tree-top snipers picking off anyone foolish enough to ventured from their holes. Horses, cannoneers, and officers made tempting targets.

Hupp recorded these observations which capture the flavor of those awful days and nights in the Georgia "wilderness."

> Having completed a temporary protection for the cannoniers [sic] against sharpshooters, the guns were taken out at 6 p. m. and opened fire at once which was doubly returned by sharpshooters which lasted till darkness prevailed: our loss was 1, Gabe Suhart, shot dead and 1 horse: 8 withdrew 4 guns, leaving two howitzers in possession.
>
> Great addition was made to our works by the Pioneers [military engineers] who worked diligently all night: next day (Sunday 29th) the 2 guns remained in possession without opening fire, the other 4 laying off the line about 40 rds.
>
> Heavy skirmishing all along the line, our forces paying dearly for the little advance made in the line.
>
> Mond. p. m. our section went into position: had just laid down for a few hours sleep when the enemy made a 11 o'clock charge: the brasia lasted but ½ hr., finding they could make nothing, retreated to their holes and quiet prevailed the remainder of the night.

Sherman's decision to pull out his troops was prompted primarily by Johnston's determined resistance at New Hope Church and Pickett's Mill. But a secondary factor, of equally serious dimensions, also convinced him to move – hunger. Leaving his rail supply line had proved a costly mistake, as the northwest Georgia countryside failed to meet the needs of his enormous army. On the 28th, his army began the slow and arduous pullout to the northeast. McPherson's troops were ordered to leave the New Hope Church area under cover of darkness for Ackworth on the Western and Atlantic railroad. But before they had time to execute the order, they were attacked and forced to do battle again.

McPherson occupied the Union left and Johnston had sent Hood there to try to flank him. Finding that the Union troops had moved back to the north bank of Pumpkin Vine Creek and had entrenched, Hood pulled back and canceled the attack. Instead, Johnston gave orders to attack the Union right, east of Dallas. At 3:00 P.M. on the 28th, the Confederate attack was launched, led by Bate's Division of Hardee's Corps. The Federals, led by General Logan, brought up reinforcements and were able to beat back the rebel troops leaving Johnston with his only defeat in the Dallas area – and Sherman's only victory. The Union commander later claimed to have emerged victorious, although in truth Johnston bested him at Dallas.

In spite of intense harassment, Sherman's troops finally succeeded in slogging their way through the muck and tangle east toward the Western and Atlantic railroad, reaching the town that was to become their temporary base, Ackworth. On June 1, Federal Cavalry took over Allatoona Pass, left unguarded by the Rebels, and by June 6 Sherman's army began staggering into Ackworth.

During this Union pull back, Hupp's battery was sent back to Kingston where they helped guard the supply trains from Confederate cavalry. The following passage, written after his company had left Kingston to join up with IV Corps, reflects the importance of the rail line for supplying this huge army, and suggests that Hupp was personally involved in fighting off Confederate skirmishers (probably cavalry).

> The [rail] cars ran through to Etawa [Etowah River] on Tuesday: the place was occupied by McPherson on Monday.
>
> The battery is in good fighting condition: forage has been rather scarce for the past wk. as well as rations, but the heavy trains which arrived yesterday will furnish ample supplies for some time and as the cars are up with the army there will be no danger of our starving: weather still continues lowery with now and then a shower.
>
> Charley and I have been busy all forenoon fighting Gray Backs: came off victorious and hope to remain masters of the field during the remainder of the campaign.

For the duration of the Atlanta Campaign, Sherman would not forget the lesson of Dallas. From that point on, he maintained close contact with

Figure 7-1 – Union works at the foot of Kenesaw Mountain (from A Photographic History of the Civil War in Ten Volumes, *vol. 3, p. 117).*

the rail line. He did so out of necessity, but that task was made less risky by Forrest's decision not to invade central Tennessee. With that major threat to his rear communications eliminated, Sherman was able to concentrate the majority of his troops for his principal objective, the taking of Atlanta. At Ackworth, he was less than thirty miles from his prize.

Pine Hill to Kenesaw Mountain

With the railroad bridge over the Etowah finally repaired, the supply trains could pour south to feed Sherman's hungry invaders. At Ackworth he made preparations for the next phase of operations. Before moving out, Sherman was reinforced by XVII Corps late of Cairo, Illinois, and led by General Francis Blair whose brother, Montgomery, was Lincoln's postmaster general. Troop strength still favored Sherman over Johnston at a 3:2 ratio, although Johnston persisted in regarding the odds as much worse, forcing him to cling tenaciously to a defensive strategy. Accordingly, in early June he now occupied a series of prominent heights northwest of Marietta, which today is a northwestern suburb of Atlanta. This move was perceived in Richmond as a clear retreat, one of a long progression of retreats that left Atlanta ever more vulnerable. Johnston, however, was unmoved by the entreaties of Bragg and others that he launch an offensive.

The hills and "mountains" on which Johnston decided to build his entrenchments form an arching line convex toward Ackworth extending from Brush Mountain to the north, bulging north to Pine Hill (also called Pine Mountain or Pine Top), and then southwest to Lost Mountain. Southeast of this line is Kenesaw Mountain, just north of Marietta, and it was there that Sherman expected to meet the most resistance. He was right about that, but the rebels also threw a few punches at him before he arrived at Kenesaw. Between the time Sherman moved out of Ackworth on the 10th and the climactic Battle of Kenesaw Mountain, his forces would engage in a whole series of battles and skirmishes, the results of which mostly favoring the Union side.

The 5th Indiana Light Artillery was heavily engaged in many actions during the June campaigns against Johnston's mountain line, but one action stands out among all the rest: Pine Hill. Pine Hill was the forward outpost of the Confederate line; in fact, it was too far forward as they were to discover. By the 14th, both Palmer's XIV Corps and Howard's IV Corps had made their way around the eastern base of the hill threatening to surround the Confederates of Bate's Division entrenced on the hill from the rest of Hardee's Corps. Sherman arrived on the scene that morning and, while inspecting the lines with Howard, noted a group of three Confederate generals at the crest of the hill peering at the Union lines with binoculars. They were Joe Johnston, William J. Hardee (one of whose divisions occupied the vulnerable salient), and Leonidas Polk, the Episcopal bishop. Hardee had asked Johnston to the hill to convince him to abandon the hill in the face of a possible Union envelopment, and Polk came to inspect his own newly established line on Brush Mountain, within easy view of Pine Hill.

Upon spying the three generals peering down on his lines from the hill, Sherman exclaimed to Oliver Howard, "How saucy they are!", and ordered him to direct some artillery fire their way to teach them some manners. Although the three Confederate generals had been warned not to stand where their appearance would draw fire, they persisted in their reconnaissance until the morning was abruptly shattered by an explosion of cannon fire from below. Howard had obeyed Sherman's order by ordering Captain Peter Simonson, for some time now Stanley's Chief of Artillery, to direct the nearby 5th Indiana Light Artillery to fire some volleys at the impetuous rebel officers. The initial shot caused Hardee and Johnston to flee from their observation post for cover. Polk, however, refusing to be intimidated, walked slowly from the precipice, too slowly as it turns out. According to official reports – and legend – the second shot fired by one of the 5th's 3 inch Rodman rifled guns struck General

Leonidas Polk in the left side, continued at an angle to the right tearing out his lungs and heart and hideously mangling both arms. Johnston and Hardee viewed his body in utter shock and horror. Johnston cried, "We have lost much! I would rather anything but this."

If, in fact, it was a shell from the 5th Indiana that dispatched Bishop Polk to his Maker, Hupp's comrades could be excused for feeling some satisfaction in having avenged the thrashing dealt them at Perryville. For it was Polk's forces who ultimately overran their positions on the Union left, and it was one of Polk's batteries (Calvert's of Cleburne's Brigade) who fired the shell that would provide Private Hupp an unplanned furlough in New Albany. But did the 5th fire the shot that ended the life and career of Jefferson Davis' personal friend, Leonidas Polk?

Most popular accounts of the battle do point to the 5th Indiana as the battery that fired the fatal shot. They do so because the overwhelming majority of official reports of the battle give the honor to Hupp's battery. But at least two other batteries have also laid claim to the feat. In his lengthy summary report to the Adjutant General of XX Corps dated September 15, 1864, General John W. Geary gives the credit to Captain McGill's Battery. Geary claims to have given the order for the artillery barrage himself:

> I noticed a group of rebel officers collected near some tents near the summit; calling Captain McGill's attention to it, I directed him to bring his battery to bear on the spot. The shells struck in the midst of and around the group, causing evident consternation among them and their immediate retreat. Prisoners afterward taken point out that as the spot where Lieutenant-General Polk was killed.

Another battery given credit for the fatal shot is Captain Hubert Dilger of Battery I, 1st Ohio Light Artillery. His role in the affair was championed by Shelby Foote in Volume 3 (*Red River to Appomattox*; p. 355-356) of his excellent Civil War trilogy. Foote gives no reference for this claim, although no doubt he must have had good reason to propose it. On the other hand, the *Official Records* shows no connection between Dilger and Polk's death.

Typical of reports linking the 5th Indiana Battery to Polk's demise is this one penned by Brigadier General Walter C. Whitaker, 2nd Brigade, IV Corps in his Report of Operations May 3-June 30:

> On the 14th a shell from the Fifth Indiana Battery, command-

Figure 7-2 – Union batteries (including the 5th Indiana) pound Pine Hill where Confederate General Leonidas Polk was killed by an artillery shell June 14, 1864. (Cannan, 1991)

> ed by Lieutenant Morrison, fired from a 3-inch Rodman gun, from the section commanded by Lieutenant Ellison, killed Lieutenant-General Polk of the rebel army, who in company with Generals Johnston and Hardee, was surveying our lines from Pine Mountain.

Brigadier General William Grose (3rd Brigade, 1st Division, IV Corps) wrote in his September 5 report:

> . . . advanced upon the mountain early on the morning of June 14. On this mountain is where Bishop Polk, general of the rebel army, fell by a shot from the Fifth Indiana Artillery, Captain Simonson. The battery was in position at the front and right of my lines.

General George H. Thomas in his summary report of the Atlanta Campaign wrote:

> . . . we learned subsequently, the second shot fired from a rifled section of the Fifth Indiana Battery exploded in a group

> of rebel generals, killing Lieut. Gen. Leonidas Polk. Early the morning of the 15th it was found the enemy had abandoned his works on Pine Top.

In addition to the above official reports, Hupp's diary makes reference to Polk's death: "The second volley fired from our section yesterday is said to have killed L. G. Polk . . ."

Obvious from the many reports of the "Polk incident" is the fact that more than one battery participated in harassing the three Confederate generals on Pine Hill on June 14th. Simonson, McGill, Dilger, or someone else may have fired the fatal shot; we can never know for sure. By the sheer weight of the many reports pointing to the 5th Indiana, coupled with Hupp's assertion, that particular company probably deserves credit for the deed. On the other hand, this may demonstrate how battlefield rumor can evolve into historical "fact."

On June 15, the day General Polk was buried in Atlanta, Union forces surveyed Pine Hill to find the Confederates, now temporarily under General William Loring, had withdrawn. Tacked to a tree by one of the men of Bate's Division at the crest of "Pine Top" was a note reading, "You damned Yankee sons of bitches have killed our old general Polk."

On this same day, Sherman issued orders to McPherson to threaten the Confederate right at Kenesaw, and for Schofield to attack the left at a place called Gilgal Church and to threaten Lost Mountain. Thomas was to attack the center between Pine Hill and Kenesaw Mountain. He moved up his troops but found the rebels well entrenched and fortified along a ridge between Marietta and Gilgal Church. Although Thomas was under orders from Sherman to break through the Confederate center, he decided to form an entrenched line west of the rebel works after assessing their strength as formidable.

The next morning, the 16th, Thomas ordered his batteries to pound the Confederate lines. During the bombardment Captain Simonson, in an effort to get a better view of the rebel works, crawled forward toward the skirmish line hidden behind a log he rolled ahead of himself. Suddenly the log stopped rolling and Simonson lay motionless, felled by a rebel sharpshooter who fired three shots before hitting him squarely in the head. Hupp's diary entry recorded the tragic event:

> . . . our corps (the 4th) lost many in killed and wounded on the 17th: Capt. Simmons [Simonson] was killed with a musket ball while on the skirmish line overseeing works that were

> being constructed for our battery: his loss is greatly felt with us boys as he has been to us as a father since we enlisted.

In his summary report for May 3-July 26, General Stanley wrote this tribute to Simonson:

> While laying out a position for a battery this day, Capt. Peter Simonson, Fifth Indiana Battery, chief of artillery, was instantly killed by a sharpshooter. This was an irreparable loss to the division. I have not in my military experience met with an officer who was the equal of this one in energy, efficiency, and ingenuity in the handling of artillery. He never missed an opportunity and allowed no difficulties to deter him from putting in his batteries in every position that he could prove annoying or destructive to the enemy.

Over the next few days, the Union armies continued a slow advance as Johnston's legions retreated, entrenched, and then retreated some more. On the 17th, the Confederate left and right flanks dissolved and Thomas' army in the center drove the rebels in their front back beyond Noyes Creek, about 2½ miles southeast of Pine Hill. Stanley's Division was in reserve as the enemy works were bombarded by forward artillery. A later attack by Wood proved unnecessary as Walker's Division had already retreated from their red clay trenches. Sherman would later criticize Thomas' troops for not having swept forward with more vigor, as he was anxious to break through to the rebel rear beyond Marietta. However, these Union soldiers were wary of charging headlong into Confederate entrenchments, remembering the results of similar assaults around Dallas. By the 19th, amidst unrelenting rain, Johnston was backed up and his line contracted to the last real high ground between the Union lines and Atlanta, Kenesaw Mountain. There the Union troops established entrenchments after severe skirmishing with the rebels. On the 20th, Ormond Hupp wrote:

> 8 a. m. have not taken position yet: boys are scattered around through the batt. mostly sheltered behind some object to turn the bullets: before us lies a large mountain covered with Rebels and Reb. Art, which it is thought will be tried today: if it should, the loss of life will undoubtedly be great.

The last line was prophetic; after much exchange of artillery fire,

Figure 7-3 – Confederate defenses with picket fenses and chevaux-de-Frise *(crossed sharpened stakes) (from* A Photographic History of the Civil War in Ten Volumes, *vol. 5, p. 199).*

sharpshooter's balls, and musketry, Sherman finally tired of trying to dislodge the Confederates by attrition. He resorted to the favorite tactic of frustrated generals, the frontal attack. Like Picket's Charge and numerous assaults before it, this one would add more widows and orphans to the already burgeoning ranks on both sides.

From the point of view of the Confederates, Kenesaw Mountain was their last and best hope of stalling Sherman's drive toward Atlanta. As in times before, they would win the great battle, but would fail to stop Sherman. In the east, however, Lee had stopped Grant's assault on Petersburg, inflicting staggering losses on the veteran Federal troops. Although Sherman had his problems with Johnston, Grant never won a single battle against Lee.

For the 5th Indiana and the rest of Whitaker's brigade, the time between their arrival in the shadow of Kenesaw (actually three peaks descending in elevation from N.E. to S.W.; Big Kenesaw, Little Kenesaw, and Pigeon Hill) and the climactic battle was mostly spent in minor skirmishing, maneuvering, and laying low behind earth works from enemy sharpshooters.

This brigade and the rest of Stanley's division operated west of the low hills extending southwest from Pigeon Hill, where the rebels were well entrenched in the heavy red clay. On the 20th, however, they saw heavy action as they fought in the pouring rain to retake some hills, previously captured by the rebels. The battle, finally won by Stanley's troops, continued into the next day.

In his diary, Hupp mentions "Ewell" as being in command of the Confederates. In fact, General Richard S. Ewell was badly wounded and rendered unfit for field service while fighting Grant at Spotsylvania Court House in May. The troops facing Hupp and the boys at the Confederate center belonged to Hardee's Corps. However, Hupp did predict that the site of the "decisive battle" was close at hand.

On the 26th of June, frustrated by failed attempts to flank Johnston, particularly by Hooker on the Confederate left, Sheridan decided the time had come for a frontal assault, culminated by the taking of Marietta and a crossing of the Chattahoochee. This river was the last appreciable natural barrier between Sheridan and Atlanta. He ordered McPherson to attack around the southern flank of Kenesaw Mountain (Pigeon Hill), and gave Schofield the relatively easy task of keeping the rebels busy on their (Confederate) extreme left in the hope that Johnston would move troops from his center to counter the threat. Thomas was to attempt a breakout south of McPherson in the heavily entrenched low hills southeast of Noyes Creek. The attack, to commence the next morning, would be led by Newton's division with Stanley in reserve.

Today, the area where Stanley's division assembled for the "decisive battle" is a housing subdivision within the city limits of Marietta. To this day, residents of Marietta occasionally find cannon balls and shell fragments in wooded areas of the city.

At 9:00 A.M. on the 27th, the battle commenced with an artillery barrage, bugles blaring, and bands playing, the usual obligatory fanfare preceding most Civil War battles. Newton's ranks with Davis on his right surged forward and quickly overran the Confederate pickets. But from there the situation quickly soured for the Federal troops. The gray troops were well concealed behind their log-reinforced trenches fronted in many areas by tanglefoot traps and rows of crisscrossed pointed stakes called *chevaux-de-frise*. Some were concealed behind, or lay above, nearly vertical walls of rock. Advancing Union columns on all fronts were mowed down by musket fire and smashed by exploding cannon shells, with hand-to-hand combat at the few spots where the blue soldiers were able to mount the rebel parapets.

By afternoon, the results from north (Logan's assault) to south (Davis and Newton) were the same; the confederates had scored a resounding – and very predictable – victory and had inflicted massive casualties on the

Union brigades. Over 3,000 Federals died or were seriously wounded (compared to about 700 for Johnston) in the futile assault, including the devastating loss of Charles Harker and Dan McCook, both mortally wounded as they tried to rally their bloodied troops. It so happened that Thomas hit the Confederate lines where some of Johnston's best and most tenacious veteran troops were waiting, the divisions of Cleburne and Cheatham (the hills in the area were subsequently named after the latter). General Stanley also lost another chief of artillery, the officer who replaced Simonson in that capacity, Captain McDowell of the Independent Pennsylvania Battery. Whitaker's brigade saw no action in the assault owing to the rapid repulse that followed the initial assault. Rather than add even more meat to the grinder, reserve troops were held back from the futile struggle.

Obviously, this frontal attack was not one of Sherman's greatest moments, but some good news finally trickled in. It was from Schofield who had made rather surprising progress in pushing back the Confederates holding their extreme left all the way to a point overlooking the Chattahoochee River. This was all the more remarkable because his mission was to carry out a mere diversionary feint. After much fretting about the consequences of moving south around Johnston (and possibly severing Sherman's rail communications to the north), Sherman decided on a flanking strategy. In retrospect this should have been his original plan, as attested by the hundreds who died at "Cheatham's Hill" during the ill-fated charge that morning. Hupp's diary provides an enlightening description of the events at Kenesaw (see pages 100-102).

Over the next few days, after the battle at Kenesaw, truces were called to bury the dead rotting in the hot Georgia sun, and McPherson was resupplied by rail from Allatoona with provisions for the next phase of the campaign. McPherson was to pull out of line on the north and march south around the Union lines to join Schofield in a flank attack of Johnston's left. From the tree tops, observers could easily see the church spires of Atlanta seventeen miles to the southeast. Sherman's objective was now only a day's march away.

The Chattahoochee and the Siege of Atlanta

On the 3rd of July, the Union troops awoke in the morning to find that the Confederates had withdrawn once again, this time to the Methodist Camp at Smyrna. Later in the morning, the first Federal troops marched into the nearly abandoned Marietta, a year to the day after the Federal victories at Gettysburg and Vicksburg. The troops found the town much to their liking, relatively neat and clean in spite of the recent battles to the west, with fine old mansions and well kept businesses. Despite officer's warnings to the contrary, many of these troops could not resist vandalizing and looting the abandoned dwellings.

Just down the road in Atlanta, rogue Confederate soldiers were engaged in similar activities against their own people, a situation that caused many a citizen to actually welcome the idea of Union occupation. Others, sensing that the end was near, began packing their belongings on wagons and rail cars for the trip to Macon or other safe points. As time progressed the choice of havens gradually narrowed, particularly in the fall after Sherman pushed beyond Atlanta toward the Carolinas.

On the 4th, Stanley's division, in pursuit of Johnston, encountered a strong rebel line of rifle pits ("Johnny's golpher holes," as Hupp called them) supported by artillery just east of the railroad near Ruff's Station (also known as "Ruff's Mill"). They lost about 100 men in the ensuing battle to unseat the entrenched "graybacks." Private Hupp's account of the battle shows that the 5th Indiana Battery was heavily involved in the fighting, using two rifled guns recently exchanged for their worn out and damaged Rodmans at Big Shanty.

On the 5th, the Rebels fled toward the Chattahoochee with IV Corps in pursuit using the rail line for transportation. They reached Pace's Ferry on the Chattahoochee that day where Hupp and the boys went into camp until the 10th, occasionally shelling the rebels on the other side to alert them of their presence. During that time, Johnston again decided to retreat back toward Atlanta, even though to do so meant that he was virtually admitting that the city could not be defended. In abandoning first the heights of Kenesaw and now the rain swollen Chattahoochee, he was left with only Peach Tree Creek, an eastern tributary of the Chattahoochee, as a natural obstacle to Sherman's advance.

At the Chattahoochee, the Confederates, under the supervision of General Francis Shoup, had constructed earthworks, centered on the railroad bridge, with extensive log palisades and guard towers designed for extended resistance against a Federal crossing. Shoup and Johnston hoped that Sherman could be delayed at these works long enough for Stephen Lee to send Forrest from Mississippi to harass Sherman's northern supply lines. Of course, this move depended on the inclinations of President Davis who had to balance the situation of the threatened Confederate forces in Mississippi with the tenuous situation in Georgia. Ultimately, Davis balked at sending any aid to Johnston, who characteristically took a gloomy view of his prospects and retreated yet again. He did so in the face of Federal crossings of the river in the north where he had failed to post adequate pickets.

Figure 7-4 – Bank destroyed by Sherman. He concentrated on demolishing financial and government building, sparing most civilian buildings like those shown (from A Photographic History of the Civil War in Ten Volumes, *vol. 3, p. 215).*

By July 8, elements of Schofield's command (Cox's division) had forded the river just upstream from Soap Creek where a hastily constructed pontoon bridge later allowed the passage of more Union troops, among them, Ormond Hupp and company.

On the 9th, Garrard was successful at fording the river near Roswell. The Union crossing of the Chattahoochee had been effected with a minimum of skirmishing and little bloodshed. But for Johnston, it was reason enough to "skedaddle" and he established his new headquarters at the Dexter Niles house, only 3 miles from downtown Atlanta. In the Richmond "White House," this was deemed one skedaddle too many. Johnston's further command of the Army of Tennessee now fell under administrative review. Neither his foes nor his supporters would be surprised at the outcome.

This juncture in the history of the war deserves some reflection. As Johnston lay pressed up against the gates of Atlanta, the progress of the war on most other fronts clearly favored the Confederates in the summer of 1864. Conventional wisdom cites Gettysburg as the "high watermark" of the Confederacy, where a victory may have saved the Southern cause, and a defeat would have crushed any hope of salvation. But one year after

Meade defeated Lee (with skill, and no short supply of luck), the South was anything but defeated.

During the first half of 1864, Lee was inflicting staggering losses against Grant in the Wilderness, Cold Harbor, and Petersburg. Forrest continued his brilliant maulings of invading Federal armies in Mississippi, and the U.S. capital itself had been threatened by a bold invasion of Maryland by General Jubal Early. Democrats were jubilant with the prospects that the bad war news and resulting drop in Northern morale would destroy the Republican "war party." The only front where the South was clearly losing ground was northwest Georgia, and Johnston, with his constant retreats, seemed to Davis quite willing and able to give up Atlanta to Sherman. Consequently, on July 17, Johnston relinquished command to John Bell Hood, whose daring (or foolhardy?) management of the Army of Tennessee eventually led to the inevitable fall of Atlanta, and the near total collapse of a once great army. Had Johnston made better use of his own cavalry to cut Sherman's supply lines, or attacked at Cassville instead of breaking off the assault, or held out longer at Kenesaw and the Chattahoochee, we Yankees might now need a passport to visit Atlanta.

It was not long before Sherman discovered the difference between Hood's style of command and Johnston's. Hood's temperament, however, was not unknown to the Union side; both McPherson and Schofield had been his classmates at West Point. Thomas had commanded him before the war in Texas. These Union generals were fully aware of his aggressive style and impatience with the defensive tactics favored by Johnston. Shortly before Johnston's sacking in favor of Hood, Sherman had decided to depart from his usual tactic of attempting to flank the Confederates to his right, but wheeled his armies to the left instead. His goal was to sever the rail line entering the city from Decatur on the east, possibly break the Confederate lines with the help of artillery, and enter the city.

On the July 17, Sherman set his army in motion, moving McPherson to the far left to cover the Georgia Railroad near Decatur, with Schofield to his right. Thomas moved down to Peach Tree Creek where he commenced to cross on the 19th. This deployment divided the Union army with a wide 2-mile gap between Thomas and Schofield, a development that did not go unnoticed by the new rebel commander. Hood recognized this as a chance to defeat Sherman's divided army in detail before it had a chance to reunite. Thomas' forced moving across the creek from the north would be attacked by Hardee and A. P. Stewart (Polk's permanent replacement). General Ben Cheatham, with the help of some Georgia Militia and

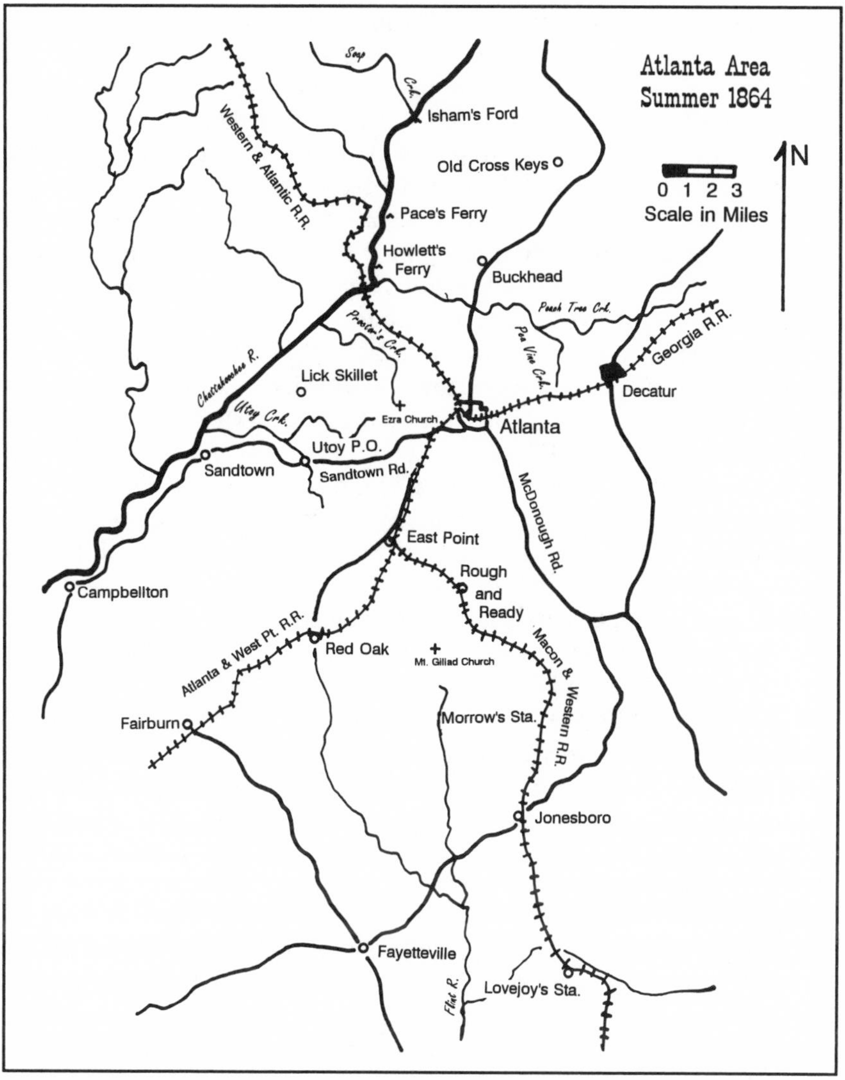

Wheeler's cavalry, was to attack Schofield and McPherson on the Confederate right.

At 3:00 P.M. on July 20, Hood sent Stewart and Hardee north after Thomas in what is now known as the Battle of Peach Tree Creek, or "Hood's First Sortie." There were four of these "sorties," and they represented a wholly new and aggressive style of fighting for the Confederates; from henceforth, Hood intended to attack the invaders with unmitigated fury whenever he smelled an opportunity.

Ormond Hupp and the 5th Indiana Battery were, of course, with Thomas' army about to be attacked from the south. He notes in his journal that they were attacked on the 20th and that his company was in the vanguard with the forward skirmishers. His description of events suggests that he was positioned near the left flank which would mean that the 5th was engaged primarily with Hardee's troops.

Note that on the 21st, the 5th Indiana fired its first shots into the city of Atlanta, from its rifled Rodman guns. This should indicate how close Sherman's army was now positioned relative to the prize of his campaign. All troops were now well within the modern city limits of greater Atlanta.

Hood's First Sortie ended in a repulse as the "Rock of Chickamauga" again stood firm against the onslaught by Hardee and Stewart's charging rebels. Cheatham was similarly thwarted after a day of hard fighting on the Confederate right. Hood's "Second Sortie" was launched two days later (also called the "Battle of Atlanta"), and although it too was repulsed, the consequences for the Union military leadership was as devastating, as it was tragic. For it was during Hood's second furious attack on the blue invaders that the army and the nation lost one of its finest leaders and greatest gentlemen, General James B. McPherson.

Hood's plan involved striking McPherson's left flank, which had been left "in the air" during his continued march southeast, past the Georgia Railroad tracks. Wheeler's cavalry would also ride into Decatur down those tracks to the northeast and raid McPherson's considerable supply train parked in the town center. Hood modeled his attack on the exposed Union flank on Lee and Jackson's brilliantly successful tactic at Chancellorsville (May 1-4). There, after a long night march, Jackson's troops attacked and routed Oliver Howard's corps on Hooker's exposed right flank.

In the present battle, Hood sent Hardee beyond the defenses of Atlanta (where his army was now entrenched) on a looping path south, then east and finally north to catch McPherson unawares on his left flank. Stewart and Cheatham were to keep Thomas and Schofield busy from their entrenchments on the north and east sides of the city, to prevent them from sending reinforcements to the beleaguered left. This part of the battle was recorded in Pvt. Hupp's diary.

This second major engagement within sight of Atlanta, like the first, eventually went sour for the defenders. After very heavy fighting on the 22nd, Hardee's men were pushed back, although Cleburne had some success near a prominent hill locally known as Bald Hill, (now named Leggett's Hill after General M. D. Leggett whose division held the hill against Cleburne's assaults). Ironically, it was on this prominence that

McPherson had on that day proposed to Sherman that some big guns be placed for the purpose of reducing sizeable portions of Atlanta to ruble. It was hoped that this measure would reduce the will of the defenders and populace to continue the fight. However, the noise of the battle on this hill prompted McPherson to jump on his horse after conferring with Sherman over his bombardment plans, and ride toward the commotion along with an orderly. Before reaching the fighting, however, he and his aide inadvertently rode into a party of Confederates who ordered them to halt. McPherson tipped his hat, swung his horse around and fled only to be shot from his saddle by a ball in the back. He died only moments later in the arms of his orderly, who had struck a branch while in flight and had fallen near the mortally wounded general. News of McPherson's death spread quickly among the troops. Sherman himself is said to have wept as the body was laid out in his headquarters.

General Logan was given temporary command of the Army of the Tennessee, but on July 27 Oliver O. Howard became its permanent commander. General David Stanley, formerly in command of Hupp's division (1st), succeeded Howard to the command of IV Corps. Thoroughly embittered that Howard was chosen over himself to replace McPherson, "Fighting Joe" Hooker departed for an inactive assignment (to no one's dismay or regret) to be replaced soon after by Maj. General Henry W. Slocum.

McPherson's loss to the Union was incalculable. Considered one of the North's most brilliant and capable leaders, Sherman firmly believed that McPherson would someday outshine both Grant and himself, and would come to lead all Union armies. His life and great promise were ended at age thirty-five; one of a multitude of bitter tragedies in this most tragic war.

Sherman's next move was to try to out flank his Confederate opponent to the west and south of Atlanta for the purpose of severing her last rail ties to the outside world. Schofield and McPherson had torn up a fair stretch of track along the Georgia road from Decatur, and the Federals were now using the Western and Atlantic as their northern supply line. The Macon and Western line, entering East Point from the southwest and southeast and, thence, serving Atlanta from the southwest, was Sherman's next target. General Lovell Rousseau, who had commanded Hupp's division (3rd) at Perryville, had torn up the southwest branch of the Macon and Western during a recent raid into Alabama, so only the southeast branch, connecting Atlanta to Savannah, remained. With that last lifeline cut, the city's imminent fall would be all but assured.

The day Howard was given command of the Army of the Tennessee

(July 27), Sherman ordered him to swing his army in back of Schofield to the north and then west around the city. Thomas would then follow behind. At the same time, Sherman gave his two cavalry commanders crucial roles to play in this phase of the siege. Edward McCook was to lead his horsemen south around the western side of the city to attack the Macon and Western below Jonesboro, 20 miles from Atlanta. George Stoneman was to attack the same target but would ride around the eastern perimeter from Decatur. Stoneman, however, was a man with a mission beyond wrecking railroads. He asked for, and received, permission to ride farther south after accomplishing his original objective for the purpose of freeing Union prisoners of war held at Macon and Andersonville.

Andersonville, whose name still conjures up images of unimaginable inhumanity, housed over 30,000 prisoners (mostly enlisted men) in an outdoor inclosure with no sanitary system, starvation rations, and little protection from the elements. The Macon prison (Camp Oglethorpe) was also an open stockade, but it housed officers, many sent there from the infamous Libby prison in Richmond. The North had its own versions of overcrowded, poorly administered prisons, such as the one at Elmira, New York, but Macon, and particularly Andersonville, represented especially vile examples of man's potential for inflicting cruelty on his own species. Stoneman wanted to free the prisoners there for humanitarian purposes, but he also knew that success in this adventure could hardly damage his career prospects. Quite the contrary, and given the added bonus of a morale boost for war weary northern citizens (including Republican politicians), the effort was well worth the risks.

Unfortunately, Stoneman, consumed by his passion to free Union prisoners, failed to stop at his primary objective and turned south toward Macon without damaging so much as a foot of rebel track; McCook was left to undertake the task on his own. Upon reaching Macon, Stoneman was overwhelmed and captured by Wheeler's cavalry who promptly threw him in the very prison he had come to liberate. The enlisted men were sent to Andersonville.

McCook did reach his objective and managed to tear up some track, burn the railroad station, and destroy a supply wagon train (and murder its 800 mules) at Lovejoy Station seven miles south of Jonesboro. However, he was later pursued north by Confederate cavalry who inflicted severe losses to his ranks. To add insult to injury, the rebels had the track he destroyed repaired in about two days. Sherman never again relied heavily on his cavalry to carry out important operations during the rest of the siege of Atlanta, and used them sparingly during his subsequent "March to the Sea."

Stoneman's raid had indeed been a "grand move," but an unsuccessful one. His folly of dividing his cavalry from McCook's mounted division, and in believing that his often less-than-competent troops could actually break through the rebel defenses at Macon and Andersonville, had cost Sherman almost two thirds of his cavalry effectives. In addition, Stoneman had made no plans for what he would do with the freed prisoners, most of them starved and sick, once he managed to liberate them. Most would have surely perished on the long march to Union lines, or left to their own devices, would have been quickly recaptured.

Stoneman, incidently, was released in a few months from Macon and went on to lead some other raids in support of Sherman in Virginia and North Carolina. He retired from the army in 1871 and in the 1880's was elected governor of California, as a Democrat.

Howard's movement around the north and west of Atlanta was going quite nicely until his troops approached a point almost exactly due west of the beleaguered city. Although Sherman expressed doubts that Hood would attempt another of his "sorties," given the utter failure of the first two, Hood, in fact, was quite willing and able to give it another try. Hood saw Howard's flanking movement (around the Confederate left) as a golden opportunity to once again strike hard at a detached segment of Sherman's army. To that end, he enlisted the services of General Steven D. Lee, recently arrived from Mississippi to take Cheatham's command, to strike Howard's vulnerable right (outer, in relation to the city) flank. A devastating blow there would set Howard up for a knockout punch on the other flank from A. P. Stewart.

On July 28, Lee attacked as planned on the Lickskillet Road west of Atlanta. The attack centered around a small rural chapel known as Ezra Church, which lent its name to this battle, also known as "Hood's Third Sortie." Unlike Sherman, Howard – a friend of Hood's at West Point – knew that his brash opponent was not yet out of gas. Based on his knowledge of Hood's character and a premonitory hunch, Howard had his troops build temporary log works in anticipation of Lee's strike. Lee's orders from Hood were to attack the next day, but faced with the prospects of turning Howard's right, Lee decided to take the initiative.

Around noon, Lee ordered Brown's Brigade to move forward against M. L. Smith's division (Logan's corps) on the far right flank of Howard's bulging U-shaped line. Ezra Church was at the forward cusp of the bulge where Wood's division waited, some Union troops sprawled hidden behind commandeered church pews. Repeated but ever weakening charges by the screaming Confederates were beaten back by the numerically superior blue troops half hidden behind their hastily constructed log

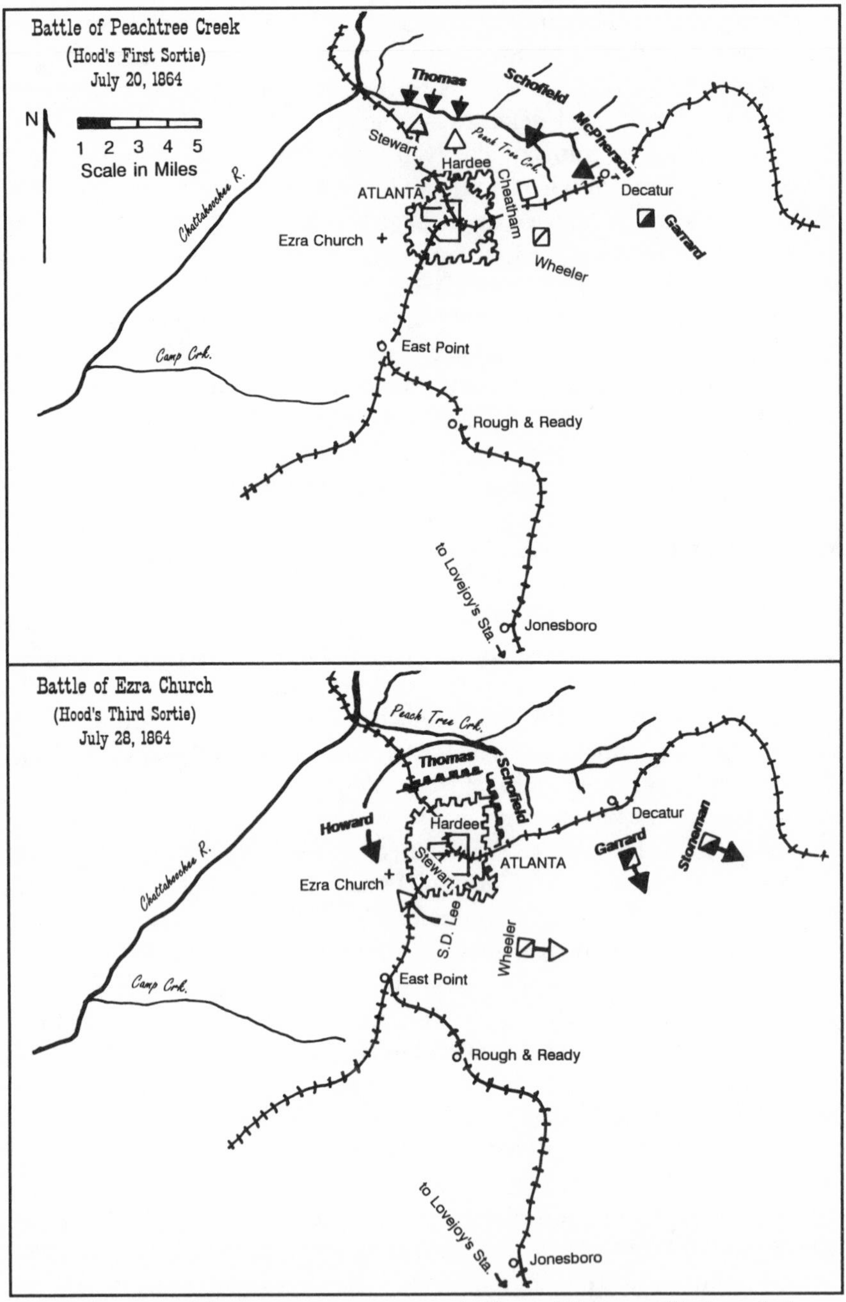

Battle maps of final engagements around Atlanta (Union = filled symbols; Confederate = open symbols; after Griess, 1986).

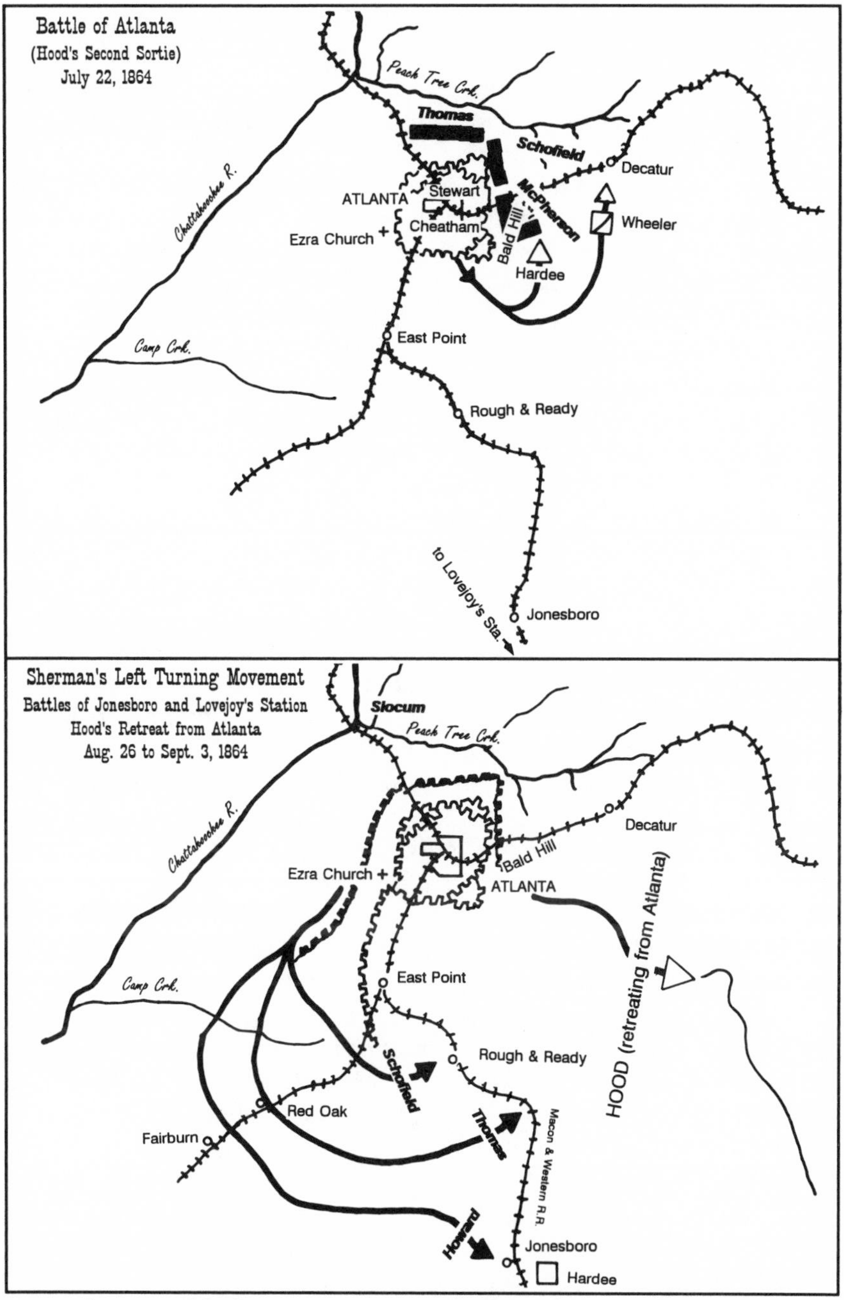

Battle maps of final engagements around Atlanta (Union = filled symbols; Confederate = open symbols; after Griess, 1986).

works. As befell sorties one and two, this one turned into a monumental disaster for the Confederates. As in the previous encounters, their losses were staggering, but more importantly, their morale was now badly shaken. The Federals seemed virtually unbeatable, and they were rapidly enveloping the city, east and west.

Thomas' army, still situated north of the city, was attacked on the 28th by Hardee's troops who occupied the northern defensive works on the city perimeter (now well within the city limits, near downtown). This attack, and those against Schofield farther east, were basically diversionary in nature, an attempt to keep Thomas from going to Howard's aid in his fight with S. D. Lee at Ezra Church. But Hardee's efforts proved unnecessary, because Howard needed no help in pushing back the increasingly demoralized and worn out butternut troops. Hupp described the attacks on his position north of Atlanta and stated that Rebel losses amounted to 10,000, while the Federals lost only 2,000

Pvt. Hupp's casualty figures are somewhat inflated. Later estimates show about 3,000 Confederates killed and wounded to about 630 Federals. Interestingly, his ratio of Union/Rebel casualties is very close to later tallies.

Hupp also refers to the Confederates opening up "a 32 lbs.", which may (or may not) refer to the shells lobbed into the Union lines by some three inch Rodman guns that Joseph E. Johnston had earlier secured from Mobile Bay for the defense of the city. When some duds were weighed, these shells proved to be twice the weight Hupp stated: 64 pounds.

During the month of August, Sherman could taste the victory that he had been seeking for so many months. He sent a note to Howard stating, "Let us destroy Atlanta and make it a desolation," and to help make good that resolution, he brought in 30 pounder Parrott rifles and other large siege guns from Chatttanooga and began to pulverize the business district and residential areas in ernest.

For his part, Hood was still hopeful of holding the city, but by now he had played out most of his options; most had not born fruit. He had some successes: notably, a bloody repulse of Schofield at a place called Utnoy Creek, and Wheeler's daring raid behind Sherman's lines.

With about half his cavalry command (the rest stayed near Atlanta), Wheeler left on August 10 to tear up rail tracks, burn bridges, destroy supply trains, and generally make things hot for Sherman where it would hurt the most – his supply bases. The raid was wildly successful, and yet Sherman was not moved to panic by these attacks in his rear, but viewed Wheeler's departure as something of a gift. With his cavalry diminished by half, Hood's "eyes and ears" were severely compromised just when he could have used all the intelligence (the information kind, and otherwise) he could employ. Sherman's final move to envelope Atlanta and close off her last life line to the rest of the Confederacy would be much easier without Wheeler in the equation.

This grand western flanking movement (left wheeel), begun in late July but stalled at Ezra Church, was ordered into motion again in August. Ormond Hupp penned some entries in his journal suggesting that, even before Wheeler's raid, Union soldiers entrenched around Atlanta were not pleased with the rations they were receiving (see page 112).

With the sweet news of Faragut's surprising victory in Mobile Bay (August 5) still ringing in their ears, Sherman's armies continued on their grand wheel beginning August 25. It was the beginning of the end for Confederate Atlanta. Sherman ordered Howard's Army of the Tennessee to Jonesboro, about 20 miles south of Atlanta on the Macon Railroad. Thomas' Army of the Cumberland was to move to a point on the railroad about 6 miles north of Jonesboro, and Schofield's Army of the Ohio (actually, barely a corps) was sent to Rough and Ready, just a few miles southeast of East Point. Slocum's corps (XX) of the Army of the Cumberland (Joe Hooker's former command) was left in the trenches north of Atlanta to keep an eye on the railroad. All three marching armies were charged with the task of tearing up as much rebel track as they could, and particularly to cut the Macon line permanently, the last supply route to the south.

By the end of the month, Hood had played most of his cards, but he saw in this movement of Sherman's three armies another chance to defeat them in detail. The old military admonition, "never divide your forces," was commonly ignored during the Civil War by all manner of leaders on both sides. Robert E. Lee, in particular, was a master of using the technique to his advantage, as Grant, McClellan, Hooker, and others could readily attest. Here at Atlanta, Sherman commonly divided his forces for convenience or to gain some tactical advantage, usually with impunity. That he could so boldly resort to this tactic without fear of risking annihilation of his armies speaks for the overpowering Union force he now had at his disposal. By contrast, Hood's depleted forces simply could not muster the sheer numbers necessary to beat any of Sherman's armies in detail and still leave enough men in the trenches to guard the city. This was about to be demonstrated at Jonesboro.

Hood's fourth (and last) sortie involved another plan to catch Sherman's armies in a divided state, and called for Hardee to attack Howard at Jonesboro early in the morning on the 31st. Pat Cleburne and S. D. Lee's corps were the major Confederate participants in what proved to be the last major engagement of the campaign. Facing them in an eastward bulging line near the Flint River were Howard's veterans, mostly Logan's XV Corps, with Judson Kilpatrick's cavalry for support.

Serious deployment delays caused the attack to commence at 2 P.M. instead of the early morning hours as ordered. The battle was over almost before it started. Mistaking the sound of distant skirmishing as a signal to advance, Lee moved his troops out prematurely and was soon stalled by withering Union fire. Cleburne had some success in driving Kilpatrick's horsemen across the river, but it was soon apparent to Hardee that Logan's troops were too numerous and too well entrenched to dislodge. He called off the battle to lick his wounds. The Confederates later learned that the bluecoats had reached the Macon road at Rough and Ready and were massing at other points between Hardee's army and Atlanta. Hardee was cut off, so it was Hood's army that was now dangerously divided.

Hardee's predicament did not escape Sherman's notice, and he now moved to nail the coffin lid shut by wiping out Hardee's forces once and for all. Both Schofield and Thomas were issued orders to move on Jonesboro for a combined attack against Hardee. Once he was neutralized, the city would be ripe for picking, its defenders unable to resist the sheer numbers that Sherman was about to bring against them. But Schofield was late in arriving, having taken it upon himself to tear up track on the way, and most of Thomas' corps were either late, or in the case of David Stanley's IV Corps, very late. Stanley had gotten lost on the way south and did not arrive in Jonesboro until way past sundown. These delays proved costly for they helped allow Hardee to escape to near Lovejoy Station. Sherman pursued him that far, but decided to call off the chase when he saw the strong entrenchments waiting for him there. Besides, at that point he had a bigger prize in mind.

On September 1, a series of explosions could be heard from the direction of Atlanta at Sherman's headquarters. The commanding general was almost sure that Slocum had been caught in a Confederate trap, separated as he was from the rest of the army. But his anxieties were relieved a few days later when he received word that Slocum's XX Corps was, in fact, inside Atlanta, having occupied the city on the 2nd. The explosions heard for miles around on the 1st were trapped ammunition cars and locomotives, and other materiel and facilities being blown to bits to prevent capture. Hood ordered the evacuation of Atlanta on September 1. After being greeted by the mayor and other city dignitaries, Slocum and the troops of XX Corps marched into the destroyed city on September 2, thus ending the bloody campaign that had started in April, nearly five months before. Ormond Hupp described his impressions of the city he had helped to destroy in some of the last passages in his diary.

After resting his troops in Atlanta, Sherman would continue across Georgia on his famous "March to the Sea," which started on November 15 and ended in Savannah on December 21. But neither Ormond Hupp nor the rest of the 5th Indiana Light Artillery went with him. Sherman, it seems, never forgave their corps commander, David Stanley, for his tardiness at Jonesboro. For better or worse, most of Stanley's troops were sent back to Tennessee, and some groups were disbanded. This included the glorious Fifth Indiana Battery, the battery that held out to the last at Stones River and Chickamauga, the battery credited with killing Leonidas Polk, the battery led by the valiant Captain Peter Simonson. After Atlanta, with most of their veteran enlistments due to expire in November, the company was split up with newer recruits transferred to other batteries. In his last daily entry, September 17, 1864, Hupp described the deactivation of the battery:

> At present we are preparing to turn over the Batt.: this morning everything went but the horses and camp equipage, we are to be relieved of the H______ this p. m. and by the first of the week it is said we are to start for Indianapolis.

On September 20, the battery turned over its guns, equipment, and horses to the ordinance officer at Atlanta. Those men with three-year enlistments, like Hupp, were ordered to Indianapolis for muster out. Arriving on the 18th, they were mustered out on the 26th of November, 1864. All others were transferred to the Seventh Battery to which they became permanently attached in April, 1865. Final muster out for these troops was July 20, 1865.

We know from one of the very last lines of his diary that Hupp was ill in late September, the cause unknown (certainly unmentioned). His muster records show that he was admitted to a military hospital in Chattanooga on October 6, 1864, but had probably recovered and was discharged by the time he was mustered out of volunteer service in late November.

Now, as Sherman marched to the sea, Hupp travelled back to LaPorte, his duty done. On November 8, just three weeks before Ormond again trod the fertile soil of Center Township, Lincoln was re-elected president, largely on the strength of Sherman's great victory at Atlanta. In no small measure, Sherman's success was instrumental in saving the Union; the

South would have fared much better under a Democratic administration, perhaps even gaining independence. While few of the individual "common" soldiers who marched with Sherman are remembered to history, they bore the brunt of the toil, torture, and sacrifice of this crucial campaign. Without their devoted and mostly skilled execution of the great Generals' plans, history would have certainly taken a different turn, with perhaps disturbing implications for the progress of human rights.

Hupp was just one of hundreds of the "boys of '61" who returned to farm, shop, and factory in 1864, as the war ground on. But now the fate of the South was virtually sealed, in spite of Grant's failure to subdue Lee and take the Confederate capital (Richmond finally fell on April 3, 1865). Nevertheless, Sherman had triumphed and would continue to roll like a giant voracious locust across Georgia as northern towns and villages welcomed home their blue-clad, battle worn heroes. They who had defended the flag of the Union, were home at last.

After September 17, 1864, Ormond Hupp never again kept a diary.

Chapter 8
HOME AGAIN!

Others may praise what they like;
But I, from the banks of the running Missouri;
praise nothing, in art, or aught else,
Till it has well inhaled the atmosphere of this river – also
the western prairie-scent,
And fully exudes it again.

Walt Whitman (1865)

The Christmas of 1864 was the first one that Ormond Hupp spent at home since 1860. Reunited at last with his father and mother, brothers and sisters, he returned to northern Indiana a hero. In November, Sherman put the torch to what was left of proud Atlanta and began his March to the Sea (Savannah campaign). Four days before Christmas, he accomplished his goal, and Savannah, too, fell under the cruel boot of "total war." Earlier, Gen. John Bell Hood's desperate re-invasion of Tennessee was turned back and his Confederate army routed at Nashville. The war would last another four or five months, but by that Christmas of 1864, the Confederacy was on the ropes and dying. The "second American revolution" would this time be won by the "mother country."

In the spring, Ormond, still recovering from his Perryville wounds, harnessed his father's plow horses and made the fertile ground ready for planting as Richmond fell, and Lee and Grant met at Appomattox Court House to seal the end of the Army of Northern Virginia.

But this idyllic scene was not without its dark side. Ormond found that his ability to perform heavy labor was progressively reduced compared to his pre-war years. The pain in the joint of his left shoulder also pervaded his back, vastly reducing latitude of movement and strength. He also suffered from a severe case of "piles" (hemorrhoids) and a fistula (abnormal tube or cavity) in the lower bowel acquired during his military service. The fistula became abscessed during his hospitalization in New

Albany necessitating an operation by A. S. Greene, the assistant surgeon at Hospital no. 1 (not mentioned in Hupp's diary). These combined maladies continued to torment Hupp for the rest of his life.

One year after the war had ended, Abram Hupp decided to leave the family homestead in LaPorte County. The family packed and left what had been the only home the Hupp children had ever known and made the slow, over four-hundred-mile trek to northwestern Missouri. No one can say for sure why they would have taken on this journey, but Abram no doubt considered the rewards worth the sacrifice. Like many farmers of the time, he was probably aware that more fertile soil could be found farther west. Not that northern Indiana didn't have abundant soil of high quality, but Missouri had one advantage over the glacial soils of northern Indiana: big rivers with wide and naturally fertilized flood plains. Ormond's father had heard that abundant, reasonably priced land could be had in western Missouri and he rushed to stake his claim. He may have viewed this area as presenting better prospects for his sons to buy farms as they came of age. The Hupp family's new home was a large plot of hill country snuggled within the large, concave-south bend of the Missouri River where "Big Muddy" ventures to its farthest northern extent within the state. It lay in Saline County, near the small Missouri river town of Miami, northeast of Marshall, the county seat.

All of Ormond's brothers and sisters had been born by the time of their western migration, and all made the trip except the eldest, Anelizabeth. She stayed behind in LaPorte with her husband, a Mr. Rapogle. In later life, she made several visits to Saline County to see her parents (while they lived), siblings, and ever increasing numbers of nieces and nephews.

Saline county gets it name from the numerous salty springs in the area, some of which were exploited to produce commercial salt products using evaporation techniques. Miami, the Hupp family's new mailing address, was named for the Miami Indian tribe that had occupied the nearby bottom lands as early as 1815. The town itself was founded in 1838 by Henry Ferrell, an early pioneer, who named it "Greenville." The name was changed to Miami in 1843. By 1860 it had a population of 14,699, one third of which was slaves.

Before the Civil War, Miami Township had been one of the wealthiest areas in Missouri, principal crops being hemp for rope and fabrics, corn, wheat, and livestock. A thriving slave trading center was only a few hours up-stream at Lexington. Much of Miami's success stemmed from its location on the Missouri River, a major agricultural shipping artery to the markets in St. Louis. It also served as a rail station for the St. Louis, Kansas City, and Northern Railroad. Ormond Hupp and other area farmers used both river barges and the railroad to ship their products. In recent times, unfortunately, Miami has fallen on hard times. The current population has plunged to about 150, and the crumbling downtown is virtually deserted, a victim of progress.

During the Civil War, Saline County and Miami Township could boast of a colorful, but at times, blood-stained history. During the crucial 1860 election, not one vote was cast for Lincoln. Bell and Everett carried the county and Douglas carried Missouri, the only state he won. Missouri, although harboring a mixed sampling of Union versus Confederate loyalists, was more Southern in its overall sympathies than not, and Saline County certainly had its share of Confederate bushwhackers, guerrillas, and fellow travellers. The notorious guerrilla William C. Quantrill is known to have visited Miami twice, and "Bloody Bill" Anderson made frequent forays into town.

Quantrill was the consummate Confederate bushwacker whose murderous band included the likes of "Bloody Bill," and the James and Younger brothers. His most famous exploit was the sacking and massacre of Lawrence, Kansas, (August 21, 1863) in which over 150 men, boys, and old men were indiscriminately shot to death. Much of the town was burned to the ground. Bill Anderson later went off on his own campaign of cold blooded murder and pillage in central Missouri and elsewhere. It was to this area, where many of the local folks at least sympathized with the aims of Quantrill and his ilk to punish the "Free Soilers" in Kansas, that Abram Hupp moved his family in 1866.

From the above we can be sure that Ormond did not immediately don his old uniform upon arrival, and march down the streets of Miami waving Old Glory. Although Missouri was under Union control, guerrilla activities and depredations by former guerrillas turned bank and train robbers (*a la* the James and Younger gangs) continued for many years after the war. Over-zealous demonstrations of Union patriotism in the northwest Missouri of 1866 held potentially dire consequences for life and limb. Thus we can be fairly sure that Ormond used some discretion in discussing his service record with his new neighbors.

In 1878, Ormond acquired his own farm by purchasing the farm formerly owned by Dr. William Lacy on County route F. His younger brother, Theodore (called "Teed"), was given forty acres worth $1,200, and brother Arthur obtained a farm near Marshall. Sister Julia eventually married into the Crane family and was given the old Abram Hupp farm after her husband deserted her.

Ormond later moved to another farm (now owned by the Franklin family) just down the road from the first one, and later acquired three

Figure 8-1 – Ormond Hupp (c. 1923) as he appeared a few years before he died. This picture was included in his printed Civil War diary.

other farms encompassing over 1,000 acres of prime Missouri farm land, a little over 100 acres lying in the Missouri River bottom lands. His personal holdings were reduced toward the end of the century as Ormond parcelled out 160 acre units to his sons and daughters at the time of marriage. These farms were not gifts; each child was expected to pay him back as they were able. As a farmer, Ormond primarily raised cattle and grew corn for their sustenance. He was renowned for his skilled management and frugality, although he could be very generous, particularly with his children, if sufficient need were demonstrated.

Ormond's partner in producing their twelve children (counting Mary Louisa and Lotus who died in infancy) was Laura Margaret Campbell, a native of Greene County, Tennessee (childhood home of Davey Crockett), whom he married on November 9, 1873. Laura was ten years Ormond's junior but died well before he did, in 1907 at age 57. Although speculative, her early demise could be at least partly attributable to the fact that Ormond kept her pregnant during much of their married life. Particularly in the 1880's, he would get Laura pregnant and then depart on an out-of-state trip that would conveniently allow for his absence at the moment of birth. Many of his trips were to the far western states, including Montana, California, and Oregon. The names of some of Ormond and Laura's children reflect the colorful localities where Ormond was away on business when they were born. Thus were concocted the names Montana ("Montye"), Oakland ("Oakye"; my maternal grandmother), and Willamette ("Willye" or "Billy"), the latter named for the Willamette valley of Oregon.

The occasion for Ormond's western excursions is a matter of great mystery. All who would have been personally familiar with the reasons

Figure 8-2 – Laura Margaret (Campbell) Hupp (1850-1907), wife of Ormond Hupp.

for these trips are now departed from this world, and Ormond did not leave much of a paper trail. In a postcard and letter to his friend and lawyer, Louis Benecke, he asks Benecke's pardon for not answering a letter with the vague excuse that he "was absent for some time." The postcard was probably mailed about 1879; the letter is dated 1881.

Trips to the far western states were no small matter in those days, particularly considering that major rail lines did not reach the area until the late 1870's. Eventually, however, Ormond could have taken a train from the station at Slater, 10 miles southeast of his farm, to Kansas City, and from there would have made his way west (the transcontinental railroad was completed in 1869). But what would have compelled a Missouri farmer to make such long and arduous journeys?

Conjectures about Ormond's travels offered by Hupp descendants have proliferated over the years. By some accounts he was fighting Indians (doubtful; he quit the army for good in 1864); buying and selling horses or mules (he was indeed a "horse trader," but that trade could be plied locally); or he was giving recruitment or pension rights speeches for the Grand Army of the Republic (G.A.R.). Only the last hypothesis deserves serious consideration.

Ormond Hupp's Civil War journal reveals a man whose patriotism and devotion to the Union were beyond compromise. Membership in the G.A.R. would have been a logical progression for such an ardent soldier and patriot. The G.A.R. was a fraternal organization of Civil War Veterans, similar to the American Legion or Veterans of Foreign Wars. Besides providing a forum for maintaining camaraderie among veterans, the organization pursued political ends, lobbying Congress for more liberal pension rights and other benefits. Numerous documents, mostly correspondence between Ormond and his lawyer Benecke, show that Ormond attempted to have his own pension increased several times between 1881 and 1915. He was receiving $2 per month in 1881, but by the time of his death the sum was up to a respectable $65 per month. If his passion for increasing his own pension extended to his fellow war veterans, he may have been recruited to speak on the topic in the west, or may have served as a recruiting agent.

But can a case be made that Ormond ever even belonged to the G.A.R., much less served as an important spokesman? The closest posts to Hupp's farm were Col. Cornine Post 163 in Slater, founded in 1885 and commanded by A. B. Babbit. By the following year, however, the post's charter was suspended, probably for lack of interest. In 1890, a new post was founded in Slater to supersede the now defunct 163. The new post was the Gen. George Crook Post 470 commanded by William Davis. It, too, lasted only a few years and then slid into decline. None of the Missouri Annual Encampment (annual meeting of state posts) proceedings lists Ormond Hupp as a representative or alternate to these meetings, nor is he mentioned in any other leadership capacity. However, an "Osmond" Hupp is listed in the 1927 Proceedings as having died in 1926, the year of Ormond's death. The "Osmond" entry is alone among an extensive list of departed comrades in having no military unit noted, but his post is given as the George H. Thomas Post 8 in Kansas City.

If Ormond wanted to join the G.A.R. shortly after arriving in Saline County, he would have had to wait almost twenty years for the first post in Slater to open, and a similar period for the post in nearby Marshall (Post 106). Post 8, although seventy miles distant in Kansas City, was available with the added draw of being named after one of Hupp's old commanders during the Atlanta campaign, George Thomas, the "Rock of Chickamauga." But clearly Ormond was not a major player in this post; they did not even have a record of his very distinguished military unit to place in his obituary, and misspelled his name to boot. In addition, not one of the existent bibliographic sketches on Ormond written from 1881 to 1910 contains any mention of activities with the G.A.R. or any similar organization. But they do mention land speculation.

Owing to the richness of the soil in Miami Township and Ormond's sound management of it, he amassed a significant fortune well before the turn of the century. But in addition to his large land holdings in Saline County, at one time he also owned one sixth interest in 3,000 acres of valuable land in Canada, and some excellent farm land in Texas.

Illustrative of his wealth is the fact that all of the Hupp children had a live-in governess who tutored them in their studies at home; not one attended public school below high school. Most of the children, however, attended college, with Ormond footing the bill.

Figure 8-3 – Rare family reunion portrait taken about 1900 in front of the Hupp home shown in 8(c). Participants are: Back Row: Mrs. "Teed" (Martha) Hupp; Maud Crane Olinger; Edith Hupp; Lula Hupp Ruppert; Otto Ruppert; Oakye Hupp Dysart; Mrs. Arthur (Martha) Hupp; Guy McAmis; James McAmis; May Hupp Sappington. Second Row: Jessie Hupp Kemper; Lloyd Kemper; Vernon Hupp; in front of Vernon, Oral Kemper, Sr.; Roy Hupp; Eula Hupp Webb; next little girl, Hazel Ruppert Cook; Arthur ("Otho") Hupp [a younger brother of Ormond]; Gertye Hupp Brown; Willye Hupp Johnson; Theodore "Teed" Hupp [a younger brother of Ormond]; Roscoe Hupp, Sr.; Anelizabeth Hupp Repogle [in rocking chair; Ormond's older sister]. Front: Mrs. Ormond (Laura Margaret Campbell) Hupp [in rocking chair]; Ormond Hupp, sitting on ground in front.

At least a part of Ormond's considerable wealth came from buying and selling land, and in the case of the Canadian holdings, there was the potential for lumber and mining profits, although that is speculative. Given his willingness to invest in lands as far flung as Canada and Texas, his trips to California, Oregon, and Montana may have been for the purpose of scouting out new prospects. Considering the geography and geology of those three states, it is probably not stretching the imagination too far to suspect that he was not considering investments in mere farm land. As for the Canadian holdings, timber and mineral resources were the likely treasures that could lure Ormond over one thousand miles from home and pregnant wife. Laura must have been a very patient woman.

As the years passed, Ormond eventually emerged as a leading citizen

Figure 8-4 – Ormond and Laura Hupp's retirement home in Slater, Missouri.

of his county. A committed Baptist and Republican his entire life, he ran for alderman (but lost) in the city of Slater later in life, and donated land for a new church in 1884, the New Prospect Baptist Church finished in 1887. Ormond's philanthropy, however, was greased a bit by self interest. The Bethel Baptist church, where he and his parents and siblings had worshiped for many years, refused to institute a Sunday school for the children. So, in essence, Ormond founded his own church with the stipulation that a Sunday school be provided. It was.

Although he was, without question, one of the wealthiest men in Saline County, Ormond liked to go into town during his farming days dressed in his old ragged overalls. The story is told that one day a stranger to Slater spotted Ormond and took him for some pitiable soul down on his luck. The stranger decided to go door to door to take up a collection for the poor old fellow, until a neighbor laughed in his face. He informed the good-hearted stranger that Ormond Hupp could "buy and sell all of us, if he wanted to."

The settlement of his will after his death in 1926 allowed that each of his children (except Jesse) were to ". . . share and share alike all of my property real, personal, and mixed, to be theirs absolutely." This division of his remaining assets to his children provided all of them the ability to buy, outright, fine homes or make other beneficial investments. Unfortunately, some of the children decided to invest in stocks and lost out to the crash of '29.

In his will he stated, "It is my intention that neither my daughter Jesse K. Kemper nor her husband [Lloyd] nor her bodily heirs shall take any part of my estate, except as provided in section 2 aforesaid in this will." Section 2 provided Jesse with $2,000, but no more. It seems that husband Lloyd was not in the same league with Jesse's father when it came to managing money. Lloyd squandered thousands on failed business ventures, whereupon Jesse would go to Ormond to plead for one more loan. Apparently she went to the well once too often. Jesse died in December of 1926, one month after her father. Thus she was afforded little time to spend the $2,000, however we may surmise that Lloyd made good use of it.

Ormond Hupp's sense of humor was legendary in Miami Township. He was known to enjoy a good joke, particularly the "practical" variety. One of his favorites was to stand behind someone and to use his left leg to kick their hat off. The paralysis that left his foot deformed, also created a "double joint" feature in the leg allowing him to swing it freely 180 degrees. Ormond was also fond of "a little wine," a taste he likely acquired in the army judging from his diary.

As mentioned above, Ormond was a "horse trader", and an accomplished one at that.

The following story, reproduced nearly exactly from an account by my second cousin, Robert Ruppert (grandson of Luella Hupp and William O. Rupert), tells of one of the few times anyone got the best of "Grampa Hupp," and lends some insights into his personality.

> Ormond was a shrewd horse-trader. The only person the family knew of who bested him in swap was a poor old black man who traded Ormond a mule for an old mare horse. Ormond asked him if the mule would pull.
>
> The old fellow heartily said, "Mr. Hupp, tickle you to death to see dat mule pull!"
>
> He was a beautiful animal, so Ormond figured he'd skinned someone else. When he got the mule home, and hitched him up, he found he was "wind-broke" and would not pull "the hat off your head." He charged back to the old black man, threatening to "cause you trouble."
>
> The old fellow answered, "I was born in trouble, raised in

trouble, had trouble all my life. I reckon any trouble you can cause me wouldn't hardly matter."

Then gramps accused the man of lying to him, "You told me that mule would pull!"

Reply: "No suh, Mr. Hupp! I told you it would tickle you to death to see dat mule pull. It'd tickle me, too, cause he won't do it".

Grampa Hupp burst into laughter, recognizing a fellow scoundrel who had bested him, and told the story on himself across the years afterward.

In 1899, Ormond and Laura bought their retirement house in Slater at 303 Euclid. Slater is located about 10 miles southeast of the Hupp farms, and with the retirement of Ormond there, became the center for family activities.

Founded in 1878 by Josiah Baker, Jr., the town was named for John F. Slater of Norwich, Connecticut, a major stockholder in the Chicago and Alton Railroad. Slater was founded specifically to serve as a station on that railroad, later sporting a roundhouse and other repair facilities that could accommodate twenty steam locomotives at one time. Today, Slater's grain elevators serve as a storage center for local farmers (including some of the Hupp descendants), and the town can also boast of supporting some "high-tech" light industries.

As patriarch of the Hupp family in Missouri, Ormond and Laura (and after 1907, just Ormond) hosted Sunday family dinners for nearby relatives, including his surviving offspring and their children. Dinner inevitably featured fried oysters, a taste for which he likely acquired during his convalescence in New Albany during the war. My mother recalls that "Grampa" liked to kick at the children with his orthopedic boot, after which he would laugh with delight. She found the experience a bit disconcerting, but knew that Grampa meant no harm. He also delighted in taking the children to the candy store in a buggy pulled by old "Prince," the horse. She suspects that he also owned a car, but kept it out of sight in the barn most of the time. He took the train on longer trips, and was a frequent guest at daughter Willye's (Willamette) house in Odessa, Missouri, near Kansas City. His diary was printed there in 1923, bound in suede leather and distributed to his sons and daughters, and their children. It is upon the now battered copy that he presented to my mother when she was about eight years old, that much of this book is based.

In later years, Ormond made frequent visits in his horse and buggy to the farm of his daughter Gertye and her family, husband Elliot Brown and children Clyde, Ormond, and Ruth. Clyde's son (with Virginia Page Brown), C. Gary Brown, now owns the greatest share of former O. Hupp holdings in the region (145 acres; about one third of his total holdings).

One day after one of Ormond's visits in late November 1926, he complained of illness and was driven home to Slater by automobile. His grandson and namesake, Ormond Brown, later drove the buggy back to Slater. A few days later, Gertye was alerted by two of Ormond's neighbors, T. M. Smith and George Haines, that they had not seen Ormond for a few days and feared for his well-being. Using her key, they entered the cold and silent house on Euclid Street and found Ormond dead. He had died on November 26, the specific cause of death never determined, although "old age" will suffice. He was 86 years old.

The crippled boy who had served his country, his community, and his family with immeasurable sacrifice, devotion, and skill was finally at peace. He was laid to rest next to Laura in the Slater Cemetery, another recruit for the "phantom army" of departed Civil War veterans.

Thank you, Grampa.

* * *

The last survivor of the "Grand Army of the Republic" – and the last Civil War veteran – Albert Woolson, died in Duluth, Minnesota on August 2, 1956, at age 108.

* * *

This dust was once the Man,
Gentle, plain, just and resolute - under whose cautious hand,
Against the foulest crime in history known in any land or age,
Was saved the Union of These States.

Walt Whitman: This Dust Was Once the Man *(1871)*

BIBLIOGRAPHY

Amster, Betty Lou (1963) New Albany on the Ohio: Historical Review 1813-1963: The New Albany Sesquicentennial, Inc., 151 pp.

Benecke Family Papers, 1816-1989: Collection 3825, folders 844, 1101, 3252; Western Historical Manuscript Collection, University of Missouri and State Historical Society of Missouri, Ellis Library, Columbia.

Boatner, Mark M. (1991) *The Civil War Dictionary*: Vintage Books, Random House, Inc., New York, 974 pp.

Cannan, John (1991) *The Atlanta Campaign, May-November, 1864*: Combined Books, Conshohocken, PA, 176 pp.

Castel, Albert (1992) *Decision In The West, The Atlanta Campaign of 1864*: University Press of Kansas, Lawrence, 665 pp.

Chapman, Elizabeth Humes (1989) *Changing Huntsville 1890-1899*: Historic Huntsville Foundation, Inc., P.O. Box 786, Huntsville, AL, 196 pp.

Cogons, Jack (1962) *Arms and Equipment of the Civil War*: Broadfoot Publishing Co., Wilmington, NC, 160 pp.

Coleman, Helen: Collected information about military hospitals in New Albany during the Civil War: Collection of the Stuart Barth Wrege Indiana History Room, New Albany-Floyd County Public Library, 180 West Spring Street, New Albany, IN 47150-3692.

Cozzens, Peter (1992) *This Terrible Sound: The Battle of Chickamauga*: University of Illinois Press, Urbana & Chicago, 675 pp.

Cozzens, Peter (1991) *No Better Place To Die: The Battle of Stones River*: University of Illinois, Urbana & Chicago, 281 pp.

Davis, William C. (1975) *The Battle of New Market*: Louisiana State University Press, Baton Rouge, 249 pp.

Dyer, Frederick H. (1979) *A Compendium of the War of the Rebellion, Vol. 2*:Morningside Press, Dayton, OH, p. 1112-1113.

Foote, Shelby (1986) *The Civil War: A Narrative, Vol. I; Fort Sumter to Perryville*: Vintage Books, Random House, New York. 840 pp.

Foote, Shelby (1986) *The Civil War, A Narrative, Vol. II; Fredricksburg to Meridian*: Vintage Books, Random House, New York, 988 pp.

Foote, Shelby (1986) *The Civil War, A Narrative, Vol. III; Red River to Appomattox*: Vintage Books, Random House, New York, 1106 pp.

Funk, Arville I. (1976) *Clark County hospital treated 16,000 in Civil War* (newspaper column: the Hoosier Scrapbook): Louisville Times, p.B1, May 3rd.

Funk, Arville I. (1967) *Hoosiers in the Civil War*: Adams Press, Chicago, 100 pp.

Grand Army of the Republic, Proceedings (of) Annual Encampments, Department of Missouri, 1-46 (1882-1927).

Griess, Thomas E., Ed. (1986) *Atlas for the American Civil War; The West Point Military History Series*: Avery Publishing Groups, Inc., Wayne, NJ, 58 maps.

Guernsey, Alfred H. and Alden, Henry M. (1866) *Harper's Pictorial History of the Civil War*: The Fairfax Press (Crown Publishers, Inc., New York), 836 pp.

Hafendorfer, Kenneth A. (1991) *Perryville, Battle for Kentucky*: K H Press, Louisville, 515 pp.

History of Saline County, Missouri: Carefully Written and Compiled from the Most Authentic Official and Private Sources . . . Illustrated (1881): St. Louis, Missouri Historical Company, 966 pp.

Hupp, Timothy A. (1986) *Hupps from the Shenandoah Valley, Virginia after the American Revolution*: (privately published genealogical study).

Hurt, Douglas R. (1992) *Agriculture and Slavery in Missouri's Little Dixie*: University of Missouri Press, Columbia, 334 pp.

Jones, Archer (1992) *Civil War Command and Strategy: The Process of Victory and Defeat*: The Free Press, Macmillan, Inc., New York, 338 pp.

Marszalek, John F. (1993) *Sherman, A Soldier's Passion For Order*: The Free Press, Macmillan, Inc., New York, 635 pp.

Marvel, William (Feb, 1991) The Great Imposters: *Blue and Gray Magazine*.

McConnell, Stuart (1992) *Glorious Contentment: The Grand Army of the Republic, 1865-1900*: The University of North Carolina Press, Chapel Hill, 312 pp.

McPherson, James M. (1988) *Battle Cry of Freedom: The Civil War Era*: Oxford University Press, New York, 904 pp.

Miller, Francis T., Ed. (1911) *The Photographic History of the Civil War in Ten Volumes*: The Review of Reviews Co., New York.

Mitchell, Reid (1993) *The Vacant Chair; The Northern Soldier Leaves Home*: Oxford University Press, New York, 201 pp.

Morrison, Olin Dee (1961) *Indiana at Civil War Time*: E. M. Morrison, Athens, OH, 269 pp.

Reid, Richard J. (1987) *They met at Perryville*: West Kentucky Printing and Office Supply, Central City, KY 42330, 77 pp.

Reid, Richard J. (1986) *Stones River Ran Red*: Commercial Printing Company, Owensboro, KY 42301, 79 pp.

Report of the Adjutant General of the State of Indiana, 1861-1865: (1867) Samuel M. Douglas, Indiana State Printer, Indianapolis, Vol. 3, p. 397-400; Vol. 7, p. 709-712.

Scribner, Benjamin F., *How Soldiers Were Made*: p. 150-151.

Sifakas, Stewart (1988) *Who Was Who in the Civil War, Vol. I; Who Was Who in the Union*: Facts On File, Inc., New York, 479 pp.

Sifakas, Stewart (1988) *Who Was Who in the Civil War, Vol. II; Who Was Who in the Confederacy*: Facts On File. Inc., New York, 324 pp.

Slater Area Centennial 1878-1978, Slater News-Rustler, Slater, Mo., 104 pp.

Smith, George Winston and Charles Judah (1966) *Life in the North During the Civil War: A Source History*: University of New Mexico Press, Albuquerque, 397 pp.

Steenburn, Donald H. (1993) *Gunboats of the Upper Tennessee*: in Civil War Times Illustrated, V. 32, no. 2, 38-43.

Thomas, Dean S. (1991) Cannons: *An Introduction to Civil War Artillery*: Thomas Publications, Gettysburg, PA, 72 pp.

Thornbrough, Emma Lou (1989) *Indiana in the Civil War Era 1850-1880*: Indiana Historical Society, Indianapolis, 758 pp.

War of the Rebellion, Official Records of the Union and Confederate Armies (1880-1901): 128 vols., U. S. Government Printing Office, Washington, D.C.

Wills, Brian Steel (1992) *A Battle from the Start; The Life of Nathan Bedford Forrest*: HarperCollins Publishers, Inc., New York, 457 pp.

Appendix I
Genealogical Chart

Phillip (or John?) Hupp – wife, Elizabeth. Original immigrant from Germany, c.1740's or 50's; birth-death dates unknown.

Balser Hupp (mid 1750's?-1829)-wives, †Mary, Barbara. Balser was one of the first American born Hupps in America. In 1776 he bought a large tract of land just north of New Market in the Shenandoah Valley, Virginia. Ironically, New Market was the site of a Union defeat in May, 1864 during the Civil War.

Abraham Hupp (born?-1829) – wife, Elizabeth Knopp (1774-1864). Abraham was Ormond Hupp's grandfather. His mother was Mary, above. Abraham is buried near New Market, Virginia; Elizabeth is buried in Lakeville, Indiana.

Abram Hupp (5/6/1805-4/23/1895) – wife, Elizabeth Gardner (11/28/1815-1904): married 6/9/1837. Abram and Elizabeth Gardner Hupp were Ormond's parents. After his father's death, Abram moved with his mother and 3 brothers (Jacob, Michael, & George) to Mad River Township, Champaign County, Ohio (1831). In 1836 Abram, Jacob and Michael moved to northern Indiana. Abram settled in Center Township, LaPorte County where Ormond was born in 1840. He moved with his family to Saline County, Missouri, near Slater in 1867. Children: Anelizabeth (1838-?), **Ormond (1840-1926)**, Mary Emily (1842- ?), Julia Ett (1844-?), Arthur (Otho; 1846-?), George (1848-1849), Orlando (1848-?), Harriet (1853-?), Theodore F. ("Teed"; 1855-?), John Wesley (1857-1872).

Ormond Hupp (9/10/1840-11/25/1926)-wife, Laura Margaret Campbell (8/19/1850-4/1/1907): married 11/9/1873 Children: Mary Louisa (8/15/1874-4/2/1876), Jessie Kay (1876-1926), Charlie Chauncy (1877-1949), Luella (1878-1949), Gertrude (1880-1978), Montana (1881-1957), Elbert Abram (1885-1966),‡Oakland Cozetta 1886-1930), Lotus (1/13/1888-3/27/1888), Willamette (1890-1939), Ormond Roy (1892-1953), Vernon Estil (1893-1949).

†Balser Hupp was married twice. His first wife, Mary, is Abraham's (Ormond's grandfather) mother.

‡Oakland is the author's maternal grandmother. She married William Ozwin Dysart on 5/31/1911. Their children were William, Jr. (Mike), Margaret Lyons (author's mother), and Virginia.

Appendix II
Roster of the 5th Indiana Volunteer Battery

Captain Peter Simonson
(Three year service enlistments)

Name & Rank	Date of Muster (1861)	Remarks
Lieutenant		
Alfred Morrison		Promoted to Captain June 1864
1st Sergeant		
Ellison, Jacob F.	November 22	Promoted 2nd Lieutenant
Q.M. Sergeant		
Briggs, George A.	November 22	Promoted 1st Lieutenant
Sergeants		
Allen, Joseph M.	November 22	Discharged Nov. 10, 1864
Brown, Smith	November 22	**Died at MURFREESBURO, 4/13/62**
Donley, David R.P.	November 22	**Killed acci'ly HUNTSVILLE, 6/25/62**
Freman, Samuel P.C.	November 22	Mustered out Nov. 26, 1864
Marshal, John	November 22	Discharged Dec. 15, 1862
Tollerton, James	November 22	Discharged Nov. 12, 1863
Corporals		
Aumack, Josephus	November 22	Discharged Nov. 18, 1862
Baker, Luman A.	November 22	**Died at Lisbon, IN, 7/23/62**
Bricker, Henry	November 22	Mustered out Nov. 26, 1864 as Artificer
English, John J.	November 22	**Died at LOUISVILLE, KY, 11/18/62**
Guisinger, Wilson	November 22	**Killed at PERRYVILLE, KY, 10/8/62**
Jones, William W.	November 22	**Died at MURPFREESBORO, TN, ? 1863**
Kendall, Henry M.	November 22	Discharged Jan. 5, 1863
Mayer, George	November 22	Mustered out Nov. 26, 1864

McCallum, Benjamin F.	November 22	Mustered out Nov. 26, 1864
Miles, Richard P.	November 22	Discharged Jan. 19, 1863
Mock, Henry	November 22	Mustered out Nov. 26, 1864
Robertson, William G.	November 22	Mustered out Nov. 26, 1864

Buglers

Hulse, William L.	November 22	Mustered out Nov.26, 1864 as 1st Sergeant
Miller, Claud C.	November 22	Discharged

Artificers

Chandler, Daniel H.	November 22	Promoted 2nd Lieutenant
Knapp, Sylvester	November 22	Discharged May 1, 1862
Kuntz, Jasper N.	November 22	Mustered out Nov. 24, 1864
Prickett, John T.	November 22	*Deserted Aug. 18, 1862*
Spear, John R.	November 22	**Died at MURFREESBORO, 4/16/62**

Wagoner

Broughton, Samuel	November 22	*Deserted Jan. 15, 1862*

Privates

Acker, George	November 22	Mustered out Nov. 26, 1864
Akely, Lawrence W.	November 22	Mustered out Nov. 26, 1864
Alms, Michael	November 22	**Died at Indianapolis**
Amos, Wesley	November 22	Transferred †V.R.C. April 30, 1864
Backhaus, Charles	November 22	**Died at MURFREESBORO July 1863**
Barr, Isaac	November 22	Mustered out Nov. 26, 1864
Barth, Samuel	November 22	*Deserted Nov. 15, 1861*
Baumgartner, Albert	November 22	Mustered out Nov. 26, 1864
Beckler, Henry	November 22	Discharged Nov. 12, 1862
Beckner, Joel	November 22	Mustered out Nov. 26, 1864
Blenk, Joseph	November 22	Mustered out Nov. 26, 1864
Blowers, Harrison	November 22	**Died at NASHVILLE (date ?)**
Bodle, Alonzo K.	November 22	**Died at NASHVILLE, 4/8/63**
Bolton, Robert	November 22	Mustered out Nov. 26, 1864 as Corporal
Bricker, Conrad	November 22	Mustered out Nov. 26, 1864 as Sergeant
Bricker, David	November 22	Mustered out Nov. 26, 1864
Brue, Nicholas	November 22	Discharged Nov. 14, 1864
Cassel, Solomon	November 22	**Died at MURFREESBORO, 3/29/62**
Clark, Jacob C.	November 22	Mustered out Nov. 26, 1864
Cole, Thomas	November 22	Discharged Jan. 6, 1863
Cool, David	November 22	Mustered out Nov. 26, 1864
Craig, Alexander	November 22	Mustered out Nov. 26, 1864 as Sergeant
Cramer, Harrison	November 22	Mustered out Nov. 26, 1864

Crance, McAdo	November 22	Veteran; transferred to 7th Battery
Crance, Michael	November 22	Mustered out Nov. 26, 1864
Culver, Daniel	November 22	Veteran; Transferred to 7th Battery
Culver, Samuel	November 22	Mustered out Nov. 26, 1864
Darlington, Wilson M.	November 22	Discharged (Date ?)
Davis, Joseph	November 22	Mustered out Nov. 26, 1864
Donly, Joseph H.	November 22	Mustered out Nov. 26 as Sergeant
Douglas, John E.	November 22	Mustered out Nov. 26, 1864 as Corporal
Eaton, John	November 22	*Deserted Aug. 18, 1862*
Egner, John	November 22	Mustered out Nov. 26, 1864
*Ehrich, Frederick	November 22	**Killed at PERRYVILLE, KY, 10/8/62**
Eustice, John	November 22	Transferred to V.R.C., April 30, 1864
Evans, Thomas	November 22	Mustered out Nov. 26, 1864
Everhart, John	November 22	**Died at LaPorte, IN, 6/1/62**
Fisk, Harlow	November 22	Mustered out Nov. 26, 1864
**Forry, Abraham	November 22	Discharged Jan. 29, 1863
Fullerton, John	November 22	Mustered out Nov. 26, 1864
Gaddis, Philip	November 22	**Killed at STONES RIVER, 12/31/62**
Geiger, Jacob	November 22	Mustered out Nov. 26, 1864
Ginger, John C.	November 22	**Died at NASHVILLE, 10/5/62**
Gould, Wallace	November 22	Transferred to V.R.C. Sept. 20, 1863
Gruesbeck, Peter V.	November 22	Mustered out Nov. 26, 1864 as Corporal
Gwin, Henry	November 22	Transferred to V.R.C. Nov. 13, 1863
Hackett, Henry	November 22	Transferred to V.R.C., Sept. 30, 1863
Hall, Alexander	November 22	Discharged, Aug. 3, 1862
Hall, Nelson W.	November 22	Mustered out Nov. 26, 1864
Harvey, James R.	November 22	Mustered out Nov. 26, 1864
Heath, Otis	November 22	Discharged
Henry, William	November 22	Transferred to V.R.C., March 15, 1864
Hoffman, Jacob	November 22	Discharged Jan. 23, 1863
Holm, David D.	November 22	Mustered out Nov. 26, 1864
Homsher, Albert	November 22	Mustered out Nov. 26, 1864
Homsher, Benjamin F.	November 22	Mustered out Nov. 26, 1864
Hornbeck, Peter L.	November 22	Mustered out Nov. 26, 1864
Houston, John	November 22	**Died at LEBANON, KY, 12/28/62**
HUPP, ORMOND	**NOVEMBER 22**	**MUSTERED OUT NOV. 26, 1864**
Hutchinson, John	November 22	**Died at Camp Chase, OH, ? 1862**
Imbody, Harrison	November 22	Veteran; Tranferred to 7th Battery
Johnson, Benjamin	November 22	Mustered out Nov. 26, 1864
Jones, Daniel	November 22	Discharged April 29, 1863
Jordon, Alexander	November 22	Mustered out Nov. 26, 1864
Kates, John E.	November 22	Mustered out Nov. 24, 1864 as Corporal
Keen, Norfet	November 22	*Deserted August 18, 1862*

Kehlor, Joseph	November 22	**Died at LOUISVILLE, 2/9/62**
Kelley, Stephen	November 22	Veteran; Transferred to 7th Battery
King, William D.	November 22	**Died at Indianapolis, 12/24/61**
Klocksin, Charles	November 22	Mustered out Nov. 26, 1864
Kramer, Anthony	November 22	Discharged
***Kurtz, Jacob	November 22	**Killed at DALLAS, GA 5/27/64**
Malone, Adam	November 22	Mustered out Nov. 26, 1864
****Marshall, William F.	November 22	Veteran: Transferred to 7th Battery
McCarty, Michael	November 22	**Died CHATANOOGA 11/30/63**
McGuire, Thomas	November 22	Mustered out Nov. 26, 1864
McKinzie, Stephen	November 22	Mustered out Nov. 26, 1864
Mellyers, Daniel	November 22	Discharged July 10, 1863
Mendenhall, Isaac	November 22	Discharged Dec. 15, 1862
Mendenhall, John	November 22	Mustered out Nov. 26, 1864
*****MIller, Charles W.	November 22	Mustered out Nov. 26, 1864 as Corporal
Miller, David E.	November 22	Mustered out Nov. 26, 1864
Milliman, Curtis V.	November 22	Mustered out Nov. 26, 1864 as Corporal
Ney, Patrick	November 22	Discharged Jan. 19, 1863
Parker, Simon	November 22	Discharged Nov. 8, 1863
Peabody, Arthur	November 22	**Died at LOUISVILLE, 2/5/62**
******Pettit, Andrew	November 22	Mustered out Nov. 26, 1864
Richards, Simon	November 22	*Deserted Aug. 18, 1862*
Rickard, Daniel	November 22	**Killed at STONES RIVER, 12/31/62**
Rollins, William J.	November 22	Mustered out Nov. 26, 1864
Rolly, John J.	November 22	Mustered out Nov. 26, 1864 as Corporal
Shaffer, Christian	November 22	Mustered out Nov. 26, 1864
Shaffer, George	November 22	Mustered out Nov. 26, 1864
Shoemaker, Jacob	November 22	Veteran; Transferred to 7th Battary
Shoup, Joel	November 22	**Died at NASHVILLE, 4/1/63**
Shoup, Solomon	November 22	*Deserted Nov. 15, 1861*
Sickafoose, George W.	November 22	Mustered out Nov. 26, 1864
Sickafoose, John	November 22	**Died 7/17/64 of wounds**
Simons, George	November 22	Mustered out Nov. 26, 1864
Simons, Solomon	November 22	**Died at LOUISVILLE, 1/27/62**
Sims, William	November 22	Veteran; transferred to 7th Battery
Snyder, William	November 22	**Died at NASHVILLE, 3/23/63**
Stewart, John H.	November 22	Mustered out Nov. 26, 1864
Swaize, William A. F.	November 22	Mustered out Nov. 26, 1864
Taylor, Leander P.	November 22	*Deserted October 1, 1861*
Thomas, George	November 22	Mustered out Nov. 26, 1864
Vizina, Louis T.	November 22	Veteran; Transferred to 7th Battery
Wade, John S.	November 22	Veteran; Transferred to 7th Battery

Wallace, Edward A.	November 22	Mustered out Nov. 26, 1864
Walton, John C.	November 22	Mustered out Nov. 26, 1864
Wamptner, Frederick	November 22	Mustered out Nov. 26, 1864
Ward, Perry	November 22	Transferred to V.R.C., Sept. 30, 1863
Washburn, Alanson	November 22	Mustered out Nov. 26, 1864
Waters, James M.	November 22	**Killed at STONES RIVER, 12/31/62**
Waters, Samuel	November 22	Mustered out Nov. 26, 1864
Weckerlin, Henry J.	November 22	Veteran; Transferred to 7th Battery
Wigent, John C.	November 22	Mustered out Nov. 26, 1864 as Corporal
Wilson, Joseph	November 22	Discharged Jan. 8, 1862
Worley, Oscar	November 22	Mustered out Nov. 26, 1864

Recruits

Bair, Albion	March 20, 1863	Transferred to 7th Battery
Donley, William H.	January 11, 1862	Transferred to 7th Battery
Felt, James	March 20, 1863	Transferred to V.R.C. April 10, 1863
Galentine, Henry	April 12, 1864	Transferred to 7th Battery
Goble, Abner D.	March 12, 1864	Transferred to 7th Battery
Green, William	March 20, 1863	Discharged Oct. 24, 1863
Gruesbeck, Omer	Feb. 11, 1864	**Died at CHATANOOGA, 8/19/64**
Hartsock, George W.	March 20, 1863	Transferred to 7th Battery
Holt, William	March 20, 1863	Transferred to 7th Battery
Hufford, James H.	March 20, 1863	Transferred to 7th Battery
Hughey, Joseph	Nov. 23, 1861	Mustered out Nov. 26, 1864 as Q.M. Sgt.
Kermaston, Albion M.	Feb. 11 1864	Transferred to 7th Battery

†V.R.C. stands for "Veteran Reserve Corps." Wounded men who were unfit for battle field duty, but well enough to handle desk jobs, guard duty, nursing, and hospital cooks were assigned to the V.R.C. It was established in April of 1863 to free able-bodied men for combat service. In December of 1863 the corps had grown to over 20,000 men.

*Frederich Ehrich was killed after being struck in the head by shrapnel during the explosion that wounded Ormond Hupp.

**Abraham Forry is probably "A. Farg", one of the four men wounded in the artillery shell explosion that also wounded O. Hupp. Note that Forry was discharged a few months after Perryville, perhaps as a result of his wounds.

***Jacob Kurtz is probably the soldier referred to as "J. Countz" who gave aid and confort to Hupp after his wounding at Perryville. This aid very likely contributed to saving his life. Pvt. Kurtz was later killed during the Atlanta Campaign.

****Charles W. Miller is the "Charley" Miller who is named throughout the Hupp diary. He was wounded in the same explosion that wounded Hupp at Perryville. Hupp and Miller became fast friends during the war and remained so for many years. After the war Miller lived in Florence, Marion Co., Kansas.

*****William F. Marshall is the "W. M. Marshall" who loaned Hupp a blanket during the long wagon ride from Perryville to Louisville and New Albany.

******Andrew Pettit was one of four soldiers wounded in the explosion that wounded O. Hupp at Perryville.

Data from *Report of the Adjutant General, the State of Indiana*, Vol. VII, (1867).

Appendix III
Brief Company History:

5th INDEPENDENT BATTERY LIGHT ARTILLERY
Captain Peter Simonson
(after 6/1864: Capt. Alfred Morrison)

ORGANIZED: Indianapolis, officially mustered in November 22, 1861.

Left Indiana for Louisville, KY, November 27:

Attached to **3rd Division, Army of the Ohio** to September 1862.
Attached to **9th Brigade, 3rd Division, 1st Corps, Army of the Ohio** to November 1862.

Duty at CAMP GILBERT (Louisville) to December 20, 1861;
Duty at BACON CREEK, KY, to February 1862.

ADVANCE on BOWLING GREEN, KY, and NASHVILLE, TN, February 10-25;
OCCUPATION of BOWLING GREEN on February 15; of NASHVILLE on February 25.

Moved to MURFREESBORO, TN, March 18. Reconnaissance to SHELBYVILLE, TULLAHOMA, and McMINNVILLE, March 25 to 28.

ADVANCE on FAYETTEVILLE and HUNTSVILLE, AL, April 7 to 11.
CAPTURE of HUNTSVILLE, April 11.

ADVANCE on and CAPTURE of DECATUR, AL, April 11 to 14.

Duty at Bridgeport, AL, and along Nashville & Chattanooga R.R. to August.
Moved to STEVENSON, AL, August 24. From there to NASHVILLE, and then to LOUISVILLE in pursuit of Bragg, August 31 to September 26.

BATTLE of PERRYVILLE, KY, October 8, 1862 [O. Hupp wounded; transported to New Albany, IN to miltary hospital]

****

March to NASHVILLE, October 20 to November 9, duty to December 26.
ADVANCE on MURFREESBORO, TN, December 26 to 30.

Attached to **3rd Brigade, 2nd Division, Right Wing 14th Army Corps, Army of the Cumberland** to January 1863.

BATTLE of STONE'S RIVER, December 30, 1862 to January 3, 1863.

Attached to **Artillery, 2nd Division, 20th Army Corps, Army of the Cumberland** to October 1863.

Duty at MURFREESBORO till June 1863.

MIDDLE TENNESSEE (Tullahoma) CAMPAIGN June 22 to July 7, 1863. Including **LIBERTY GAP** June 22 to 24.

Occupation of Middle Tennesse until August.

CHICKAMAUGA (GA) CAMPAIGN, August 16 to September 22, Including **BATTLE of CHICKAMAUGA**, September 19 to 20, 1863.

Attached to **Artillery, 1st Division, 4th Army Corps, Army of the Cumberland** to July 1864.

SEIGE of CHATTANOOGA, TN, September 24 to October 26.

Reopening of the Tennessee River, October 26 to 29, 1863.
Outpost duty at Shellmound, TN, until February, 1864.
Demonstrations on DALTON, TUNNEL HILL, BUZZARD'S ROOST GAP, and ROCKY FACED RIDGE, GA, February 22 to 27.
STONE CHURCH, near Catoosa Platform, GA February 27, 1864.

****

[O. Hupp returns to his regiment, April 12, 1864]

ATLANTA CAMPAIGN, May 1 to September 8, 1864.

TUNNEL HILL, May 6 to 7.

Demonstrations at ROCKY FACE RIDGE and DALTON, May 8 to 13.

BUZZARD'S ROOST GAP, May 8 to 9.

BATTLE of RESACA, May 14 to 15.

Skirmishes near KINGSTON, May 18 to 19; near CASSVILLE, May 19.
ADVANCE on DALLAS, May 22 to 25.
Operations around PUMKIN VINE CREEK;

BATTLES near DALLAS, NEW HOPE CHURCH, and ALLATOONA HILLS, May 25 to June 5.

Operations near MARIETTA and against KENESAW MOUNTAIN, June 10 to July 11; PINE HILL (Pine Top), June 11 to 14 (Leonidas Polk killed, June 14), LOST MOUNTAIN, June 15 to 17.

ASSAULT on KENESAW MOUNTAIN, June 27;

RUFF'S STATION, JULY 4;
CHATTAHOOCHEE RIVER, July 5 to 17.

Attached to **Artillery Brigade, 4th Army Corps** to September 1864.

BATTLE of PEACH TREE CREEK, July 19 to 20.

SIEGE of ATLANTA, July 22 to August 25.

Flank movement on JONESBORO, August 25 to 30;

BATTLE of JONESBORO, August 31 to September 1.

BATTLE of LOVEJOY STATION, September 2 to 6.

Ordered to Chattanooga, TN, September 20, 1864.
Garrison Artillery, Department of the Cumberland to November 1864.

Veterans and recruits transferred to the 7th Indiana Battery. Mustered out November 26, 1864.

****

According to Dyer (1979) the battery lost during service 1 officer (Capt. Simonson, during the Atlanta Campaign) and 11 enlisted men killed and mortally wounded; 24 enlisted men by disease. Total 36.

Appendix IV Armaments of the 5th Indiana Battery

Ormond Hupp's unit was a six gun light field artillery battery, considered a company (a subdivision of a regiment) in terms of standard army battle order. The battery was led by Captain Peter Simonson, with the company divided into three, two-gun sections led by lieutenants: Lt. Jacob Ellison, Lt. George A. Briggs, and Lt. Alfred Morrison. Morrison was promoted to captain and commanded the battery after Simonson's death on June 16, 1864, during the Atlanta Campaign. Morrison, himself, was wounded during the latter parts of the campaign, replaced temporarily by Briggs.

The battery deployed a fairly typical compliment of "light" field cannons, each transported by six-horse teams. Each cannon was attached for transport to a two-wheeled cart called a *limber*, on which was placed an ammunition chest. The explosion of such a chest sent the wounded Hupp to the rear during the Battle of Perryville. In addition, each cannon would normally be followed by a *caisson*, another two-wheeled vehicle carrying two ammunition boxes and a spare wheel on the back. The caisson was attached to a limber (with ammunition chest) and the combined four-wheeled device was pulled by another six-horse team. During transport, the "cannoneers" (the team which actually operated the guns), generally enlisted men with ranks of corporal and sergeant, rode on the ammunition chests on the limbers and caisson, or had their own mounts. The "Drivers," like Ormond Hupp, rode the team horses, always on the left side, one man to each of the three rows.

The 5th Battery began the war with the following cannons:

Two six-pounder smoothbores (Napoleons)

The Napoleon (named for Napoleon III; Fig. A-1) was one of the most popular Civil War cannons. Variants were used by both sides. The Federal version can be recognized by the conspicuous muzzle swell; Confederate versions had straight, unadorned muzzles.

Figure A-1 – A Napolean. Note the muzzle swell indicating Northern manufacture; Confederate models had plain muzzles (Perryville Battlefield State Historic Site).

Two twelve-pounder howitzers

Howitzers were short barrelled versions of smoothbore Napoleons, with a narrow chamber in the breech for containing a small powder charge. They were designed to lob shells in high, arcing trajectories. By the middle of the war, most howitzers in Union hands had been replaced by Napoleons.

Two six-pounder rifles (3-inch Ordinance rifles; Rodmans)

The Rodman (see Fig. A-2) was a sleek rifled gun with 3-inch muzzle diameter used to hurl elongated, spinning projectiles long distances. They were probably the most common rifled gun in field use, competing for that honor with the James rifle and Parrott rifle.

Other field pieces included:

James rifles

This rifled gun is similar in outward appearance to the Rodman, and fired a special grooved projectile invented by Rhode Island militia General Charles T. James. By the time of the Battle of Perryville, James projectiles had come into disfavor, but the guns could be fired effectively using other types of ammunition.

Figure A-2 – A 3-inch ordinance gun or "Rodman." Note the sleek, unadorned appearance (Gettysburg National Battlefield Park).

Figure A-3 – A parrott rifled gun. Note the reinforcing band around the breech (Manassas National Battlefield Park).

Parrott rifles

Field models of this gun (Fig. A-3) came in 10 and 20 pounder varieties. This rifled gun was invented and manufactured by Robert P. Parrott in Cold Spring, New York. They are easily identifiable by the wrought iron reinforcing band around the breech. Most cannon with this band are Parrotts, but not all. The Confederates also produced a copy.

"Light" artillery units carried field pieces which were easily transported over all but the most rugged terrain, as opposed to the heavier siege, garrison, and seacoast guns that normally remained in one place for a lengthy period of time (siege guns could be moved by rail or hauled by teams of draft animals). The "pounder" designation for cannons refers to the approximate weight of the heaviest shell it could fire. These shells traveled down two basic barrel types, *smoothbore* and *rifled.* Rifled barrels were scored down their lengths with spiraling grooves and ridges designed to impart spin to the elongated shells they fired. This spin made rifled guns more accurate than smoothbores and also increased their range. The Rodmans, noted above, had a maximum range of about 1800 yards, while six-pounder Napoleons could fire a cannon ball a little over 1500 yards. Howitzers were short-barrelled smoothbores with a special *powder chamber* in their breech. They were generally aimed at a fairly high angle and used a relatively small charge of powder to lob shells in high arcing trajectories. Their trajectories were intermediate in arc between a standard, long barrelled cannon and a mortar.

Field reports from Perryville note that the 5th Battery used two 12 pounder howitzers, two James rifles, and two 10 pounder Parrott rifles. At Stones River, they reportedly used two 12 pounder Napoleons and four Parrott rifles. In his journal entry of April 8, 1863, Hupp notes that the battery turned in some guns for new James rifles. On June 28, 1864, in front of Kenesaw Mountain, he mentions that four Napoleons had been deployed. He mentions the use of Rodmans all through the Atlanta Campaign. This was reportedly the type of rifled gun that killed Leonidas Polk on Pine Hill on June 14, 1864. These references suggest that adjustments were made to the battery's compliment of guns during its existence, but the original mix of smoothbores to rifles remained, more or less, in-tact.

If the battery did, in fact, acquire some James rifles in spring of 1863, they were apparently back to using Rodmans by the next year. Rodmans were a much more popular gun, and it is possible that James and Parrott rifles lost in action were replaced by Rodmans in time for the Atlanta Campaign. Also, most twelve-pounder howitzers had been replaced by the more popular twelve-pounder Napoleons by 1864. So it is very possible that Hupp's disclosure that four Napoleons were in use by the 5th battery in the summer of 1864 is accurate. Lt. Briggs' report of September 7 to the acting assistant adjutant-general (L. D. Immell), notes that the battery was using "3-inch rifles" (Rodmans) and "light 12-pounder guns," probably twelve-pounder Napoleons. This means that the two six-pounder Napoleons with which they started in 1861, had been replaced by larger smoothbores by 1864.

Index